FREEING SOMEONE YOU LOVE

from ALCOHOL *and other* DRUGS

REVISED AND EXPANDED

FREEING SOMEONE YOU LOVE

from

ALCOHOL

and other

DRUGS

A Step-by-Step Plan
Starting Today!

Ronald L. Rogers
and Chandler Scott McMillin
Foreword by James R. Milam, Ph.D.

THE BODY PRESS/PERIGEE
Produced by The Philip Lief Group, Inc.

The Body Press/Perigee Books
are published by
The Putnam Publishing Group
200 Madison Avenue
New York, NY 10016

Produced by The Philip Lief Group, Inc.
6 West 20th Street New York, NY 10011

Library of Congress Cataloging-in-Publication Data

Rogers, Ronald, date.
   Freeing someone you love from alcohol and other drugs : a step-by-step plan starting
today! / by Ronald L. Rogers and Chandler Scott McMillin ; foreword by James R. Milam.
      p.   cm.
   Includes bibliographical references and index.
   ISBN 0-399-51727-8
   1. Alcoholism—Treatment.   2. Substance abuse—Treatment.   3. Alcoholics—Family
relationships.   4. Narcotic addicts—Family relationships.
I. McMillin, Chandler.   II. Title.
RC565.R565   1992   91-27000 CIP
616.86—dc20

All information in this book is given without guarantees on the part of the author or the
publisher. This book is intended only as a general guide and is not a substitute for sound
medical advice from a doctor. Each individual's personal medical history may cause any
person dependent on alcohol or other drugs to react differently than described in this
book. Only a doctor can weigh these variables in designing an effective treatment plan.
Final decisions about treatment must be made by each individual in consultation with his
or her physician and family. The author and publisher disclaim all liability in connection
with the implementation of this information.

Printed in the United States of America
1   2   3   4   5   6   7   8   9   10

This book is printed on acid-free paper.

For our families, with love.

Contents

Foreword

For years the diseases of alcoholism and drug addiction have been surrounded by myth and misinformation. With the publication of *Under the Influence* in 1981, the valid truths about the hereditary, biological basis of alcoholism were finally assembled and presented to the public. The result has been spectacular; the whole field of addiction treatment is shifting over to this new awareness.

Centuries-old myths do not die easily, however, and there is an enormous amount of inertia still to be overcome. Understandably during this transition period, many unwittingly try to have it both ways. On the one hand they try to rid the alcoholic and addict of the stigma—the lingering guilt, shame, and resentment that so often contaminate and jeopardize sobriety. On the other hand they continue to heap on stigma, for example, insisting that the alcoholic *became* alcoholic in the first place because he or she carelessly, willfully, irresponsibly, or otherwise shamefully drank too much.

The terms "alcohol abuse" and "substance abuse" are modern codewords for blaming the victim of alcoholism and addiction, for keeping the stigma firmly in place. The belief that such a person ought to be able to restrain his "abuse" of alcohol or drugs keeps him trying to control consumption—and failing—long after the time when, with the truth, he could have been helped to stop altogether.

In practice, the distinction between "abuse" and disease is not an easy one to make. I have noticed in my travels and correspondence that most treatment programs still reflect the older view in some measure, the view that addicted people have an underlying character defect, a behavior problem that needs forgiveness and correction, rather than a primary physical disease that needs healing and restoration.

Now, Ronald Rogers and Chandler Scott McMillin have, with remarkable clarity and simplicity, presented a program of intervention and treatment based firmly on this new understanding of addiction as hereditary, progressive, chronic disease. This approach is a reversal of traditional "common sense." For example, rather than holding the alcoholic responsible and blaming him for having the disease—which in his ignorance he had no way to understand, prevent, or control—Rogers and McMillin show that he can be fully exonerated from all blame, and then introduce the moral imperative *where it really belongs in alcoholism;* in a nutshell, their message to the addicted person might be: "Now that for the first time in your life you are learning what your primary problem really is, that you are permanently addicted and can never again drink safely, you are morally responsible to do what is required to maintain and protect your sobriety."

With this one caveat, that with full understanding he or she can and must maintain continuous total abstinence from alcohol and other drugs, the victim of addiction is brought back into the larger arena of society. Absolved of guilt and shame, with dignity and self-respect restored, he becomes a responsible full participant in society rather than a second-class citizen.

Of at least equal importance, Rogers and McMillin focus attention on the concerned family members. Despite the frequent complaints of frustration and powerlessness over a loved one's addiction, the fact remains that over 40 percent of people who enter treatment are referred by someone in the family. As an agent of intervention the family can be far superior to the judge, the employer, or the physician. The authors show that simply by changing the way they view and react to the disease, family members can have a powerful impact on the sick alcoholic or addict. And in recovery, with the new understanding, the family can join the addicted person in blaming not each other but the primary disease for causing them all so much suffering.

More than just another "good read" for the family, this book is pivotal in the final liberation of families—and society as a whole—from the tyranny of addictive disease.

James R. Milam, Ph.D.
Addiction Recovery Center
Seattle, August 1988

Preface

We believe that our approach to addictions treatment is substantially different than most. We don't, however, claim credit for originating it. For that we thank two very innovative clinicians, Morris Hill and Dr. James Milam.

The key to our *task-centered* approach lies in the formulation of clear goals for treatment. This is the contribution of Morris Hill, who realized that during the period of early recovery, the recovering person underwent a process of (1) learning about the disease, (2) identifying its symptoms in his or her experience (self-diagnosis), and (3) discovering how to treat the disease on an ongoing basis, usually in a Twelve Step group. These goals then became our focus in treatment.

The core of the program—what we have come to call the Chronic Disease Model—is adapted from the work of Dr. James Milam. His classic writings on alcoholism, from the pioneering monograph "The Emergent Comprehensive Concept of Alcoholism" (now out of print), to the continuing best seller, *Under the Influence*, have provided the first coherent view of this disease.

Milam is that rarity: an "original thinker." Where others had vainly tried to fit alcoholism into preconceived notions, he allowed the facts to shape his perception, and in the process, truly described and defined the disease of alcoholism. We gratefully acknowledge that Milam profoundly changed both our lives and our approach to treatment.

Acknowledgments

We want to thank Robert Markel and Philip Lief for their great help in making *Freeing Someone You Love* . . . a reality. If this book is fun to read and easy to understand, it's because of the editorial talents of Douglas Gower and Paula Cizmar. We are also grateful for the support and encouragement of Douglas Morrison. For their work on the revised edition we would like to thank Eugene Brissie, Laura Shepherd, Lee Ann Chearneyi, and Julia Banks.

To all of the above, we offer our lasting appreciation.

PART I

FACING FACTS

Chapter One

Recognizing Addiction

Why did we write this book? Because last night, all over America, something like this happened:

Mary Louise Delaney has had a *very* bad day. In fact, she's beginning to wonder if she's going insane.

It's midnight. She's sitting at the kitchen table, drinking left-over coffee. Sleep is impossible, anyway. A single question turns over and over in her mind. *Why do I put myself through this?* she wonders. *After all these years . . . why don't I ever seem to learn?*

On the counter is the mess from her ten-year-old's birthday party. Mary Louise watches her own grim reflection in the darkened kitchen window. "Some party," she says aloud, wincing at the sound of her voice in the empty room. *Where's Daddy?* the children kept asking. *Isn't he bringing the cake?* Everyone waited for him: the boy and his sisters, and six of his friends. And of course, as always, Mary Louise, who'd busted her back making the party special for him. *He's such a lonely child, anyway,* she thinks. *It was hard to find six kids to invite.* So she'd decorated the house and wrapped his present in some of that weird paper that he loves, with the pictures of Sylvester Stallone all over it.

And then came her big mistake: insisting that Jack pick up the birthday cake at the bakery. *Well, he'd been better lately. Not drinking so much, and really a lot easier to be around. Even the kids said so.*

Besides, she remembers, *I thought he should do his share. It's his kid, too, isn't it?*

She stirs more sweetener into the coffee, trying to erase the sour taste from her mouth. In her mind she still sees the boy's face watching the clock, at first with anticipation, then with that sad, curiously adult look of resignation as the hours passed and his father failed to appear.

Eventually she made excuses, sent everyone home early. The kids were terrific; they all pretended to believe her story. *They knew, though. You could see the embarrassment in their faces.*

She studies her reflection once again. *My face used to show the disappointment, too,* she thinks. *Now I just look sort of . . . bitter.*

And then much later, when Jack finally did come home, he looked the way he does when he's been out drinking: maybe not staggering or slurring, but with that mean glint in his eye, quick to jump on anyone who gets within reach and savage them with criticism. Spoiling for a fight. *And of course, there I was, mad as a hornet and ready to give him one . . .*

Ruefully, she puts a palm to her cheek, rubs the place where he'd slapped her. *You'd expect I would learn not to fight with him when he's like that,* she thinks. *And the hitting isn't even the worst part. It's the things he says . . . the names he calls me . . .*

Tomorrow she knows she'll find him at the breakfast table, smoking a cigarette and acting as though nothing happened. *I can't believe he doesn't remember these fights. He acts as though I'm crazy when I try to tell him.*

As a matter of fact, Mary Louise is beginning to think he may be right. Her mother's voice is in her head a lot these days. "Fool me once," her mother always said, "shame on you. Fool me twice—*shame on me.*"

And to be perfectly honest, how many times had Jack lied to her, deceived her, while she just stood there and took it? It had taken years to find the nerve even to tell her friends. Most of them advised her to leave. But as the months passed and things got worse, she was still there, still miserable, but making no move to change things . . .

Even your friends get tired of listening, she realizes. "You already know what I think, Mary Louise," Alice from the office told her just last week. "There's really no point in going over it again, is there? There must be something in you that *likes* being abused . . . "

Is there? she wonders. *Is Jack right? Am I the crazy one around here?* She glances up at the wall clock, sees that she's been sitting there for more than an hour. *I don't even notice the time,* she thinks. *I just sit here with my head spinning, and I can't think of any way out. I can't even put it out of my mind anymore . . .*

She thinks about Jack again, how he'd taken the keys and left the house after their argument. *At least I know where he is,* she says to herself. *In some bar getting plastered and bitching about me to the bartender.* A little prayer skips through her mind: *Oh God, please don't let him get into an accident and die, or kill somebody else.* She thinks briefly about calling around the bars and maybe sending a taxi for him. And that makes her laugh out loud at the ridiculousness of it all. *He probably wishes I was dead. And I'm still worrying he'll hurt himself.*

Mary Louise finally realizes what bothers her about the face in the kitchen window. *I look so old,* she decides. *When did that happen?*

Suddenly, from some underground spring, tears fill her eyes. She sits, immobile, letting them run down her cheeks, not even bothering to wipe them away.

She has only one thought. *What am I going to do? In a few hours, it's going to start all over again.*

Now she puts her head down on her folded arms and gives herself over, for the thousandth time, to the weeping. *I have never in my life,* she thinks, *been so alone . . .*

Of course, Mary Louise isn't alone at all. Just around the corner, Ben Dreyfus is sitting in front of his television, pretending to watch "The Johnny Carson Show" while he waits for his eighteen-year-old son to come home. Ben knows the boy will be stoned or flying high on some unimaginable substance, knows he will deny it bitterly when Ben confronts him, knows that they may come to blows tonight, as they have before. And yet somehow he is unable to stop this from happening.

Not a half-mile away, Sylvia Denton props herself up in bed and turns on her tiny book light to read her fourteenth article on the symptoms of alcoholism. Her husband is downstairs by himself in the den, drinking Scotch whisky and gradually losing contact with reality.

Sylvia has spent the past year trying to decide whether or not her husband is an alcoholic. *He goes to work every day,* she tells herself. *How could an alcoholic be such a wonderful provider?* She wishes there was someone who could help her make up her mind. Then she looks at her watch: in a few minutes she'll sneak downstairs and make sure he hasn't fallen asleep again with a lighted cigarette in his hand.

Next door to Sylvia is the Barrett household, where Mrs. Barrett goes on a binge at least twice a year and has to be committed, and her eldest daughter is a drug addict who has been arrested twice for stealing. Mr. Barrett has been promising himself he'll get a divorce as soon as the children are all grown, but he is terrified his wife will die if he leaves her.

And in an apartment complex down the road lives Jennifer Strong, twenty-two years old and pregnant. At the moment, she's waiting up for her husband to come home so she can ask him why a thousand dollars is missing from their joint bank account and if he perhaps spent it on drugs again.

. . .And so on and so forth. There are thousands of people like these in every city. People of all kinds and from all backgrounds, afflicted with the very same problems. All immobilized, and alone.

It would be difficult for Mary Louise and Sylvia and Ben and the others to believe that, as different as their situations seem, they are all living with and suffering from the same disease. A disease that, if left untreated, will probably prove fatal to the majority of their loved ones, and in some cases, perhaps to them as well.

The disease goes by many names: alcoholism, cocaine addiction, narcotics dependency, to give just a few. You can see it in its different stages—early, middle, and late—in the same neighborhood. The extent of the damage is intimidating: if you add together its medical and nonmedical consequences (such as auto accidents, fires, suicide, and homicide), you are looking at what may be the preeminent killer among diseases.

Yet despite its remarkable complexity and variety of form, this disease *can be treated.* In fact, the treatment isn't even particularly complicated.

In order to recover, what is the alcoholic or drug addict asked to do? First: learn some new information and change a few crucial things about the way he or she lives. Second: follow certain key directions, whether or not they seem convenient. And last: once the disease is in remission, make sure he or she doesn't stray too far from a treatment regimen.

But in return for this, the victim of addiction is given something unusual in the treatment of fatal illnesses: *a virtual guarantee* of survival and the opportunity to live a normal life.

There are a lot of cancer patients who would sacrifice anything for a chance at that kind of outcome.

The Impossible Task: Fighting Addiction without Help

Most people, like Sylvia Denton, spend months or years trying to decide whether or not their loved one is an alcoholic or drug addict. Then they spend additional months and years trying to decide what to do about it.

For them, these are questions of infinite difficulty. But once you understand the dynamics of the disease, you can read its symptoms as easily as you are reading this book. And when you do, it becomes clear what must happen for your situation to have any chance of improvement.

This book will give you an enormous amount of information about addictive disease. You'll begin to build the understanding you need in order to face up to your dilemma and take positive action.

But first, let's suppose that you decide to improvise your own response to the emotional roller coaster that is addiction. To see what happens, look at our friend Mary Louise. With the best intentions, considerable effort, and extensive planning, she's managed to do almost everything possible to make her situation worse. For example:

> ***Error 1: She gives the drinking alcoholic responsibilities and then gets angry when he doesn't fulfill them.***

Mary Louise makes the mistake of letting her resentments dictate her behavior. She knows her husband will have been drinking before he comes home; after all, he's stopped for a drink every night for the past three years, and there's no reason to expect him to change now. Yet she gives him an errand that is crucial to the success of her son's birthday party. With two or three drinks in him, that cake will lose its importance. So will his wife and son. It's happened before.

So why did she do it? Because she felt he *should* bear some of the responsibility—that she was unfairly burdened.

Understandable, but unrealistic. The real question is: will his disease *allow* him to bear it? Or will he once again have trouble stopping once he's started drinking?

Error 2: *She is fooled by apparent lulls in the drinking or drug use.*

Mary Louise allowed herself to believe that her husband was "getting better" because he was a little less irritable and difficult to be around for a few weeks. Alcoholism frequently produces *plateaus* during which things seem to improve and drinking may actually decrease. Eventually, these periods are followed by still more severe problems.

The reality: she's been living with alcoholism for most of their marriage. If her husband were going to experience a spontaneous recovery, it would have happened by now.

Error 3: *She makes excuses for the alcoholic.*

In other words, she becomes a voluntary participant in the denial syndrome when she makes up some feeble excuse and ends the party early. The message to her kids: *don't acknowledge the major force in that household*—their father's drinking. She can see the effects already: an almost adult sadness and resignation in the face of a ten-year-old boy.

Error 4: *She gets in arguments when the alcoholic has been drinking.*

The picture of futility: attempting to express anger to someone whose brain is distorted by powerful chemicals. It doesn't matter how valid her arguments may be. He won't hear them. And what is the point of arguing with someone who won't even recall it the following day?

It's a good way to get hit, though. And that's what happens.

Error 5: *She gets advice from friends who don't understand alcoholism either.*

Mary Louise's friends and co-workers probably know less about alcoholism than she does. They'll simply advise her to leave—a recommendation she'll reject—and then get increasingly frustrated with her refusal to abandon her husband. Eventually, they'll stop listening, stop offering suggestions. And Mary Louise will find herself even more isolated.

Error 6: *She questions her own sanity.*

This is a natural byproduct of Mary Louise's approach. Because she obtains little factual information and takes Jack's drunken criticisms to heart, she'll eventually reach the point where *she* needs psychotherapy—even if Jack decides to stop drinking.

Error 7: *She tries to protect the alcoholic from danger.*

Suppose she does locate Jack at his favorite haunt and sends the cab after him. Suppose even—wonder of wonders—he decides to accept the ride home. Would that prevent the same thing from happening *tomorrow* night?

Of course not. Until something is done about the disease that causes these problems, they will continue to occur.

Jack has been in danger every night he's gotten behind the wheel after he's been drinking—which is nearly every evening for the past three years. And he will continue to endanger himself and others as long as he drinks in this fashion. There is absolutely no way that Mary Louise can protect him. It's foolish to try.

Error 8: *She tries to handle problems without help.*

It's no wonder Mary Louise feels alone. She's isolated herself from any real guidance.

She's sought no assistance beyond gossiping to her friends. Their advice, though well intentioned, is virtually useless. It's a little like asking your mother-in-law how to treat diabetes.

And so Mary Louise's problems continue. In fact, they're going to get worse. She has no way of knowing that in another hour she's going to get a phone call from the local police. Her sixteen-year-old, Jason, has been in an auto accident. Earlier he'd taken the family car to a friend's house to study and then stay overnight. A kid in the other car is seriously injured. Her son's blood alcohol level was .18.

To Mary Louise, this will seem like punishment from God. But in reality, it's just the natural result of untreated alcoholism. This is the kind of thing that happens in families where alcohol and drug problems exist.

Or look at it this way: it's just the beginning of another bad day.

If Addiction Is a Disease, Why Don't We Treat It Like One?

What can be done to get the ruptured lives of families like Mary Louise's back on track?

Let's put our cards on the table. One point of this book is to convince you that addiction is best treated as a disease (see Figure 1 below).

You may be thinking, "What's new about that? People have been saying it for years." And of course, you're right.

Opinion polls tell us that in the past few decades Americans have changed their minds about alcoholism and drug dependency. Where once these were regarded as signs of *moral* weakness, they are now seen as a disease process.

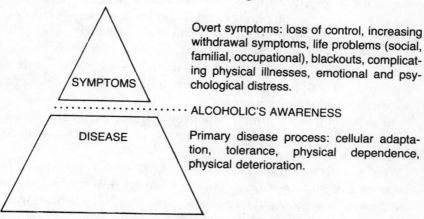

SYMPTOMS

Overt symptoms: loss of control, increasing withdrawal symptoms, life problems (social, familial, occupational), blackouts, complicating physical illnesses, emotional and psychological distress.

.... ALCOHOLIC'S AWARENESS

DISEASE

Primary disease process: cellular adaptation, tolerance, physical dependence, physical deterioration.

Figure 1. The disease model of addiction links observable behavior with hidden physiological adaptation.

Accordingly, treatment programs exist in almost every city of any size. Virtually all of these programs are predicated on the view that addiction is a disease.

So what's the problem? It's this:

There's a big difference between knowing that something is a disease and actually treating it as one.

And as a matter of fact, it is rare in America today to find any form of addiction treated as a disease.

Take alcoholism, for example.

For years, medical people have noted the striking similarities between alcoholism and diabetes. Both conditions are *chronic* (long-lasting). Both are *progressive.* Both can be potentially *fatal* if untreated.

There seems to be a hereditary component involved in susceptibility to each disorder. People can develop either condition at different points in life. Some become alcoholic or diabetic as children or adolescents; others first show signs at an advanced age.

In each case, ignorance of symptoms interferes with early identification. As a matter of fact, both alcoholics and diabetics experience a certain level of *denial* that prevents them from recognizing their illness until it's fairly well advanced.

Of course, we have at present no cure for either disorder. We do have effective treatments that help to arrest its course, making it possible to survive diabetes or alcoholism. Ultimately, though, we cannot presently restore victims to their predisease state.

One key for both alcoholics and diabetics involves adherence to a regimen of treatment: in particular, *avoidance of certain substances that aggravate the disease* (alcohol for the alcoholic, foods with high sugar content for the diabetic). And when further problems in treatment do occur, it's usually because the patient has abandoned this regimen.

Quite a number of similarities, aren't there? Accordingly, we might expect treatment programs for alcoholism and diabetes to have a lot in common.

We'd be disappointed. In reality, we'd encounter vast differences. We go into this in detail in Chapter 4, where we show you how to find the right treatment program. But for now, we'll simply summarize the problem.

Most treatment for alcoholism and drug addiction is geared to exploring psychological and interpersonal issues, when in fact—because addiction is a chronic disease—it should be devoted to the completion of *tasks.*

Task-centered treatment is designed to accomplish specific objectives, particularly in the realm of changing behavior (such as drinking and drug use). A task-centered program is most effective where the principal goal involves teaching someone to live within the boundaries set by a disease.

Issue-oriented treatment, on the other hand, is built around the presumption that the patient needs to identify and deal with a variety of hidden issues, ranging from internal conflicts to unresolved feelings about the past to communication difficulties with other people. The issue-oriented approach is the basis for much of modern psychotherapy.

Task-centered programs are focused and intense. They try to get a lot done in a short period, so as to have the maximum positive impact on the patient.

Issue-oriented programs are diffuse and exploratory. They attempt to address many diverse problems and concerns, some of which may take years to resolve.

In our view, too many alcoholism programs follow the issue-oriented approach (what we call "psychoanalysis in sheep's clothing"). This is often a prescription for failure.

The first turning point in effectively dealing with alcoholics and drug addicts comes when you truly recognize the condition for what it is—a chronic, progressive, and potentially fatal disease. Not simply pay lip service to that idea, but accept it.

That's what Dr. James Milam calls a "paradigm shift"—a fundamental change in the way you look at what's wrong with the alcoholic.

And to our way of thinking, effective treatment *begins* with this change in attitude.

How This Book Can Help

Maybe your alcoholic or addict has already been through treatment, and failed. It's easy to understand why families who experience relapse lose faith in the possibility of recovery. But don't give up hope yet. *Addictive disease can be effectively treated at nearly any point in its progression.*

As you read *Freeing Someone You Love,* you'll begin to understand why relapse occurs. And you'll learn why the simple concepts described here can hold the key to *effective* treatment.

In the rest of this book—and in a special **Guide to Addictive Disease** at the back—we'll show you how to identify addiction and assess its extent and severity. We'll present a straightforward, practical plan for the recovering addict, *and for you*. A plan that simplifies the essential elements of recovery into step-by-step tasks that both of you can understand.

We'll show you how to get through the first critical months of recovery, when the danger of relapse is greatest. And we'll give you a simple way to measure progress, so you'll know—every step of the way—how well you're doing, and how far you have to go.

But first, we'll show you how to get your loved one to take that first major step into treatment. We'll offer suggestions for transforming yourself from an enabler or provoker to an *intervener*—a potent agent for change in the life of someone you love.

Now let's take a brief look at some of the general patterns of addiction, regardless of the particular drug being abused.

The Nature of Addictive Disease

There are four characteristics that mark addictive disease in all its forms. It's **chronic, progressive, primary,** and **potentially fatal.**

Chronic diseases are long-lasting. *Progressive* diseases are those which worsen over time. There may well be extended periods (known as "plateaus") during which the disease appears to hold steady, or even go into temporary remission. View it over a sufficient span in the victim's life, however, and progression should be evident.

A *primary* disease is one that doesn't depend on some other condition for its origin. Contrary to popular belief, for example, the presence of alcoholism doesn't necessarily indicate the existence of an underlying depression.

The term *potentially fatal* should require no explanation. Just remember that addiction kills in a variety of ways—some medical, some not—and that most recovering addicts can point to at least a dozen incidents during their active addiction which might easily have proven fatal.

In most cases, addictive disease develops in early adulthood or in adolescence and continues to progress through its various stages until the addict draws his or her last breath. "Treatment" can only arrest this progression. The central tenet of the disease model is that the disease persists—in its dormant state—even when the addict abandons drugs and alcohol.

Some people learn this the hard way: they resume their primary drugs, even after years of abstinence, and rapidly redevelop signs of addiction.

Chronicity is by no means exclusive to addictive disease. It's shared by forms of heart disease, cancer, and diabetes, all of which are characterized by an extended course.

And because we have no cure for most chronic diseases, the role of medicine is simply to provide methods for regulating and controlling the disease to the point where its victim can live a normal life.

In the case of diabetes, such methods include insulin supplements, dietary control, exercise regimens. For heart attack victims, various medications, once again combined with diet and exercise, reduce the likelihood of a second attack. Cancer patients are a bit less fortunate: even with available treatments, the chances of recurrence are generally high. For addictive disease, recommended treatments center around abstinence and involvement in a program of recovery.

Some people protest bitterly at the inclusion of addiction in this company. "In the first place," they insist, "somewhere along the line, the alcoholic chooses to drink alcohol. Nobody forces him. Whereas the diseases you mention are involuntary. There's no choice involved."

True, the alcoholic does make an initial choice to drink. But then, haven't billions of people, throughout history, made exactly the same choice—but with vastly different results? Isn't it a fact that many people in our society believe there's something odd about a person who *doesn't* drink?

You might as well criticize the diabetic (as people did, not so terribly long ago) for having eaten too much candy. Or the heart patient for being overfond of fried foods. Or the lung patient for having started smoking thirty years earlier.

If you do, you'll get much the same answer as you will from the alcoholic. "Sure, if I had to do it all over again, I'd change some things. *But I never thought it would come to this.*"

Maintenance and Loss of Control: The Dominant Patterns

As we explore addiction, we will encounter two common patterns of addictive use. The first is the **maintenance pattern**. Here, the drug is used primarily to control *withdrawal symptoms,* and therefore is seen by the addict (and perhaps by others) as a medication. Though maintenance addicts may consume prodigious quantities of a given drug over an extended period, they are often protected by their elevated tolerance and may exhibit few signs of obvious intoxication. Their lives, nevertheless, are increasingly dominated by their addiction.

The second pattern features signs of **loss of control**, usually in three key areas: *the amount consumed,* the *time or place where the drug is used,* and the *duration of an episode of drug use.* These addicts are much easier to spot; loss of control creates identifiable problems.

Of course, the patterns mingle. A longtime maintenance drinker, let's say, develops symptoms of loss of control which finally motivate treatment. He's been alcoholic for years, but those around him didn't recognize it until they saw obvious social problems that fit their preconception of alcoholic behavior.

"We always thought he drank too much," they'll explain later, "but he was able to *handle* it until recently."

On the other hand, families of those in the loss of control pattern sometimes fail to identify addiction because their loved one may not use drugs daily. Addiction, they mistakenly believe, is confined to those who "have to have the drug" on a daily basis.

"She's able to go for days without a drop," they insist. "So how could we call her an alcoholic?"

As we discuss the forms of addictive disease, note the interplay between these patterns. See how they influence not only the addict's behavior, but also his or her experience of the disease (both physiological and psychological), the defenses used to thwart treatment, and even the response of those around the addict.

Above all, notice how incredibly predictable addictive behavior becomes as the disease progresses. A diagnosis of addiction allows us to predict the future with remarkable accuracy. Despite profound differences in background, character, education, and social standing, all addicts will have, to a remarkable degree, a similar experience of addiction (see Figures 2, 3, and 4).

And of course, one of the most predictable features is its ultimate endpoint: a tragic death. Untreated, this disease is routinely fatal. There's no use beating around the bush. Simply doing nothing can be a death sentence.

But paradoxically, this very predictability turns out to be our one significant advantage in the battle against addiction. *We already know what is going to happen.*

Even if the addict doesn't.

Therefore, we can plan. Whatever our involvement with the addict—as friend, family, or clinician—we can use this knowledge of the disease to develop a strategy for intervention, for treatment, for recovery.

Or, if you prefer: for survival.

That's what this book is about.

Using This Book's
Guide to Addictive Disease

So far we've outlined some of the basic characteristics of addictive disease. Addiction is far too complex a subject, however, to explain in a few short paragraphs or diagrams. You'll find the elements of the story of addiction interwoven throughout every chapter. You'll also want to consult the comprehensive **Guide to Addictive Disease** that you'll find at the back of the book. In it, we review addictive syndromes associated with various drugs, one by one. If you're interested in a particular substance— alcohol, cocaine, narcotics, marijuana, PCP, and so forth—flip back to that section and you'll find much more detailed information there. You'll also find a discussion of "multiple" addicts— people who use more than one drug. So for instance, if you're interested in what happens to people who mix cocaine and alcohol, first read the section on each drug, then follow up with the section on multiple drug use.

As you continue through the book, you may want to pursue other topics by reading about them from the perspective of the effects of a specific drug. So feel free to flip back to the Guide at any time. It's arranged by major drug headings for easy reference.

ALCOHOLISM:
PROGRESSION AND RECOVERY

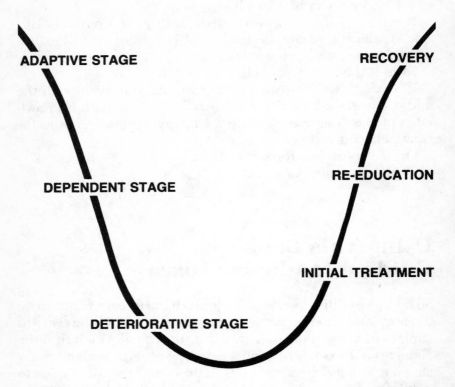

ADAPTIVE STAGE

RECOVERY

DEPENDENT STAGE

RE-EDUCATION

INITIAL TREATMENT

DETERIORATIVE STAGE

Figure 2. Disease of Alcoholism: Progression and Recovery. The course of addictive disease if unchecked is highly predictable. This diagram details the alcoholic's descent from maintenance drinking to complete loss of control. Compare Figures 3 and 4 which illustrate similar patterns of addiction for cocaine and narcotics dependency. (See pages 36 and 82.)

ADAPTIVE STAGE
Drinks to feel better
Drinks to relax
Drinks to feel stimulated
Drinks for any reason
Frequency of drinking increases
Drinks with improved functioning

Feels lucky to be able to drink
   without getting drunk
Mild irritability the "morning after"
Nausea early in day
Mild shakes which "cure"
   themselves

Preoccupation with next drink
Daily drinking
Gets drunk more frequently
Night sweats
Loss of other interests
Drinks inappropriate amounts
Drinks at inappropriate times
Drinks in inappropriate places
Begins taking "the hair of the dog" or tranquilizers
Blames drinking on problems

DEPENDENT STAGE

May seek psychological help for problems
Drinks with other "sadder cases"
Shakes increase
Is questioned by others about drinking
Efforts to quit fail
Blackouts
Suffers seizures or DT's
Thinking confused
Work, family, personal problems increase
Memory lapses

DETERIORATIVE STAGE

Increase in colds, flu, infections
Severe physical penalty if drinking is stopped
Notices swelling, puffiness, numbness, or tingling in arms, legs, feet
Loss of appetite
Blood in urine or stools
Digestive problems
Pain in stomach or back
Heart racing
Broken blood vessels, particularly in face
Bruises easily
Yellow eyes or skin
Seeks medical help
Life becomes unpredictable
Loss of control over alcohol intake

INITIAL TREATMENT

Enters treatment because of physical illness or is coerced into treatment because of social–job–behavioral problems
Patient is detoxified
Medical condition is treated
Patient feels guilty, angry, depressed over his/her situation

RE-EDUCATION

Re-education begins
Learns alcoholism is a disease process
Denies alcoholism—"compares out"
Emotions are augmented
Compares experience with learning
Self-diagnosed with some minimization
Admits having the disease without reservations
Learns how to treat it
Begins to take personal responsibility by changing thinking and behavior
Makes commitment to treat illness
Anger, depression, guilt subside

RECOVERY

Begins working in groups
"Compares in" at AA meetings
Becomes hopeful
Becomes willing to go to any lengths for sobriety
Helps fellow patients
Accepts oneself as nondrinking alcoholic
Signs for aftercare
Not drinking becomes unconditional
Maintains recovery program

Chapter Two

Gaining Leverage:
Becoming an Intervener

If you're involved with an alcoholic or drug addict, you most likely spend a good portion of your time trying to figure out how to get him or her into treatment.

If you haven't found an answer, it's probably because you're asking the wrong question.

Consider the problem from a different perspective. Ask yourself: how does the alcoholic or drug addict manage to avoid treatment?

Because the real mystery is how people get so deeply involved in a potentially fatal disease without ever confronting the need for help.

This idea might seem a bit strange at first. You may have become convinced that nothing short of a miracle could deliver your alcoholic or drug addict into a treatment program. Here we are, telling you it's a minor miracle he isn't there already.

Think of it this way: Are most addicts able to drink or use drugs throughout their lifetimes without experiencing a variety of problems?

Of course not. If they were, people like you would not be trying to get them into treatment programs. You seek help precisely *because* drinking and drug use cause trouble.

Remember that addictive disease is progressive in nature. Over the course of time, seemingly isolated incidents link together to form a coherent picture of a disease that is growing worse.

"Problems" related to alcohol or drugs turn into "crises" that disrupt everyone's life. The gaps between crises grow shorter and shorter. The effects of drinking on the alcoholic's mental and physical health become unmistakable.

Nevertheless, despite their difficulties, alcoholics and drug addicts successfully resist treatment.

Why?

There are three principal reasons. These form the obstacles that stand between the addict and treatment.

1. Defenses

Addicted persons are masters at using defense mechanisms to explain away negative aspects of their own behavior. The most famous such defense is *denial:* the inability to recognize a problem in the face of compelling evidence.

Examples: "I don't care what that Breathalyser reads, Officer, I have not been drinking"; "I don't know whose bottles you found in the basement. I told you I stopped drinking, and I have."

Another favorite is *rationalization:* developing excuses for problems caused by drinking or drug use.

For instance: we talked to a law student in his mid-twenties who'd been arrested three times within a twelve-month period for driving while intoxicated. He insisted we "couldn't hold those against" him because they weren't "real" DWI's. When we asked him what wasn't "real" about them, he explained: "In each case, I'd been drinking in my favorite pub downtown. I'd come out at closing time, get in my car, and drive across the parking lot. There'd be one of those damn Sobriety Checkpoints across from the entrance, and some cop would pull me over and give me a breath test. I'd blow a .20 or whatever, and he'd bust me. It just isn't fair. I mean, I hadn't even driven anywhere."

"Bill," we pointed out, "you've managed to get three DWI's in one year, and you haven't even hit traffic yet."

Then there's *externalization*—blaming your behavior or problems on forces outside yourself. As in: "If *you* were married to you, you'd drink, too."

It's also tempting to *minimize* events until they seem insignificant. Example: "Okay, I yelled at her, but I didn't hit her." Or later on: "All right, I hit her, but I didn't *kill* her."

Whatever the defense, the addict is exhibiting behavior common among people who have chronic illnesses. If you're afraid of what you might find, you can always refuse to look.

2. Stigma

Don't be misled by the publicity accorded to celebrity alcoholics like Betty Ford and Liz Taylor. It's still not a status symbol to be the first person on your block to wind up in detox.

Alcoholism and drug addiction are stigmatized disorders. This lends a moral aspect to diagnosis that isn't present when the doctor identifies diabetes or heart disease. Alcoholics are, quite unnecessarily, ashamed of their addiction.

Thus it becomes a matter of personal pride to avoid the diagnosis. Acknowledging powerlessness over alcohol or drugs is seen as admitting personal weakness. *Other people can handle it,* the alcoholic tells himself over and over, *Why can't I? What's wrong with my willpower?*

This is ironic, because far from being weak willed, the addict is the supreme example of sheer willpower put to the wrong use: the perpetuation of a disease process that ultimately will prove fatal.

3. Avoiding the Consequences

The most important single obstacle, however, is also the simplest. Alcoholics and drug addicts successfully evade treatment because, somehow, despite the problems their addiction causes, they manage to get away with it.

How? Through considerable personal effort, of course. But more importantly, *other people help them.*

Here's an example.

We were consulted by a woman whose husband was severely alcoholic. She estimated his daily consumption at somewhere in excess of a quart of vodka. He avoided drinking during working hours but more than made up for this once he got home in the evening. The quart bottle rapidly disappeared between the hours of 6 and 9:30 P.M., when he "fell asleep" (read: passed out).

This woman had "tried everything" to convince him to stop, to no avail. Rather than listen to a catalogue of failures, we simply asked if her husband smoked cigarettes while he drank.

"Yes," she answered, puzzled.

"Well," we went on, "it seems to us that if he's putting away that amount of vodka in less than four hours, he must get pretty well bombed toward the end of the evening."

"Oh, he does. He kind of slips in and out of consciousness. He wakes up to have another drink, or to threaten me if I try to take the bottle away."

"Okay. Then if he's smoking the whole time he's getting plastered, there must be plenty of occasions when he lets the cigarette drop on the couch, or knocks the ash off onto the floor, or into his lap, and doesn't even realize it. He must be one hell of a fire hazard, your husband."

"How strange you should mention that," she said. "That happens to be my greatest fear—that he'll fall asleep and set fire to himself and not even know it."

"Wait a minute, though," we interrupted. "He's been drinking like this for years. How come he hasn't set himself ablaze already?"

"Oh, just lucky, I guess," she sighed. "They say God looks after fools and alcoholics. Plus, I keep an eye on him, of course."

"Describe what you mean by 'keeping an eye on him.'"

"Well, we have our chairs arranged next to one another, across from the TV in the family room," she explained. It was hard not to picture Archie and Edith Bunker. "He refuses to carry on a conversation, so I read or knit while he sits and drinks. When he starts to nod off, I reach over and take the cigarette from his hand. Unfortunately, this wakes him up. He snarls at me and grabs the cigarette back. Then about twenty or thirty minutes later, he starts to drift off again. I take away the cigarette, he wakes up and grabs it, and the whole procedure starts over. This lasts 'til he falls asleep for the night."

"Let's get this straight," we said. "He drinks and smokes. You spend the evening grabbing cigarettes out of his hand so he doesn't burn himself up."

She nodded.

"Pretty fulfilling existence for you," we commented. "Sitting there snatching cigarette butts from your drunken husband."

"It isn't great," she agreed. "But what else can I do? I couldn't live with myself, knowing I let him die when I could have prevented it."

"How many times would your husband have set himself on fire if you hadn't been right there to protect him?"

We saw panic in her eyes. "Oh my God. I don't even like to think about that. Any night I wasn't there, I'm sure."

Now step back from this situation for a moment. Here is a woman who is miserable because she lives with an alcoholic in the process of drinking himself to death. She does any number of things to encourage him to seek help, all of which he utterly rejects. He's unmotivated, she complains. She thinks perhaps he hasn't suffered enough to want to quit.

Yet the one thing standing between her husband and a very severe consequence of alcoholism—we consider setting oneself on fire severe—is the fact that she virtually devotes her life to preventing that from happening.

Back to our initial question: why isn't this alcoholic in treatment? *Because he's unmotivated.*

Why does he lack motivation? *His drinking has yet to produce serious consequences.*

What's keeping these problems at bay? In large part: *his wife's willingness to work overtime to prevent their occurrence.*

If his wife were to disappear—kidnapped by aliens, perhaps, and taken to another planet—how long would it be before he developed problems sufficient to shake the hell out of his denial?

One night.

Let's make it clear that we are in no way criticizing this woman for her actions. Faced with the same situation, who knows but we might not fall into the same trap? Our point is this: what she does in the name of "protecting her husband from harm" directly contributes to his ability to drink himself to death in blissful ignorance.

Our experience is that people like this woman can learn to *change their behavior* so that the alcoholic or drug addict is compelled to confront the negative aspects of the disease.

And that's good. Because it is pain—be it physical, emotional, financial, legal, what-have-you—that motivates a willingness to change.

Thus our motto: if anybody is to suffer from addictive disease, make sure it's the addict. Because he or she can be made to benefit from that suffering.

The Enabling Syndrome

There's a common name for the activities of the woman described above. It's **enabling**: behavior on the part of others that protects the alcoholic/addict from the consequences of drinking or drug use.

> *The first and most important task of intervention is to identify and change enabling behavior.*

Enablers come in all shapes and sizes. They're bosses, employees, spouses, children, friends, co-workers, neighbors, police officers, judges, doctors, ministers, nurses, social workers, teachers. All remain unaware of the extent to which their enabling undermines their ostensible goal: getting the addict into treatment. Enablers, paradoxically, may be the most vocal critics of drinking or drug use.

They may complain bitterly, even throw tantrums, at each new symptom of addiction. They may read every book about alcoholism that comes on the market; they might consult every expert in the Yellow Pages. Nevertheless, when push comes to shove, they act to protect the alcoholic from the pain of drinking, and thereby decrease his or her motivation for change.

Why do people become enablers? Once again, the reasons are fairly straightforward.

First of all, they feel sorry for the addicted person. Underneath their illness, people with addictive disease are basically as nice as anyone else. They sometimes act like monsters as their disorder worsens; still, there will be a reservoir of memories to remind the enabler how good things used to be.

Second, enablers are unable to overcome the defenses that surround drinking and drug use. If you find that any mention of drinking brings grief from the alcoholic, you'll learn to keep your feelings to yourself.

Third, just as addicts make excuses for drug use, so, too, do enablers.

Therefore, the enabler may consider the problem in terms of the addict's supposed motives for drinking or using drugs, rather than its *results*.

If the alcoholic is unhappily married, is disappointed in his children, suffers from physical or emotional problems, or is under a lot of stress, enablers customarily blame the addictive behavior on these problems, rather than on addictive disease.

That's why some of the very best enablers are psychotherapists, who were trained that addiction itself is the result of underlying psychological or relationship problems. They automatically shift attention *away* from drinking and toward other issues, sincerely believing they act in the patient's best interest.

Lastly, enablers like the woman in our example protect not only the alcoholic—but themselves as well.

At one point, we asked her: "Suppose your mother in New Jersey had a heart attack, and you were forced to go to her bedside. What would you do about your husband?"

"I've worried about that," she said promptly. "I'd get my neighbor to look in on him every night."

"Suppose the neighbor forgot? Suppose your husband got drunk with nobody there to watch him? Suppose he accidentally set himself on fire and died? Would that be your fault?"

"No," she answered. "Because I'd know I'd done everything in my power to prevent it. I would have had no choice."

"I see. And suppose he did die—would you miss him?"

She looked embarrassed. "I wish I could say I would. But the truth is, he's been hell to live with for ten years. I don't really think I love him anymore. I love the person he used to be, I guess, but that person's gone. My friends tell me I'd be better off without him. I think maybe they're right."

Note the difference: she wasn't worried about surviving his death. Her concern was having to live with guilt if his death were to occur while she could have prevented it.

If he'd set himself afire, it would somehow have been her responsibility. Secretly, she might actually wish that he would die (common enough among those who care for the very ill), but only if it could not be construed as negligence on her part.

This woman became an enabler to avoid her own excessively

harsh conscience. Other enablers strive to avoid still other consequences. To cite a widespread example: they may be afraid the alcoholic will cut off financial support.

Enabling, you see, is not truly altruistic behavior. It seems selfless on the surface. Yet one of the enabler's primary concerns is self-protection. And by preventing the addicted person from experiencing one kind of pain, the enabler unwittingly exposes him or her to another, more dangerous kind.

Death by addictive disease.

Becoming an Intervener

There's a paradox here. Those same persons whose enabling permits the disease to flourish—and who may feel completely helpless in the face of it—are the very ones who can most effectively encourage the addicted person to change.

Why? Simply because alcoholics and drug addicts become so dependent on their enablers.

Rule 1: the sicker the alcoholic, the more he or she must rely on other people to support and maintain the addiction.

Thus it follows that if enablers radically change their behavior—become what we call *interveners*—chances are that alcoholics and addicts will be forced to alter their behavior as well.

The initial task of intervention, therefore, is to identify the enabling syndrome that surrounds the addicted person, and to get the enablers to act differently.

So let's ignore the alcoholic for a moment. He isn't ready to change, anyway. Concentrate instead on what other people are doing in response to his behavior.

We're looking for two types of enabling.

First, we want to identify *primary* enablers. These are persons whose cooperation seems to be essential to continued drinking or drug use. If these enablers alter their approach, the addict should experience serious problems as a result.

In the previous case—which we came to call the Human Fire Hazard—there were two primary enablers.

One, of course, was his wife. In reality, her role was that of an unsalaried, private duty nurse. She fed, clothed, and babysat her husband while he, oblivious to her efforts, plied his brain with vodka.

Without her assistance, he would have difficulty maintaining a semblance of normalcy. Lapses in her devotion might directly precipitate crises in his life.

There was a second enabler, however, whose contribution was equally important: the alcoholic's employer.

This gentleman had hired the alcoholic on the basis of a friendship dating back to their years in graduate school. He knew something of his friend's problems but operated under the misconception (encouraged by the alcoholic) that these difficulties were the result of personality conflicts with supervisors. The boss hoped to provide a supportive environment where the alcoholic could again become a valuable contributor.

Big mistake. From the outset, our hero exhibited real evidence of impairment. Reports he wrote were sloppy and error-ridden. His behavior with customers was just this side of actionable.

It became clear the alcoholic could not function at an appropriate level. What was the boss' response?

They had several heart-to-heart talks. These produced only temporary improvement. He found himself faced with a painful decision: fire the alcoholic, or "make allowances."

Termination was out of the question. He couldn't fire a friend whose life was in such disarray. The alternative? Arrange the office around the alcoholic's deficiencies. His contact with customers was routed through more diplomatic employees. And the boss was forced to instruct his staff to send all the alcoholic's work through him, for review. Horrified at the sheer number of errors, the boss had no choice but to rewrite the reports himself, and then send them out under the alcoholic's name. He did all this without telling the alcoholic. The blow to his friend's pride, he felt, would have been too harsh.

In other words, the boss paid the alcoholic a salary, then proceeded to do his job for him. We were amazed. We wondered if this boss had any openings in his firm. *We wanted to work for him.* No wonder the alcoholic stubbornly insisted that drinking never interfered with his job performance. As far as he knew, it didn't.

What might have happened if instead of receiving special attention, he'd been expected to function at the same level as everyone else?

He'd have been in serious trouble within a month—or he'd have been forced to do something about his drinking.

Thus the wife functioned as nurse, housekeeper, cook, and safety inspector. She kept up a facade of family life that fostered her husband's delusion of normalcy. The boss provided money and the self-esteem that comes with gainful employment.

They were in fact the pillars on which his disease rested.

Have you ever seen a picture of a "sedan chair," a vehicle popular among European nobility several hundred years ago? It had no wheels of its own. No power to move by itself. It had to be carried by human bearers. When those bearers stopped moving, so did the chair. The passenger's only option at that point was to get out and walk.

The relationship between this alcoholic and his primary enablers might have been diagramed as follows:

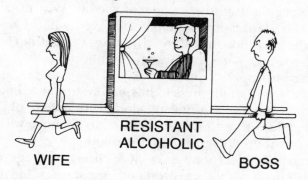

WIFE   RESISTANT ALCOHOLIC   BOSS

The enabling syndrome is a little like the sedan chair. Without enablers, the alcoholic or addict finds it difficult to continue in the manner to which he has become accustomed.

There may in addition be *secondary* enablers who play a less dramatic role in the perpetuation of the disease. Secondary enablers practice a sort of "benign neglect" that by its very passivity reinforces the atmosphere of denial. The addict thinks: "Well, if I was really as bad as all that, people would surely tell me. *Because they don't, I must be okay.*"

In this particular case, secondary enablers were numerous. The alcoholic's children, for example, complained bitterly among themselves about their father's behavior. One even moved to another city specifically to avoid seeing his father. Nevertheless, they resisted any suggestion of intervention.

"It's not our problem," said one son. "I suffered because of my father when I was growing up, and I finally got away from that house. If Mom wants to stay, that's her business. But I've been through enough for that guy already."

"I seriously doubt that we could do anything," said a daughter. "I really think Mom is the one who has to make a change. It's not our responsibility."

Then there was the family physician. He had long suspected drinking contributed to his patient's problems, yet had never issued more than vague warnings about it. Several years earlier, when an alcohol-related crisis had occurred and the alcoholic had become severely depressed, his doctor referred him for psychiatric help without mentioning—to patient or psychiatrist—that alcoholism was the real issue.

This psychiatrist hospitalized the alcoholic in a psychiatric unit. Every weekend the alcoholic was given a pass home. He drank wine on these passes. Discharged a month later, he resumed his regular nightly regimen of vodka. "Why not?" he told himself. "My depression is better. I proved while I was in the hospital that I could control my drinking. If I get nervous, all I have to do is take some of these tranquilizers."

We'd have to call this primary as well as secondary enabling. The psychiatrist's willingness to hospitalize under a diagnosis of depression instead of alcoholism, along with his use of prescription medications that the alcoholic used to alleviate withdrawal, directly contributed to prolonged drinking.

Secondary enablers may have little direct leverage over the alcoholic or drug addict but often possess considerable influence over the primary enablers.

As a result, secondary enablers who become interveners can use their influence to promote change in the primary enablers. When the primary enabler changes, so, too, will the alcoholic.

In fact it's often a secondary enabler, now converted to a new approach, who motivates (read: pushes, pulls, or shoves) a primary enabler to an intervention counselor.

The wife of the Human Fire Hazard came to see us only at the insistence of her daughter, who was sick and tired of listening to her mother's complaints.

Changing the Enabling Syndrome

How do you recognize a primary enabler?

Within the family, look for *obsessive involvement* with the addict's drinking or drug use, to the point where it intrudes into most other activities. "I'd love to [take up that activity, see that counselor, go on that vacation, etc.], but I can't"—because of the effect it would have on the alcoholic.

Or statements like: "My sister says this is all I ever think about or talk about anymore"; "It's getting so I can't concentrate at work, I'm so worried about what's going to happen when I get home."

Look for someone who seems to be immobilized: unable to act decisively to remedy their situation, yet equally unable to accept things as they are.

"I really should leave him," you might hear someone say. "All my friends say I should."

"So leave," you counter.

"I can't. I still love him, I guess. What if he were to stop drinking? I'd want to be with him, and then it would be too late. He'd never forgive me for having deserted him."

"So stay."

"I can't stay. I'm miserable."

"So leave, then."

"I can't, I told you."

And so on. Primary enablers are afraid to do anything, because they feel anything they do will make things worse.

Look for someone whose *actions contradict their stated aim.* And if you ever hear the phrase, "If it wasn't for me, I don't know what would become of [him, her, it]"—odds are you've just met a primary enabler.

Or, if any of the above describe you, you've become one yourself.

An expert on alcoholism once commented that the alcoholic has a drinking solution. It's other people who have his drinking problem. The first step in intervention is to teach the enablers to give the problem back to the alcoholic or addict. So it can motivate change.

How does one change enabling behavior? Simply by choosing to act differently in key situations.

Let's return to the case of the Human Fire Hazard.

His wife insisted that she would "do anything" to get her husband into treatment. "Just tell me what to do," she promised. "I'll go to any lengths."

"We want you to go to Alanon meetings," we said.

"I can't do that," she objected immediately. "My husband would be furious. Besides, what if he set the house on fire while I was gone? I wouldn't be able to concentrate on the meeting."

Primary enablers, as you can see, often have as many defenses as addicts. They may be every bit as terrified of change.

"Here's what you do," we advised. "When your husband gets home from work, say the following:

"'Hello, dear. I have to go out tonight to an Alanon meeting, so I left your dinner in the oven. But I thought I should tell you that most nights—you probably don't realize this—you get very care-less with your cigarettes. You let the ashes fall onto your clothes and onto the rug. That's why there are little black holes in the upholstery and carpet all around where you sit. This as you know is very dangerous. Usually I'm around to watch you, but tonight I won't be. So if you don't want to set yourself on fire, I suggest you be very careful.'"

It took her several weeks to get up the nerve. Her daughter had to stand beside her while she said it.

Nevertheless, they finally got out to an Alanon meeting.

She spent the entire time picturing her home in flames. She could see the fire trucks and the ambulance in her mind's eye. She even thought she smelled smoke. She didn't hear a thing that was said at the meeting.

We knew she wouldn't. We wanted her to go because it forced her to be out of the house during the period of time when her husband was most likely getting drunk.

When she got home, the house looked fine. No fire trucks. All was quiet.

Her husband was waiting in the living room. There was a nearly full bottle of vodka next to him. He'd consumed very little of it. As soon as he saw her, he began drinking. Within three hours the bottle was three-quarters empty, and he was uncon-scious.

What did she learn from this experience? First, that her con-stant attention was in fact a security blanket for uncontrolled drinking. Second, her activities were more important to her husband than she thought. When she changed, so did her situa-tion.

These small changes often give the enabler a sense of personal power that paves the way for still more effective action.

In a way, it's similar to what happens to an alcoholic when a counselor directs him to attend AA. Individual meetings may have little effect—he may reject most of what he hears.

Nevertheless, the act of attending—and remaining sober in order to do so—can produce an amazing degree of progress in a short time.

Like the addict, the enabler must undergo a process of "self-diagnosis," wherein he or she identifies unproductive or self-destructive behavior as part of the problem. Changing this behavior motivates further change. The enabler begins the transformation into an intervener.

An intervener is someone whose behavior forces an alcoholic or drug addict to examine the extent and severity of the problem, and thereby encourages him or her to seek help.

Most good interveners—and many good intervention counselors, to be honest—were primary enablers in the past. They learned from their mistakes.

About half the time, alcoholics and addicts become motivated for treatment simply because the people around them begin to change. No further, more structured intervention is necessary. Given time, the pressure brought about by the disease itself—without interference from enabling or provoking behavior—is enough to drive the addicted person toward professional help.

When this is the case, *outpatient treatment* can be a viable option. We'll discuss that in more detail in Chapter 4.

In the remaining cases, however, some form of confrontation is needed to get the alcoholic/addict over the hump and into treatment.

PART II

TAKING ACTION

Chapter Three

Intervention:
Confronting the Addicted Person

Suppose you've worked at changing your actions, at eliminating enabling behavior from your life. The addicted person still stubbornly refuses to believe that something's wrong with his or her behavior.

It's time to plan a formal confrontation.

This is where interveners meet the addict for the express purpose of getting him or her into a treatment program.

Let's move on to a step-by-step review of the practical aspects of developing a structured confrontation with an addicted person.

Step One

**Assess the extent and severity
of addictive disease.**

This falls under the heading of "know your enemy."

Remember this: it's really the disease you're contending with, not the person who has it. That's why alcoholic and other addicted behavior is so predictable; the progression of the disease makes it difficult for someone who suffers from it to avoid certain situations, no matter how hard he or she may try.

Likewise, resistance to treatment takes different forms, depending on the stage of the disease.

In the early stages of addiction, for example, the biggest obstacle will be the relative shortage of problems that accompany drug use. "Why should I quit?" the drug user asks. "How's it hurting me? Okay, maybe coke is addictive, but I'm not addicted to it. If I ever start to have problems, then I'll do something about it. But you want me to give up drugs before I have trouble? That's crazy. Suppose you're wrong? Suppose I never get in trouble? Then I'd have given up something I enjoy for no reason!"

In the middle stages, when loss of control is common and problems increase, resistance comes in the form of defense mechanisms. The addicted person denies, rationalizes, externalizes, or minimizes the extent and severity of the symptoms. The challenge of overcoming these defenses will require considerable preparation and effort, but interveners have an advantage: the reality of the disease is much more apparent than in the first stage.

In the late stages, the nature of intervention often shifts dramatically. Where the middle-stage alcoholic is capable of perceiving the truth—as much as he or she would rather avoid it—the late-stage alcoholic may be in the grip of a brain syndrome that renders an accurate appreciation of reality impossible. In such cases, intervention often becomes a matter of finding enough leverage to force the patient into making a choice for treatment, even if he or she never fully understands the need.

How do you assess this? The easiest way is to visit an addiction professional, describe the situation as you have seen it, and allow the counselor to evaluate its severity for you. Or read something that describes the symptoms of addictive disease as a progressive process—such as the material on the many faces of addiction at the back of this book (see Guide to Addictive Disease). Or read one of the published works recommended in the Suggested Reading section also at the back of the book.

Where on the continuum does your addict fall? (See Figures 2, 3, and 4.) Often, it's with one foot in one stage and one in another. You're considering intervention precisely *because* the disease is growing worse.

Learning about the progression of addiction serves a second purpose. You get to see what's coming next if the disease isn't arrested. That helps solidify your own motivation for intervention.

COCAINE DEPENDENCY: PROGRESSION AND RECOVERY

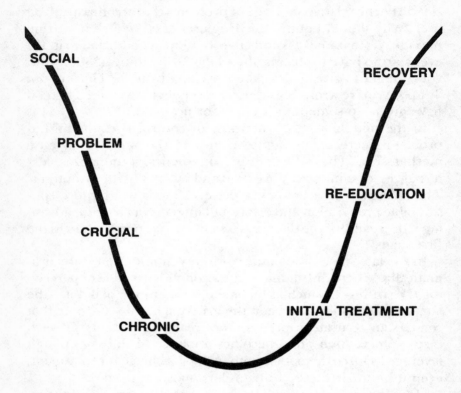

SOCIAL

RECOVERY

PROBLEM

RE-EDUCATION

CRUCIAL

INITIAL TREATMENT

CHRONIC

Figure 3. Cocaine Dependency: Progression and Recovery. Since addiction occurs in recognizable stages, the intervener's first step is to determine what stage the addict's disease has reached now. This influences the ultimate strategy of the formal confrontation. (Note, as well, the predictable course of recovery— adding a strong motivator of hope to the intervener's task.)

SOCIAL
First introduction
Use at social events for stimulation
Use only when others have and offer
Sex heightened by cocaine

PROBLEM
User starts buying cocaine
"Morning after" financial regrets
Using cocaine until sunup
Missing work & commitments
Begins to deal
Buys more quantity and hordes
Loss of other interests
Changing companions
Loss of normal willpower

CRUCIAL
Paranoia begins
Can't stop until cocaine is finished
Grandiose behavior
Using cocaine alone
Promises & resolutions fail
Missing social events because of cocaine
Inability to perform sex when high
Searching for more cocaine after original purchase is finished

CHRONIC
Work & money problems
Onset of cocaine binges: overdose, physical deterioration
Efforts to quit cocaine fail
Using cocaine with inferiors
Persistent remorse
Family & friends avoided
Frequency and length of binges increase
Intense paranoia & hallucinations
Impaired thinking at all times
Moral degradation
Loss of family
Financial ruin
Bizarre behavior
(Obsessive cocaine use continues in vicious cycles. Three options: Recovery, Insanity, Death.)

INITIAL TREATMENT
Total defeat admitted
Honest desire for help
Stops taking cocaine

RE-EDUCATION
Learns addiction is an illness
Told addiction can be arrested
Assisted in making personal stocktaking
Meets former addicts, normal and happy
Spiritual needs examined
Right thinking begins
Physical overhaul by doctor
Onset of new hope
Start of group therapy
Appreciation of possibilities of new way of life
Regular nourishment taken
Diminishing fears of the unknown future

RECOVERY
Realistic thinking
Return of self-esteem
Natural rest and sleep
Desire to escape goes
Adjustment to family needs
Family and friends appreciate efforts
New circle of stable friends
New interests develop
Rebirth of ideals
Facts faced with courage
Increase of emotional control
Application of real values
First step toward economic stability
Confidence of employers
Care of personal appearance
Contentment in sobriety
Rationalizations recognized
Increasing tolerance
Group therapy & mutual help continue
Way of life opens up with road ahead to higher levels than ever before.

Step Two

Identify the defenses you will face.

Suppose you were to go up to the addicted person right now and politely suggest he or she get treatment. What response would you get?

Negative, right?

This should give you an idea of the defenses you will encounter in a confrontation session.

It's highly unlikely you'll hear anything new during a confrontation. The old defenses have been working beautifully, so the addict won't change them.

In other words, you already know what will happen. This is a terrific advantage. It means you can anticipate problems and work out solutions ahead of time.

Some samples:

Simple Denial. The addicted person rejects every bit of evidence of the problem. As in: "I don't care what you say, I know myself, and I am not an alcoholic," or "That never happened—you've got it all mixed up."

This is easy for alcoholics because they frequently don't recall all or part of a drinking episode. The same events that are burnt into your brain may not be recorded in theirs. Thus if you're not careful, confrontation can easily degenerate into "your word against theirs"—and, the alcoholic thinks, everybody knows how crazy you are.

Temper Tantrums. When someone's addiction is threatened, you'll probably see a "fight or flight" response not unlike that of a cornered animal. Brandishing one's temper, or stalking angrily from a room, effectively silences many families for years on end. After all, the best defense is a good offense, right?

Indignation. Families feel guilty about bringing up what they regard as "shameful" topics like alcoholism or drug dependency. The addicted person may tap into this. Statements like the following are guaranteed to silence:
1. "You're humiliating me in front of everyone."
2. "How could you bring such shame to your own father?"
3. "You have no right to criticize—you drink yourself!"

4. "You don't really care about me. If you did, you wouldn't hurt me like this."
5. "I never would have believed my own family would desert me . . . go behind my back to some outsider."

Essentially, the alcoholic or drug user is climbing onto the highest horse available and acting as though he or she is surrounded by a pack of vicious dogs. In the general atmosphere of wounded pride, the issues of addiction are lost.

Hostile Silence. A favorite among adolescents and older persons. The addict thinks: "If I wait them out, they'll give up and go away." You're supposed to get the message that confrontation is useless, since you can't make the alcoholic do anything against his or her will.

Defense Mechanisms. As we mentioned, these are classic psychological defenses against an anxiety-provoking reality. Along with denial, there's rationalization, externalizing, and minimizing—there are even a few more, which we won't bother with. Examples of defenses you might hear in a confrontation session:

1. "Alcohol [drug] is the only thing that relieves my [select one: arthritis, insomnia, nerves, depression, stress-related tension, et al.]." **-rationalization**
2. "You'd drink [use drugs], too, if you had my [select one: problems, wife, husband, kids, parents, worries, childhood]." **-externalizing**
3. "Look, you're overreacting to this." **-minimizing**
4. "It's my life. I'm not hurting anyone but myself." **-denial**
5. "I hardly ever miss [select one: work, school, et al.]. I even got [select one: promoted, praised by boss, complimented by friends, swung a big deal, et al.]. How could I have a problem with alcohol [drugs]?" **-rationalization**
6. "If my drinking [drug use] is hurting me physically, why didn't the doctor tell me to stop?" **-rationalization**
7. "I'm perfectly capable of handling my own problems, thank you." **-denial**
8. "You know what the real problem is? You guys are trying to impose your values on me. Drinking [using drugs] is part of my lifestyle." **-rationalization**
9. "That only happened once. The other time, it was for a different reason." **-rationalization**

10. "You're no angel, yourself. There are plenty of things you
    do which I don't like, either. But you don't see me making a
    big fuss." **-externalizing, minimizing**

And so on and so forth. It's amazing how these simple defenses
can defeat enablers for years on end. As part of intervention
training, interveners learn to puncture them.

Step Three

Analyze flaws in previous approaches.

Most families have, on their own, made attempts to convince the
alcoholic or drug addict to do something about his or her problem. These have been unsuccessful. Why?

Untrained interveners tend to make three simple mistakes that
almost insure failure.

They're vague about the effects of drinking or drug use. This is a fatal
flaw, because the purpose of intervention is to overcome defenses that exist specifically for the purpose of denying these
effects. If you can't provide specific, indisputable evidence of
problems, you can't get past defenses.

For example, the distraught wife of a cocaine addict may cry
for hours in a therapist's office about the misery she suffers at the
hands of her husband's addiction. But when asked to provide
specific examples, she may lapse into inarticulate rambling.

"Well, he's just using drugs all the time . . . and he's completely
changed, for the worse . . . he's not at all nice, and he says things
that are so mean . . . "

"You mean he's abusive."

"Oh, no, I wouldn't call him abusive, more just sarcastic,
although sometimes, he's pretty abusive, I guess . . . I don't
know, what exactly does 'abusive' mean, anyway?"

"And you say he uses drugs all the time."

"Absolutely. Well, not all the time. But a lot, anyway. Although
I'm not sure how much. Just more than he used to, I guess."

"Is this what you say to your husband when you confront him
about his drug use?"

She nods. "And you wouldn't believe it: he still doesn't think
it's a problem."

No wonder. Her approach is long on emotional appeal, short
on concrete evidence.

Don't make broad statements like: "You've been drinking a lot lately," or "You just don't act like the Bob we know and love."

For example, when you tell an alcoholic he's "always drinking," he thinks: *I was sober for three days last month.* If you tell him he's "not the person he used to be," he says to himself: *Neither are you.* Then he cancels out the rest of your speech.

Another mistake involves *approaching the addict individually, instead of as a united front.* This greatly reduces your power and makes you relatively easy to deflect.

Families spend years discussing someone's addiction among themselves, but when it comes to confrontation, they tend to dispatch emissaries who they imagine will be able to "talk some sense" into the addict.

In fact, this may be the family's primary strategy, and much of their effort will go into an elaborate search for someone to whom the addict will listen. "Maybe if we get his old college friend up here for the weekend," they muse. "We could give him a little briefing beforehand. Maybe Dad won't be so defensive with a buddy."

This is what some families mean when they tell a counselor they've "tried over and over to talk to" the alcoholic. As in: "Uncle Jack talked to him at Christmas, and Grandma talked to him at Easter . . . none of it did any good."

It never will, either. Any alcoholic or drug addict worth his salt can handle a one-on-one confrontation with anybody.

It's the group that's hard to ignore. There's an old, oft-repeated saw: If one person tells you you're a horse, laugh at him. If five people tell you, go out and buy a saddle.

Lastly, untrained interveners tend to *give up too easily,* especially when confronted with overt resistance.

If the addict loses his temper, for example, or bolts from the room, it's tempting to shrug and say, "What can we do? He just won't listen." This reflects lingering uncertainty about the rightness of intervention. It's this self-doubt that can render you helpless against the disease.

You must believe in what you're doing. If you don't, you can't expect the addict to believe in it.

Unearth these weaknesses in the preparation stage. You can be sure the alcoholic will unearth them during the confrontation itself.

Somebody might warn: "Well, the last time we tried to talk with him about this, he just got up and went into the den and slammed the door."

The logical question is: what happened when you followed him into the den?

A family that gives up too easily will get a glassy look and say: "What? Followed him? Into the den? Nobody ever goes in there but him."

Precisely. That's his lair. That's why he went in there. Because every time he does, you give up.

Family members also commonly mistake aggressive statements for assertive behavior. Aggression feeds right into addictive defenses. It allows the addict to misidentify your legitimate concern as a personality dispute. Assertion involves making your point in a firm manner, without rancor, and then sticking to it.

Assertiveness is powerful. Aggression may seem powerful but usually isn't. People who employ histrionics to get their way frequently back down at the first sign of real determination.

Concerned persons often feel they must learn to overcome the alcoholic's emotions. In reality, it's their own feelings—their anger and resentment, anxiety and self-doubt—that silence and render them impotent. To become an effective intervener, you must learn to control these emotions.

And you must also follow the golden rule of intervention: persevere through resistance.

On the other side is success.

Step Four

Begin preparation for the session.

First, decide on your goal. In other words, what has to happen for you to consider intervention successful?

Does the addict have to enter an inpatient program? Outpatient treatment? Get evaluated by an addiction professional?

Base your decision on two factors: your assessment of the addict's condition (see Guide to Addictive Disease), and the likelihood of his or her response to treatment. For example, most alcoholics, given the choice, would opt for a trial as outpatients. But there's a second consideration: how sick is he or she? How far advanced is the addiction? How much control does the person have over drug use at this point? In short: even though it would be easier to talk the addict into outpatient treatment than inpatient, *will that work?*

Outpatient treatment works best for patients who have a fair degree of internal motivation. If your addict was that motivated, you probably wouldn't be preparing a confrontation.

Of course, money plays a role: outpatient treatment is always cheaper than inpatient programs. If your alcoholic is poorly motivated and inpatient treatment simply isn't affordable in your area, you'll just have to take your chances. *It can and does work—* but try to select an outpatient program with as much structure as possible, and which makes extensive use of self-help groups such as AA.

Again, there are exceptions. Once you select your goal, keep it in mind throughout the process of intervention. This is where you want to end up when all is said and done. (See Chapter 4 for more about finding the right treatment program.)

Next, each person who is involved with the intervention should list examples of the following:

1. Episodes where drinking/drug use interfered with the addict's functioning.
2. Episodes where the addict was experiencing signs of withdrawal, or alcohol/drug-related illnesses.
3. Instances where alcohol/drugs have been used in excessive amounts, at inappropriate times, or in inappropriate places.
4. Instances of financial, legal, psychological, or social problems related to drinking/drug use.
5. Any other symptoms identified during Step One of the intervention process.

Give actual incidents, complete with dates. Don't assume the alcoholic recalls the incident. Don't worry about embarrassing him or her in front of everyone. Don't worry about delivering an "emotional setback." Just stick to the facts and avoid getting angry.

It's sometimes hard for enablers to think concretely about the effects of addictive disease because they may be in the habit of bending over backward to "be fair" (read: avoid guilt). Thus some enablers focus more on the problems that don't yet exist, rather than on the many that do.

Something is wrong with this person's drinking, or you wouldn't have come for help in the first place. Until this is brought fully into the light, no real change can occur.

Step Five

Identify potential leverage and influence.

During this process, you'll get an idea of the confrontation's chances for success.

Leverage and *influence* are terms which describe what the interveners will bring to bear during the session.

They're two entirely different forms of persuasion.

Influence refers to strong, direct encouragement to seek help from persons the alcoholic/addict respects.

When your best friend says, "Julie, you know I'm on your side, and you really need help," you are being influenced to do something that is ultimately in your own best interest.

Those who frequently have influence are physicians, pastors, trusted friends, and family members with whom the addict is not at war.

If the addict perceives such individuals as knowledgable, concerned for his welfare, and somehow impartial, their recommendation can go a long way toward making treatment palatable.

If the same advice comes from a spouse with whom the alcoholic has been arguing for twenty years, it will have no effect whatsoever.

Leverage, on the other hand, is something quite different.

It involves actual consequences that the interveners will bring about should the addict, despite all encouragement, continue to refuse treatment.

People with addictive disease, you'll recall, are most likely to choose recovery when the alternatives seem even more painful than the struggle involved in giving up drugs. Leverage is the measure of the intervention team's ability to create such a situation.

To determine whether or not you possess leverage, ask yourself: what do I have (or do) which the alcoholic/addict depends on—that might be hard for him or her to replace?

Suppose you weren't available? Could he immediately find a substitute to perform the same functions? Or would he be forced to face some of his difficulties? Rely on his own (probably diminished) capabilities?

On occasion, judges and employers conveniently provide

leverage. An upcoming court date or a bad employee evaluation put the heat on the addict's defenses.

Equally often, leverage is provided by those persons upon whom the alcoholic has become most dependent: the primary enablers. If the addict can be convinced that these persons are truly, at long last, committed to change, the impact can be enormous.

Suppose, despite your accumulated evidence of problems related to drinking, and the strong urging of people who care for him, the alcoholic flatly rejects the need for treatment. What will you do?

To use leverage properly, the intervention team must be prepared to offer a choice. Go into treatment. Or continue as you have been, only this time without our participation. In other words, without everything we can take away from you.

Which might be: your money. Your support. Your friendship. Your home. Whatever you decide will have impact.

Still, you leave one door open: the one that leads into treatment. "When you're ready," you tell the resistant alcoholic, "you call me, and I'll take you to the program myself."

Given a choice this clear, the vast majority of alcoholics and drug addicts will opt for the treatment program. That's because it's finally become the easier alternative.

Interveners sometimes wonder about the use of such leverage to "force" someone into treatment. Will the program do any good, they ask, if the choice is made under pressure? Will he simply go to get us off his back but remain resistant throughout?

That's always a possibility, of course. But things seldom turn out that way. Remember that most patients enter treatment programs because of some crisis brought about by their drinking or drug use. It could be the threat of divorce or estrangement from family. The prospect of losing a job. A medical illness, or crippling depression. Arrest or incarceration. Somebody after them on the street.

This crisis serves as a temporary, external motivating force. *The patient enters treatment in order to avoid the consequences.* More enduring motivation comes later—from the treatment process itself.

Intervention simply creates a "controlled" crisis to motivate the addicted person, rather than relying on the kind of "uncontrolled" crises characteristic of the disease. Instead of waiting for the next catastrophe—therefore risking a bad outcome—the interveners combine forces to maximize their chances of getting the result they want.

Usually, resistance disappears over the first few weeks of treatment. After all, what is the patient defending? The right to die of liver cirrhosis? A sacred duty to shoot dope?

Once the cycle of addiction is broken and the patient learns something about the disease, treatment becomes less painful and resistance weakens.

Step Six

Select the confrontation team.

It's time to decide who will participate in the confrontation session.

Ideally, a team consists of three to six persons who represent both leverage and influence.

Of the two, leverage is by far the more important. With enough leverage, successful intervention can occur in the absence of other factors. Without sufficient leverage, even the best-organized confrontation sometimes fails.

Most teams fall somewhere in the middle. They feature some of each, and the combination gets the desired result.

We should point out that many people commonly presumed to have influence may in fact have little.

Take the case of the woman in our initial example. She'd begged, nagged, threatened, and browbeaten her husband for years, to no avail. As a result, he'd learned to ignore everything she said. Though his lawfully wedded wife, she had less influence than the mail carrier.

In fact, he regarded her as the reason he drank so much.

Obviously, the cause of intervention would not be aided by more pleading or threatening on her part. Nevertheless, unbeknownst to her, she retained a considerable degree of leverage which, if intelligently applied, could increase his motivation for treatment.

Changing her various caretaking behaviors made it impossible for him to drink as he preferred. If she filed for divorce, he'd find himself burdened with legal fees, in danger of losing his home, and in a position where he needed to make decisions his alcoholism would not permit him to make. The increased pressure would expose all his flaws.

Her role, then, was to convince him—not through histrionics but through actions—that she was at long last prepared to cut the cord between them if he didn't get help.

In the sampling of cases at the end of this chapter, we'll show you how leverage and influence are used.

A Note: People Who Shouldn't Participate

Not everyone who cares about the alcoholic should participate in the confrontation session. People who can't help getting visibly angry, or who freeze up and can't speak in a tense situation, or who dissolve into helpless weeping—or who can't overcome their feeling that confrontation is somehow wrong—shouldn't attend confrontations.

These approaches don't work—you should already know this from experience—and therefore have no place in a session designed to succeed. There are plenty of ways to support recovery without direct involvement in a confrontation session.

Similarly, because addictive disease seems to be hereditary, it's not uncommon to find more than one person in a family with a drinking or drug problem. This means there's an outside chance that some family members who want to confront the addict about his or her drug use have a problem themselves, about which they are in denial. Assuming the addict knows this, it's generally not a good idea to include such people in a confrontation session—because the addict will leap on it with both feet, and the team will end up defending itself.

Step Seven

Rehearse the session.

In other words, practice what you'll do and say during the confrontation.

Have one team member play the part of the resistant patient. Let the others make their statements to him or her. Practice overcoming objections to treatment.

Choose one member to be a *moderator:* the team member who introduces the session and presents the options for treatment at its conclusion. The moderator ideally is someone whom the alcoholic respects but who is not so closely involved in the situation that he or she is likely to be overcome by emotion during the session.

Additionally, it's the moderator's job to prevent the alcoholic from interrupting team members as they make their statements. When the alcoholic begins defending himself, the moderator might say: "Excuse me, Jack, but why don't you wait 'til everybody has had a chance to tell you why they're here? You'll have plenty of opportunity to give your side, later. But let's get all the cards out on the table first, shall we?"

Practice handling situations that might occur. As in: "Suppose he [select one: leaves the room, yells, interrupts us, etc.]—what will we do?"

For example, imagine the alcoholic accuses his wife of "setting this whole thing up and turning the family against me, poisoning everyone's mind."

If she denies it, or apologizes, the alcoholic wins. But suppose she remains quiet while other members jump in, insisting that intervention is something they all believe in—indeed, have been putting off for years? Then the alcoholic is forced to confront the group as a whole rather than as individuals, and the team regains its power.

What if the addict simply leaves the room? Refuses to sit and listen?

Suggestion: have one or two team members with influence go with him, urging him to sit and listen to what the team has to say. "We're only asking that you listen to us," you might say. "Not that you promise anything. We think you owe us that much, at least."

Remember, addictive defenses thrive on emotion and can't long withstand the scrutiny of logic. They are at root irrational. If you get them out where everyone can see them, they'll look pretty feeble—even to the addict.

If you fall back into the familiar role of nag or adversary, however, the addict can react emotionally and cancel out your message. If you maintain your stance as a group assembled specifically because you're concerned about the addict's welfare, it's harder for him or her to dismiss your comments.

During the session, the team aims to communicate four things:

1. **Positive feelings** for the alcoholic or addict as a person
2. **Fear** that the worsening problem is doing serious and perhaps irreparable harm
3. **Concern** that he or she doesn't see this and hasn't sought help
4. **Determination** that help be obtained now.

It's always difficult for families to understand how someone who is the subject of such concern and worry can nevertheless convince themselves that "nobody cares." Still, that's exactly the way many alcoholics see it, and that's part of what has to be dealt with during the confrontation.

It's also important that the interveners separate the person from the disease. The addict tends to take any comment about drinking or drug use as a personal criticism. The remedy: alternate expressions of warm regard for the human being with direct comments about the negative effects of the addiction. You want to drive a wedge between the individual and his or her addictive behavior. You like one, you hate the other.

The team takes this position simply because the addict or alcoholic can't. Instead of fearing the damage he's doing, he may have convinced himself he has things firmly under control. Rather than viewing her resistance to treatment as a sign of denial, she may be inordinately proud of her "independence" in the face of adversity. And far from considering immediate action, the alcoholic sees treatment as a last resort, reserved for a distant future, when and if things get "out of hand."

The addicted person's perception is obviously the product of addiction. It may seem "crazy" to outsiders, but it's very real to the addict himself. It's one of the reasons addicts take so long to get help: they don't believe they need it.

It's also helpful to have each intervener identify his or her weak points. How has the addicted person silenced or deflected you in the past?

Through a display of temper? Getting you to feel sorry for him? Making excuses? Cutting the issue off? Attacking your own behavior? Simply walking out on the discussion?

How will you respond differently during the confrontation?

Because if you do what you've always done, you'll get the same result as before: no change.

Take some time to think about the kind of approach that generally elicits the best response from this person. For example, some people—at the risk of sounding sexist, usually women—

are receptive to open expressions of love and caring, and you are more likely to get a positive response if you include generous doses in your presentation. Others—often men—run for the rafters at the first hint of emotionalism, and respond much better to simple, well-reasoned arguments in favor of getting help. And of course, there are plenty of exceptions to both observations.

Some families have actually trained addicted persons to ignore them by going back on their own threats. Thus when someone promises divorce, the addict thinks, "I've heard that before." How will you convince him that this time is different? Words may not be enough.

Above all when using leverage, do not make any statements about what you will or won't do unless you are prepared to back them up with action. Don't tell an alcoholic you're going to divorce her if she doesn't get help, unless that's exactly what you're planning to do. Don't tell a cocaine addict you're going to turn him into the police for drug trafficking, unless you really mean to take that step.

If you don't intend to do what you say, then don't say it. Sure, it might sound great in the heat of the moment. But in the long run, it would just be another empty threat or broken promise.

There are occasions, however, when you can make productive use of leverage simply by pointing out what might happen if the addict keeps on using drugs. Some cocaine addicts respond very strongly to the mere suggestion that the "narcs" are watching them and a disastrous bust may be imminent. It's a way of taking advantage of the addict's natural paranoia to motivate treatment.

Some Suggestions for Dealing with Objections to Treatment

There's no single "best response" for the defenses you encounter in the confrontation. This is one of the areas where a counselor can really be of assistance (they spend all day listening to alcoholic defenses), so it's a good reason to consult one prior to attempting confrontation. Here are some examples of effective responses to typical objections.

ADDICT: *This is none of your business.*
INTERVENER: It is our business. We're the people who [live with, care about] you. Your problems affect us, whether or not you're aware of it.

ADDICT:	*You don't care about me.*
INTERVENER:	If we didn't care about you, we'd just keep our mouths shut and let you ruin your life. We're here because we do care.

ADDICT:	*I'm not hurting anybody besides myself.*
INTERVENER:	If we agreed with that, we wouldn't be sitting here right now.

ADDICT:	*You're not perfect. I've seen you have a drink.*
INTERVENER:	The issue isn't whether or not you drink. It's whether or not your drinking is causing problems. If you listen to what we're telling you today, I think you'd have to agree it does.

ADDICT:	*Look, I'll take care of this on my own.*
INTERVENER:	You've said that before, and it hasn't worked. You improve for a while, then slip right back. The professionals tell us that's the nature of the problem. You need help to stay stopped.

Here are some final reminders:
1. Don't lose your temper. Don't argue.
2. Express positive feelings for the person and negative feelings about the drug use.
3. Be specific with evidence.
4. Stick with your goal.
5. Don't accept promises to "stop on my own."
6. When one member falters, another should step in.
7. Don't back down. Don't give up.

Step Eight

Select the time and place.

Question: when's the best time to confront an alcoholic or addict?
Answer: when he's closest to sober (usually the morning).
Hint: if he knows you're coming, he won't be there. You'll have to surprise him.

Where to have the session? Preferably outside the alcoholic's home. Someplace where you'll have space, time, and privacy, but where he'll have trouble getting up and leaving, and where he won't have a hidden stash.

Plenty of successful confrontations have occurred right in the lion's den, however—the addicted person's home.

When are you ready to confront?

When you're adequately prepared, working as a team, and fully rehearsed.

When is a confrontation session over?

When you've reached your predetermined goal, or come to believe it won't happen that day. The average session lasts under an hour.

Step Nine

Have treatment prearranged.

Check out available treatment (see Chapter 4, on selecting a program). Set up admission prior to the session.

Check insurance coverage and funding arrangements. Think of all the possible logistical problems that might arise, and solve them.

As the intervention proceeds, the patient may negotiate about the when, where, and how of treatment, bringing up obstacles against going in now. Such as:

"I have to be at Kerry's wedding."

"What do I tell them at work?"

"Who'll look after the dog?"

"I can't stand being cooped up."

"I need the weekend to get organized."

"I have a trip planned to Borneo."

Of course, when this negotiation begins, you've won. The point has been made. The patient acknowledges the need for help. It's only a question of hammering out the particulars. So forge ahead.

Step Ten

Do it.

Go ahead. Take your best shot.

Case One: Day in Court

We doubt that anyone has more defenses than an alcoholic trial lawyer. In this instance, we were contacted by the wife, a veteran primary enabler who'd been asking people for help with her husband's drinking for years. She had no influence herself but was able to assemble the raw material for a confrontation team.

Included were two daughters—secondary enablers who'd married and moved out but continued to work around the touchy subject of their father's obvious alcoholism—and a son, who, as Dad's law partner, served as a primary enabler. He managed the business so his father could persist in the illusion that he was still a functioning member of a successful firm.

Their leverage: the prospect of marital separation (not very strong, in this case—the alcoholic might welcome it) and possible forfeiture of the partnership (much more effective).

In addition, since it seemed a formidable defense attorney would be protected by layers of argument, we recommended an overwhelming show of agreement. The family decided to stage a very large confrontation.

This was effective because in that community were dozens of people who had apparently been waiting for years to inform this alcoholic that something was wrong with his drinking.

The final team: his daughters and their respective husbands, two former law partners who'd left because of his drinking, a longtime Elks Club drinking buddy who was now in AA, and the two primary enablers.

The family had guessed correctly: as soon as the alcoholic saw how many people had come out on a Sunday morning to confront him, his resistance crumbled.

He knew a stacked jury when he saw one.

Case Two: One Down, One to Go

Here, initial contact was made by the alcoholic's daughter. Her mother was a matron of sixty-five who lived with her second husband in a mansion she rarely left. Her stepfather was the primary enabler. Not only did he provide financial and emotional support, he actually controlled her intake.

Though his wife was physically debilitated, she was able to get alcohol by calling a cab and having it delivered. If her husband refused booze, she obtained it anyway. As a compromise, he assumed the job of rationing her alcohol. He doled out drinks much like a nurse dispenses pills.

The husband defended his behavior by stating he would rather have his wife reasonably content than harping at him, and if he cut off the supply, she'd only get her own.

The children didn't know how to respond to this. We asked them to attend a lecture series in which they learned alcoholism is a progressive disease. They were able to identify their mother as being in the late stages.

Late-stage alcoholics drink in the morning, have all sorts of medical problems, and show signs of decreasing tolerance.

They also tend to die of the disease if they don't get treatment.

This knowledge mobilized the children. They decided that the real obstacle to getting their mother into the hospital was their stepfather. Without his support, she'd collapse in no time. They therefore focused their efforts on him.

Looking for leverage, they realized that he relied heavily on them whenever his wife's disease got out of control. When she became ill, he called them to take her to the emergency room. When she was abusive, he called on them to help calm her. When she threatened to kill herself, he depended on them to talk her out of it.

Yet he resisted any outside help, feeling her alcoholism brought shame to the family. In a sense, the children discovered they were enabling him to continue enabling her.

The family met with him one morning, ostensibly to discuss what to do about Mom. Instead, his daughter informed him they now appreciated exactly how close to death their mother was. They also believed that his behavior was contributing to its likelihood.

And they promised they would no longer respond to his requests for help. If he wasn't going to allow their mother to get professional treatment, he could take care of her by himself.

He gave in. Two days later, he packed his wife into the station wagon and drove her off to detox.

Case Three: Cocaine Intervention

Several years ago we were contacted by a psychologist whose preceptor—also a psychologist of considerable repute in the field—had developed an addiction to cocaine. As those around him confronted him with his worsening problem, the addict bitterly denied it, then threatened them with legal action.

"Spread this vicious rumor," the addict promised each of them, "and I'll slap you with a slander suit the very next day.

You'll spend the next year in court, I swear to you. My lawyers will make you look like a fool. I'll sue you for every dollar you've got. And on top of that, I'll make sure nobody ever hires you again."

This worked beautifully. "What could we do?" the psychologist asked us. "I mean, he could really screw us. We don't have any hard evidence, you know. He's got us over a barrel."

"Wait a minute," we interrupted. "You say you don't have hard evidence. What do you mean?"

"We don't have pictures of him doing drugs, or blood tests with cocaine in them, or whatever."

"Have any of you ever seen him snort coke?"

"Sure," he answered. "All of us. Many times."

"So he's going to sue you for slander," we pointed out, "and put you on the stand in open court, so that one by one you can swear under oath that he uses cocaine, and you've seen him do it."

The psychologist nodded.

"And that's going to make you look bad?" we said. "What's it going to do to his reputation in the professional community?"

"I hadn't thought of that," he reflected.

"Why don't you catch him by surprise one morning—the whole group of you at once—and tell him that if he doesn't get some help, you're going to stop keeping his addiction a secret. And if he wants to sue you for slander, go ahead."

"And while you're at it," we continued, "why don't you point out to him that cocaine is an illegal drug, and if you know all about his use of it, there's a chance the narcs are watching him as well. Ask him if he's noticed anybody suspicious following him around. Ask him how he knows they're not going to bust him for trafficking any day now. And what he thinks that will do for his professional standing."

They did. He blanched, packed his bag, and let them drive him to the treatment program.

Do We Need Professional Help to Prepare an Intervention?

It's a good idea. There are counselors attached to most treatment programs who have been trained in the intervention process. They can help you plan and rehearse.

Professionals bring knowledge and experience to the planning process, but most importantly, they bring objectivity. It's not *their* loved one. They can help you step back and see what approach is best.

Some professionals attend the confrontation session with the family and the alcoholic. This is fine as far as we're concerned. We don't attend sessions, however, for one good reason.

Of all the persons involved in the intervention process, the only one with neither leverage nor influence is the counselor. *The alcoholic really doesn't care what we think.* As much as he tries to hide it, he cares what *you* think.

So whether or not the counselor attends the confrontation, his or her real importance lies in training you to maximize your own leverage and influence. It's always tempting to think you can turn everything over to "the experts." That simply doesn't work.

We may have the knowledge. But we don't have the power. You, however, do.

The Big Fear: Will Our Marriage End?

Just as addicts depend on enablers, so too do some enablers become quite dependent on addicts.

In fact, the single most common reason given for ongoing enabling by wives is the fear of financial hardship resulting from divorce or separation. The devil you know, these wives sometimes decide, is better than the one you don't.

This is partly why intervention becomes scary for some people. It doesn't matter that intervention seldom results in divorce. The threat is always there.

There's no way we would presume to make a decision like this for anyone else. It's a choice every individual must make for himself or herself.

But we do advise: there are many behavioral changes an enabler can make which run short of actual confrontation. And many times, these changes produce the same result: an alcoholic or drug addict who becomes motivated for help.

It's a slower process, for sure. But often just as effective.

And after all—what have you got to lose?

PART III

CHALLENGE OF INITIAL RECOVERY STAGE

Chapter Four

The Keys to Finding Good Treatment

Once you've realized that intervention may be possible, it will occur to you that you need a good treatment program.

Finding one is your job for two reasons. First, your alcoholic or addict isn't in any condition to evaluate treatment himself. Left to his own devices, he'll figure out a way to avoid the whole issue. You'll be back where you started.

Second, the confrontation method is designed to lead *directly into treatment*. Any gaps between the alcoholic's agreement to accept help and his or her actual enrollment in a program will effectively sabotage the outcome.

In this chapter we're going to provide ten "keys" to identifying a good treatment program, whether inpatient or outpatient. We'll even tell you how to ask the right questions, to help you differentiate quality from the *appearance* of quality.

First, though, we'd like to talk a bit more about the crucial differences between *task-centered* and *issue-oriented* treatment.

Applying a Chronic Disease Model to Addictions Treatment

Recall from Chapter 1 our comparison of alcoholism and diabetes. Both, as we observed, are chronic and progressive. Both appear to have a hereditary component. Both often remain undiscovered in the early stages. Both require adherence to a treatment regimen which involves avoidance of certain substances.

As we noted earlier: two diseases with so much in common ought to be treated in a very similar fashion.

Unfortunately, they aren't.

To illustrate: let's take two patients, both male and in their late thirties. Assume that in recent years both have experienced a variety of persistent and puzzling symptoms: extreme irritability, pronounced mood swing, numerous medical complaints. At last, their physicians discover a hidden cause. Jerry, age thirty-eight, is a diabetic. Mack, age thirty-nine, is an alcoholic.

Neither one is particularly glad to learn his diagnosis. Mack, of course, is a little angrier, because alcoholism has a stigma attached to it. Nevertheless, both eventually ask their physicians a variation of the same question.

Jerry: "Does this mean I'm on a restricted diet for the rest of my life?"

Mack: "Does this mean I can never drink again?"

The doctor refers both on for further counseling. He motivates them to participate with vivid descriptions of the consequences of untreated diabetes and alcoholism.

Both men's families strongly support the idea of treatment. "It may sound funny," Jerry's wife says, "but I'm almost relieved to find out he's diabetic. He's been so hard to live with lately. And you can't talk to him about it—no matter how funny he was acting, he'd insist there was nothing wrong with him, and it was all my imagination. I was beginning to think I was crazy."

Mack's wife tells a similar tale. "Living with him is like being on a roller coaster," she says. "Some days, he's a wonderful man. But other times, you just can't please him. I knew it had something to do with the drinking, but he doesn't slur his speech or fall down or that kind of stuff. So how could I call him an alcoholic?"

With considerable urging, both agree to enroll in treatment programs. Jerry goes to a diabetes clinic. Mack enters a residential program for alcoholism.

The night before he's supposed to show up for admission, Mack goes out and gets drunk. *What the hell,* he thinks, *it could be my last chance.*

Jerry, meanwhile, eats most of a quart of ice cream the evening before entering the program. His rationalization is identical to Mack's.

At the clinic Jerry is assessed by a counselor. He completes a detailed history that includes an analysis of his dietary and exercise habits, his medical status, and his daily behavior patterns.

Mack also completes an intake interview. However, his assessment includes not only questions about his drinking but a thorough examination of his childhood, his relationships with his parents, his religious background, his hobbies, his vocational training, how well he communicates with his wife, the current state of his career, and his feelings about himself as a man, as a father, as a husband, as a son.

The goals of treatment are clearly explained to Jerry. Mack, on the other hand, is asked to write out his *own* goals. Not just in terms of recovering from his disease, but in nearly every aspect of his life: mental and physical well-being, professional or occupational achievement, spiritual needs, family harmony, personal growth.

Jerry's diabetes rehabilitation program includes education, reading, and supportive group counseling. He's encouraged to ask questions and take notes for further study. Every activity is related to accomplishing certain goals, which, it is explained, are regarded as essential to successful treatment. Jerry is instructed to:

1. *Learn about diabetes,* so that he understands its nature and is not burdened by misconceptions.
2. *Self-diagnose*—that is, identify the symptoms of the disease in his own experience and to accept the reality that he is diabetic.
3. *Learn to follow the best treatment regimen,* so that he can avoid further problems, especially the dangerous consequences of uncontrolled diabetes.
4. And begin taking *personal responsibility* for treatment, rather than relying totally on his doctors and nurses for motivation and monitoring.

Once again, Mack's program is very different. Although he, too, is given information about alcoholism, its importance is discounted. "Knowledge won't keep you sober," his counselor insists. "At best, it'll turn you into an educated drunk."

Likewise, the goals of treatment are not so clearly defined. A survey of activities might lead us to conclude that the program has *dozens* of goals. Mack finds himself participating in:

Group therapy sessions
Individual therapy sessions

Family therapy groups
Spiritual counseling
Crafts classes
Art therapy
Role-playing sessions
"Personal growth" groups.

Quite a change, isn't it? It's remarkable that two diseases with so much in common could be treated in such dissimilar fashion.

Jerry's program is (1) entirely focused on his presenting problem, (2) easily explained, and (3) monitored through the completion of tasks. Mack's program, by comparison, is (1) amazingly broad in scope, (2) not strongly focused on the problem which brought him to treatment, and (3) structured so as to make it nearly impossible to measure progress (or lack of it).

Even though diabetes and alcoholism both may be, as the textbooks assert, chronic, progressive, and potentially fatal diseases, an examination of treatment method would lead one to believe that *diabetes is clearly more of a disease than alcoholism.*

In Chapter 1 we defined *task-oriented* treatment as being designed to accomplish specific behavioral changes that help the patient live within the boundaries set by a disease. *Issue-oriented* treatment, on the other hand, we defined as focusing on the patient identifying and dealing with hidden issues—internal conflicts and unresolved feelings.

Clearly, Jerry's program is task-oriented while Mack's is focused on issues.

Our opinion: Mack's program could learn a great deal from Jerry's.

By borrowing some of the methods and techniques of medical rehabilitation, we can develop addiction treatment programs which do the following:

1. Maximize the impact on the addict/alcoholic.

There's a rule of thumb in changing behavior: *to increase impact, focus attention.* Where Mack's program is devoted to unearthing and clarifying a variety of issues—many of which are only peripherally related to alcoholism—we might instead choose to focus on the need to arrest the disease and to establish a stable program of recovery.

2. *Develop clear goals for the patient and the counselor.*

This is the only way to make sure that both parties are working on the same thing at the same time. When the addict asks (as they inevitably do) what treatment is supposed to accomplish, the counselor should have an answer that makes sense.

The alcoholic should be able to concentrate on solving the problems that brought him into treatment instead of unearthing ever newer and more complex issues to distract him from his primary purpose.

3. *Simplify the principal elements of successful treatment into* TASKS *that the patient can complete.*

Everyone agrees that treatment should be individualized—that is, tailored to the needs of a particular addict or alcoholic.

But we must remember that there are *two ways* to fit the treatment to the patient. One is to design the program around the personality of each individual. The epitome would be classical psychoanalysis. It sounds terrific—the idea of treating every patient as a totally unique being is an attractive one—but in practice there are many disadvantages: it's painfully slow, forbiddingly expensive, and often unsuccessful. And it's never had a good track record with addiction.

Fortunately there's another method. It involves taking everything known about effective treatment of a given disease and boiling it down into a few simple directions that anybody can follow. These are then handed to the patient as a "prescription" for recovery.

The message: *Follow this path, and you'll get where you need to go. Stray too far, and you could run into trouble.*

On paper, it might seem like everyone is lumped together, without regard for individual differences. In practice, it's just the opposite. Though every patient is involved in similar activities, based on the same principles, no two people are doing exactly the same thing. Because each person is "cutting and pasting" the program to fit his or her peculiar situation, the alcoholic is given the opportunity to use the directions in the manner that produces the most direct benefit.

In fact, that's the approach used in the Twelve Steps of Alcoholics Anonymous. It's also a widespread practice in the treatment of many other diseases. Our version: outline the activities required to stay sober in the form of tasks, which the professionals help the patient to complete. As he finishes each task, the addict brings himself that much closer to the ultimate goal.

4. *Prioritize activities in the first months of treatment.*

In an issue-oriented program, you're always having to decide what to deal with *today:* your "grief" over losing the bottle, or your conflicts with your mate, or your unresolved rage at your dead alcoholic father, or your desire to make a career change, and so on. Every time you think you've got your priorities straight, something happens that brings to mind yet another issue.

Task-oriented programs are very different. When you don't know what to do, you can work on a task. They're numbered, so you always know which one to do next.

5. *Measure progress.*

One of the big problems with issue-oriented treatment programs is that it's difficult to tell whether or not the patient is improving.

The fact that's he's working on some identified psychological issue doesn't automatically mean that he has a good plan for staying off drugs once he leaves the program. You could say he's making progress—but not in addressing the problem that brought him to treatment in the first place.

In this respect, task-oriented treatment has obvious advantages. You need only determine whether or not the patient is completing the tasks. And since the tasks themselves are designed to bring the alcoholic into a position of stable sobriety, it's also easy to figure out whether or not he's likely to succeed.

Let us clarify something: it is not our intention to deny people the opportunity to explore their many interpersonal and psychological issues. Our point is that treatment programs operate within a limited time framework. No matter how many unresolved issues exist, we have a certain number of weeks or months in which to motivate an alcoholic or addict into a program of ongoing recovery.

If that doesn't happen, the patient is going to drop out of treatment. Or, if you prefer: the disease wins another round.

Addiction treatment programs should be designed with this in mind. Treatment must have impact on behavior. And for that purpose, we regard a task-centered approach as far superior.

Task-Centered Treatment Program

What goes on in a task-centered addictions program?

Picture a very intensive training program rather than a psychiatric hospital. The patients are there to learn, and to put their learning into practice.

In essence it's a *school for sobriety.*

The task-centered model adapts well to any environment, with only minor adjustments. It fits beautifully into the average general hospital. It works equally well in nonhospital residential settings. It's easy to operate on an outpatient basis and can be provided relatively inexpensively. Almost any program that wants to use it, can.

Here's a typical day in such a program.

Classes begin right after breakfast. First, there's a brief *community meeting,* where patients hash out problems within the patient group—not emotional problems, mind you, but the problems of everyday living (who's hogging the telephone, coming late to class, and so forth). This is important because the patients themselves are responsible for running the program. When a problem arises—take lateness, for example—the staff turns it over to the patient community. The patients themselves work out a solution.

The first lecture of the day is always on some aspect of addictive disease—topics range from blackouts to heredity to the development of tolerance, to medical hazards associated with drug use, to relapse or the importance of aftercare. The patients take notes, because they are accountable for the information. They will use it in treatment assignments given to them by their counselor and in completing the *ten tasks of early recovery* (see Chapter 6).

If somebody is forced to miss a lecture—because of a scheduled medical test, for example—they can see it later on videotape. All of the school's lectures—nearly fifty at this point—are available as a "resource library" for the patient.

In the afternoon, patients attend a group therapy session. There's a difference between this group and ordinary psychotherapy groups, however. Group members are given a task that is designed to advance the goals of treatment. The patients know the task and are expected to work on it during the session. A sample task: identify the symptoms of addiction in your own experience. This relates directly to one of the most important goals of treatment: self-diagnosis—accepting the reality of addictive disease.

There's yet another lecture to come, followed by an evening foray to a self-help group, such as Alcoholics or Narcotics Anonymous. These groups form the basis for maintaining recovery, so participation is emphasized from the outset. Patients aren't just passive participants, either. Many have been given assignments that involve meeting AA members and perhaps arranging to attend AA with them following discharge.

Each patient has a primary physician, counselor, and nurse. Again, they serve as teacher and consultant rather than therapist, guru, or spiritual advisor. They help the patient identify and remedy flaws in his or her own plan for recovery and provide practical guidance where needed.

As the addict undergoes treatment, so does the family. But instead of spending time in psychotherapy groups, family members have their own *ten tasks* to complete (see Chapter 5). These are designed to make it easier to accept and deal with the changes that inevitably result when someone close to you stops drinking or using drugs.

When the intensive phase of treatment is over, addict and family enter an aftercare program designed to continue the learning process and to promote the transition from a drinking to a sober lifestyle.

The schedule looks much like that found in thousands of treatment programs, all over America. The difference lies in what happens in the lectures, groups, and individual counseling sessions. Instead of digging up issues that may be impossible to resolve, the addict devotes time and energy to learning how to treat his or her disease.

By now, you should have a clearer idea of the importance of the disease model and the task-centered approach to the creation of a good treatment program. We're ready to take a practical look at actually choosing one.

The Keys to Identifying Quality Treatment

Most people approach the selection of a treatment program as they would the task of buying a new car. And in fact, the two processes do have something in common.

Most buyers assume that all new cars of any given make are pretty much equal. And (they think) even if I get a lemon, they're going to provide me with a safety blanket: a multi-year, multi-thousand mile warranty. Thus, superficial window-dressing tends to get more attention than actual product: the convenience of the dealership to your home or place of business, ensuring easy repairs; various rebates, discounts, special packages, and generous financing; and most of all, a spectacular showroom filled with gleaming examples of technological achievement.

Things aren't much different when you go to choose a treatment program. The program itself becomes the product. The facility where it is housed is the equivalent of the showroom. If you're operating on the assumption that treatment is a "new car" kind of product, you'll be tempted to buy on the basis of location and setting.

You'll be impressed by exercise equipment, swimming pools, tennis courts, nature trails. You'll want to look at the menu to see how patients are fed. You'll examine the schedule of activities with an eye toward diversity and impressive-sounding titles.

"Oh, look, Mabel," you might exclaim. "They've got Massage every Tuesday, followed by Men's and Women's Self-Discovery Groups. Doesn't that sound therapeutic?"

Ancillary features become more important than the product itself. After all, you assume all programs are the same. You shop for the extras.

That's the problem. Your basic assumption may be incorrect. All treatment programs are not created equal—and the differences between them are more profound than the size of the swimming pool or the number of times they serve lasagna every week.

In fact, the odds are that there exist a number of very well-appointed treatment programs with plenty of great-sounding activities but with a program of treatment that is decidedly second-rate. The extras are terrific, but if that's what you're looking for, you'll get more for your money on an ocean cruise.

Here's the reality, as we see it.

Good programs can be run in almost any environment. So can bad programs. In both cases, the key features are often hidden. The automobile analogy holds: if you don't know an exhaust pipe from a transmission, you'll probably buy a car from the nicest salesman in the prettiest showroom. If, on the other hand, you know what to look for . . .

Think of it this way: treatment is a "used car" product. Variances in quality are not always obvious to the naked eye. With that warning, here is what we search for when we choose a treatment program for a dear friend or family member who lives in another area.

Key One

The program uses a disease model.

Most Americans agree with the statement, "Alcoholism is a disease." However, that statement may mean something different to each respondent. The same thing is true with treatment programs. To one, a "disease model" implies that you treat the alcoholic as you would a diabetic or a heart patient—with an emphasis on education and on changing behavior so as to avoid relapse. To another, it includes in-depth explorations of the alcoholic's childhood in the name of working through various unresolved "issues" the program believes are important to mental health.

In our view, only the first program qualifies as a disease model. Earlier we described the second as a program of "psychoanalysis in sheep's clothing."

Example of the Wrong Way to Address This Question. Simply asking the staff at a treatment program if they believe alcoholism is a disease. You'll almost always get a "yes" answer, but it tells you nothing about how that program treats alcoholics.

Example of Right Way to Address It. Bring a list of questions about the treatment itself, and compare the responses to the recommendations you find in this book or in others based on a chronic disease model (see the annotated Suggested Reading list).

Key Two

The program is oriented toward measurable goals.

Recovery is not a free-form, spontaneous exercise in self-discovery. It's a means to an end—survival and health. The only way to measure whether or not you're making any progress toward this end is through the attainment of measurable goals.

In a disease model program, these goals should include the following:
1. The addict learns about addictive disease.
2. Based on this new knowledge, the addict comes to the conclusion that he/she suffers from addictive disease.
3. Now motivated, the alcoholic receives intensive instruction in the best methods for treating this disease.
4. The addict begins to take personal responsibility for treatment.
5. Accordingly, he or she learns how to use resources in the community.
6. Lastly, the addict learns to recognize the warning signs of relapse, and learns how to reduce that risk.

These aren't the *only* goals that programs have, but they give you some idea what every program should be striving to achieve.

Wrong Way to Address This Question. Asking the program staff to tell you about their treatment philosophy. You'll hear something along these lines: "We believe in addressing the needs of the whole person"; or (worse yet), "Every patient is unique—we try to fit the treatment to the individual"; or (still worse), "We deal with the physical, psychological, emotional, and spiritual needs of the chemically dependent person." We believe it is impossible for anyone to figure out, on the basis of these statements, exactly what that treatment program intends to do during the course of treatment. They're slogans, not explanations.

Right Way to Address It. Ask them to explain how they achieve some of the goals listed above. You needn't go through the entire list; if you get a satisfactorily rational answer to one or two, you're probably dealing with a good program.

Key Three

The program emphasizes education for the patient.

The biggest stumbling block to treatment is sheer ignorance. Therefore, all good programs emphasize the importance of imparting new knowledge to the alcoholic and those around him.

Bad programs, on the other hand, teach you almost nothing of value. You leave feeling more confused than when you entered.

Wrong Way to Address This Question. "Do you educate the alcoholic?" You'll get a meaningless "yes" response.

Right Way to Address It. "What do you teach the alcoholic (or addict) about the disease?"

Key Four

The program emphasizes group counseling.

Groups are the best method for allowing patients to relate their new knowledge to their own experience and that of others. The best groups for addictions patients are *task-oriented*—in other words, designed to work toward the goals of treatment, rather than simply to give patients a chance to socialize.

Wrong Way to Address This Question. "Do you have group therapy?"

Right Way to Address It. "What is the purpose of group therapy in your program?" or "What are you trying to accomplish in group therapy?"

Key Five

The staff is selected because of their expertise in addictions treatment.

It's obvious, isn't it? Any good specialized program should be staffed by persons competent in that specialty. There are programs, nevertheless, where staff members may have little or no expertise in addictions treatment and are simply there because they have an appropriate credential to practice medicine, psychiatry, or psychotherapy.

Because addictions treatment is a "stepchild" of several disciplines, you can't tell much about a professional's orientation or philosophy toward alcoholism treatment by looking at his license or degree. You have to ask them about their approach—and you have to have enough knowledge to evaluate their answers.

Wrong Way to Address This Question. "Do you have a good staff?" (You think someone will say, "Actually, our staff is completely inadequate"—even if it's true?)

Right Way to Address It. "Does your program specialize in addictions treatment? Are the staff selected because of their expertise in this area? What criteria are used in selecting staff? What educational background or other experiences are required?"

One important point: some programs feel it's crucial that the staff be composed entirely of persons who are themselves recovering alcoholics or drug addicts. There are a number of extremely gifted recovering counselors, but from a disease perspective, making recovery a prerequisite for counseling makes no sense.

If you had cancer, would you insist that the doctor also have cancer? Wouldn't you be more concerned that he be skilled at the *treatment* of cancer?

Key Six

The program has a good method for determining who should be treated as an inpatient or outpatient.

Some patients do beautifully in an outpatient setting, in which they come in for treatment several days weekly but live at home and probably continue to go to work. For many others, this is simply a prelude to relapse.

A good program has a reliable, understandable method for differentiating promising outpatient candidates from unlikely ones. For example, patients who might *not* do well in outpatient programs include:

1. Someone with a severe psychiatric disorder as well as a drug or alcohol problem.
2. Someone with a severe *physical* disorder as well as alcoholism or drug dependency.
3. Someone with recent heavy use of sedative drugs.
4. Someone who is without a stable home or family environment.
5. Someone who has already demonstrated failure to remain sober in an outpatient program.

In a task-centered model, outpatient treatment works very much like inpatient treatment. You use the same methods to accomplish the same goals. The addict attends several sessions weekly—including education and group counseling—and works on a "treatment plan" assigned by a primary counselor. He or she also enters an aftercare program upon completion and is involved in self-help groups such as the Twelve Step fellowships.

Since outpatient treatment is by definition *less intensive* than residential programs, it takes longer to complete. Our own outpatient program, for example, does exactly the same thing as the inpatient program—but in seven weeks rather than three.

Wrong Way to Address This Question."Do you offer both inpatient and outpatient treatment?"

Right Way to Address it. "How do you decide who gets treatment on an outpatient or inpatient basis? What are your criteria?"

Key Seven

The program has good aftercare.

Because addictive disease is chronic and we have no cure, aftercare becomes a key ingredient in recovery.

An aftercare program involves attending a group session at least once weekly for a specified period following completion of an intensive inpatient or outpatient program. The aftercare program should emphasize ongoing treatment of the disease and discuss issues related to recovery, such as nutrition, avoiding relapse, using AA, and so forth.

If you or your loved one is thinking of attending a program at some distance from where you live, the most important question you can ask has to do with the program's provisions for aftercare. If the program, for example, tells you that they simply refer patients to AA instead of an organized aftercare program, that isn't a good sign. Left to his or her own devices, the average new graduate of a treatment program will attend a few meetings and then drop out. It takes some systematic follow-up to establish real sobriety.

Wrong Way to Address This Question. Simply asking the program if they offer aftercare.

Right Way to Address It. "What does your Aftercare Program consist of? Where is it located? How much does it cost?"

Key Eight

The program should use abstinence as the criterion for successful outcome.

Many people find this difficult to understand, but different programs have different definitions of "success." So when you hear that a program has such and such a rate of "successful outcome," your first question should be: What do you mean by success?

An example: we knew of one program that defined success as "measurable improvement in significant areas of life." Thus if the alcoholic was adjudged to have made progress in family relations, career, or psychological health, he could be counted a success—whether or not he was still drinking.

Still another program measured success in terms of the patient's willingness to continue in treatment. If, a year after completion of the inpatient program, the alcoholic was still trotting off to see the therapist every week, the program assumed he or she was benefiting from treatment.

Yet another program measured success in terms of the frequency of drinking episodes. If a fellow got drunk eight times a year before treatment, and only five after treatment, that could qualify as a successful outcome.

Aside from this obvious sophistry, there's a legitimate problem which haunts treatment: the need to rely on patient self-report to measure success. The flaw: *addicts who relapse almost always lie about their drug use.* And if they're successful in concealing relapses from those around them, the program will simply never find out.

Nevertheless, if you believe that addiction represents a chronic, progressive, and potentially fatal disease, the only truly successful outcome involves abstinence from alcohol and drugs. Whatever the method for achieving abstinence, it should always remain the goal.

Wrong Way to Address This Question. "What is your success rate?"

There are two things wrong with this question. First, the answer won't tell you how the program measures success. Second, since all programs have both successes or failures, how do you know your alcoholic will fall in the "success" group? (Admit it: a program that gets your alcoholic sober has a 100-percent success rate as far as you're concerned. If he gets drunk when he leaves, its success rate is zero, no matter how well anyone else does.)

Right Way to Address It. Remember that treatment outcome depends in large part on what you start with. Describe the alcoholic or addict to the staff and ask them how this kind of patient responds to the treatment they offer.

Example: "The person I'm trying to help is a forty-six-year-old employed man with a stable family [or a nineteen-year-old poly-drug user; or a twenty-six-year-old cocaine addict who lives with her dealer; or whatever]. Do you treat many patients like this? How do they respond to treatment? What percentage of patients with this profile complete Aftercare?"

And lastly: "How do you measure success?" Look for the magic word "abstinence."

Key Nine

The program should give good value for the money.

Good treatment often costs quite a bit. Unfortunately, so does bad treatment. Some of the least effective programs are among the most expensive.

Some advice: treatment programs that emphasize a view of the mountains or ocean, gourmet food, and fifteen different varieties of psychotherapy tend to turn out graduates who have a gorgeous tan, an improved backhand, and a vocabulary of the latest pop-psych phrases. But these are not in themselves very good indicators of the quality of addiction treatment. It could be terrific; it could be terrible. You can't tell by the atmosphere. You should look a little deeper into the treatment itself.

Another bit of advice: wherever the staff consists primarily of persons with advanced medical or psychological degrees, the cost goes up. The more education you have, the more you can charge for your services. Are those services necessarily better for the addictions patient than those of persons with less formal medical or psychological training? Probably not—up until the last decade, most medical, psychological, and social work training included few (if any) specific courses in addictions treatment. Most good alcoholism doctors learned how to treat alcoholism *after* they left school.

What constitutes "good value"? In our view, it's a program that does three things:

1. Sets forth a logical, organized, and effective plan for getting someone sober;
2. carries out that plan exactly as promised;
3. with a minimum of distraction and unnecessary activity.

There will be no guarantee of success, of course. After all, we're talking about sick human beings, not robots. But the chances of good outcome are always higher where these three conditions are met.

Wrong Way to Address This Question. "How much does this program cost?"

Right Way to Address It. "What do we get for our money?"

When You Can't Pay for Treatment

It's a fact of life for many people. Drug addicts tend to spend all their money on drugs before they ever consider treatment. And the segment of the population that is hit hardest by the current epidemic—eighteen- to thirty-year-olds—is the one with the fewest financial resources.

Just about every city and county in America has a number you can call to obtain free services. The principal difference between public and private resources is that there may be a waiting list. That doesn't mean you'll inevitably have to wait as long as you might think: a lot of people will drop off the list, and your name will move up rapidly. Contact your local Health Department or government office for the appropriate information.

Key Ten

_____

The program should make an effort to educate the family as well as the addict.

This should require no further explanation. Whether or not you take advantage of the services offered to the family is up to you, but the program should offer them, anyway.

Wrong Way to Address This Question. "Do you have a family program?"

Right Way to Address It. "What do you do to educate the family? Does it extend into Aftercare? What is your approach toward the family member?"

Remember: the acid test of a good treatment facility is its focus on the disease model and on clear-cut goals for the addicted person's recovery. It's not necessary that the staff answer every one of the above questions in exhaustive detail. If most of their answers are straightforward and focused on serving *your* needs rather than the institution's, you've probably come to the right place.

Chapter Five

The Ten Tasks—
for Family or
Concerned Others

We said earlier that a task-centered program focuses on the completion of objectives rather than the exploration of issues.

Given: we can't cure addictive disease. Yet we have all seen that some people are more successful at *treating* it than others. We know thousands of people complete treatment programs and go on to establish stable, happy sobriety. We also know thousands relapse.

We know too that some *families* adjust better to recovery than others. Numerous studies have indicated that the divorce/separation rate is high after one partner is treated for addiction.

Experts debate the causes of both phenomena, blaming differences in personality, upbringing, social status, environment.

Our perspective is somewhat different. We ask a simpler question: What is it "winners" do that relapsers don't? What is it some families learn about living with addiction that others seem unable to grasp—and which might make the difference between stability and dissolution?

And since the great majority of relapse occurs in the first year of recovery, we assume that this is probably where success or failure is decided—and therefore is the period where the need for clear direction and guidance is most pronounced.

That's why we created the ten tasks of recovery. They are designed to take a recovering addict and his or her family through the initial months of abstinence and to establish a stable basis for ongoing sobriety. Of course, there are any number of other activities that people can use to support recovery. The ones we present here are just the *essentials*—without which many simply won't make it.

One thing we've observed: for the recovering addict, completing these ten tasks makes it harder to fail. If someone does relapse, it's pretty easy to identify the cause, and to figure out what to do to restore sobriety.

That isn't all. Because alcoholism and drug dependency almost always involve and affect the family, there are ten tasks for you to perform as well. When you've completed them, it should be easier to live with a person who is recovering from addictive disease.

It's tempting to compare these tasks to the Twelve Steps of the self-help groups. But those represent a *spiritual* program—something to live by for the rest of your life. Our tasks are specific to the early weeks and months of recovery. They constitute a simple program of behavorial and attitudinal change, which helps addict and family through the ups and down of this crucial phase.

One important note: very few alcoholics or addicts are able to establish any kind of recovery without outside help. Therefore, we assume that the addict will get involved in professional treatment *and* in a self-help fellowship such as one of the Twelve Step groups. That's why we haven't bothered to include "seeking professional help" and "joining a Twelve Step program" among our tasks of recovery. The tasks themselves are a guide to *what should happen in the initial months of treatment*—and in fact, you'll be asked to make extensive use of others, including counselors and even "sponsors," throughout.

We've included a chapter on how to use a Twelve Step program later on in Chapter 9.

Whether you are addict or family member, it's a good idea to read both sets. You can find out what the disease looks like from the other side.

We'll begin with the ten tasks for the family member or other concerned person.

Task One

Learn about the disease—involve yourself in the treatment process.

The reason why you must educate yourself about addictive disease is obvious. All along, ignorance has been your biggest enemy. Perhaps not even ignorance: *misinformation.*

So gather accurate information about the disease. Take notes. Attend seminars. Ask questions.

We know that the bulk of the responsibility for successful treatment is in the hands of the patient. But you have to realize that there's more than one patient here.

You can't sit back and watch TV, telling yourself, "Well, I've done everything I can do. Now it's up to him."

Once in a while, we run across a family that wants to disappear completely from the scene once the alcoholic is safely in treatment.

"Why don't you come to some education sessions?" we'll ask.

"It isn't convenient," they say. "Besides, we really need a break. All we've been thinking about for I-don't-know-how-long is alcoholism. I'm burned out on the whole subject. I mean, there's nothing we can do now, anyway. We want to help, but it's really not our problem, is it?"

It isn't?

This seems to us to be a form of denial. If addiction were exclusively the addict's problem, then why do the people around it suffer? Why do they devote hours and weeks and months and years to futile attempts at dealing with it? And just suppose—for argument's sake—that the alcoholic relapses? That won't affect family members or other closely involved people?

Once again, it helps to think of addictive disease in light of similar disorders. Suppose someone in a family contracts cancer. That's an enormous shock, not only to the victim but to the whole family. But even after the initial blow, the family has to deal with the course of treatment. Surgery, chemotherapy, repeated hospitalizations, periods of incapacitation—do we really think the family is unchanged by this?

Admittedly, it isn't fair that someone else's addiction could affect our existence to such a degree. Then again, it isn't fair when cancer or diabetes or heart disease does the same thing.

The reality: this person's recovery (or lack of it) is going to exert a powerful influence on our lives, for better or for worse. The closer we are to the alcoholic, the more profound this effect will be.

And in turn, our response—no matter how we try to avoid it—will influence (positively or negatively) the addict's recovery.

So there's no middle ground here. No easy way to abdicate responsibility. We can become part of the solution—or we're likely to remain part of the problem.

In which case, *we'll probably continue to suffer.*

How to Learn about Addiction

1. Start by reading the sections of the Guide to Addictive Disease at the back of the book which relate to your loved one's addiction(s).
2. Then: take out a piece of paper and write out the definitions for:
   a. tolerance
   b. withdrawal
   c. loss of control
   d. maintenance pattern
   e. chronic
   f. progressive
   g. primary.
3. Identify the pattern of your addict's recent addiction (see Figures 2, 3, and 4). How is his or her behavior consistent with the picture of addiction described in Chapter 1 and the Guide? Where does it differ?
4. If you find you're still not sure your loved one qualifies as an addict or alcoholic—make a list of your doubts, in the form of questions, and discuss it with a counselor or someone else familiar with addiction. Do this until you feel you understand:
   a. What addiction is
   b. How the diagnosis of alcoholism or drug dependency is made
   c. Why ongoing treatment will be necessary for ongoing sobriety

d. Why it benefits you to participate in the treatment process.
5. Turn to the Suggested Reading list at the back of the book. Select two additional books of particular interest to you. Read them.

How Do I Know When This Task Is Complete?

1. You're able to explain addiction—its dynamics, terminology, even the mysteries of addictive behavior—to others who need the information.
2. You're able to list the symptoms of addiction and apply them to your own experience of involvement with an addict or alcoholic.
3. You understand the meaning of the statement, "Addiction is a chronic, progressive, primary, and potentially fatal disease," and can explain to others what that means in terms of ongoing treatment—both for the addict and for those around him or her.

Task Two

Identify enabling and provoking behaviors.

Just as the alcoholic needs to *self-diagnose* through a process of identifying symptoms, so too does the family need to identify and change enabling and provoking behaviors.

Look at it this way: suppose the alcoholic or drug addict goes through a treatment program, returns home, and begins doing everything exactly as he did before he entered treatment. What do you think will happen?

You guessed it: he'll eventually relapse. The alcoholic's lifestyle is built around drinking. It's designed to work best with a steady (or in some cases, periodic) influx of alcohol or drugs. It doesn't work very well without that influx.

Similarly, what do you think will happen if those around the addict fail to change their approach? Isn't it likely they'll once again get the same result as in the past?

Which is more drinking.

Once you realize that misguided enabling and provoking both protect and promote drug use, you'll see how changing these

NARCOTICS DEPENDENCY: PROGRESSION AND RECOVERY

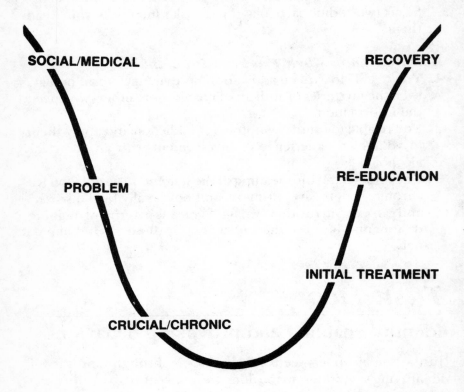

Figure 4. Narcotics Dependency: Progression and Recovery. Interveners make it their business to learn about addiction. In this example, narcotics dependency leads a predictable course toward final physical and psychological collapse. Note the course of recovery is similarly predictable. This goal of recovery is your ultimate reason for educating yourself about the addictive disease.

SOCIAL/MEDICAL
First introduction
Recreational/Medicinal use
Powerful memory effects
Increased attraction to narcotics
Developing tolerance

PROBLEM
Diminishing effect from normal
  dose
Initial signs of withdrawal
Vivid dreams, waking thoughts of
  drug
Craving for drug
Increased amount, frequency of
  use
Preoccupation with availability
Loss of interest in other activities
Involvement in criminal subculture
Abandons "lesser drugs"
Increasing financial expense
"Maintenance" pattern
Persistent strong craving
Severe withdrawal
Sexual performance deteriorates
Unable to get "high"

CRUCIAL/CHRONIC
Obsession with drug availability
Regressive, childlike behavior
Criminal activity
No tolerance for frustration
Gets arrested
Loss of "straight" friends
Loss of family
Reliance on "dope buddies"
Financial ruin
Continued use despite adverse
  consequences
Depressed, suicidal thoughts
Impaired thinking constant
Strong overdose risk
Painful, persistent withdrawal
Complete moral and psychological
  collapse
**(As narcotic addiction cycle
  continues, four options:
  Recovery, Multiple Relapse,
  Jail, Death.)**

INITIAL TREATMENT
Total defeat admitted
Desire to give up drugs
Detoxification

RE-EDUCATION
Learns addiction is disease
Abandons moral approach to
  illness
Self-diagnosis
Learns about treatment of disease
Meets recovering addicts
Begins working in groups
Regular nourishment taken

RECOVERY
Begins working Twelve Steps
Physical health improves
Examines own defenses
Craving diminishes
Natural rest and sleep
Increase of emotional control
Appreciates possibilities of new life
Decreased defense mechanisms
Assumption of responsibility for
  own actions
New interests develop
Others begins to appreciate efforts
Facts faced with courage
Recovery program becomes first
  priority
Continues to new life

behaviors greatly increases the addict's chances for recovery. And how failing to make changes greatly increases the chance for relapse.

Here's a list of common enabling and provoking behaviors.

Enabling. Behavior that protects the alcoholic or addict from the consequences of drinking or drug use.
1. Making excuses for problems caused by drinking or drug use.
2. Pretending to accept the alcoholic's excuses simply to avoid conflict.
3. Protecting the alcoholic from potential crises associated with drinking, such as:
    a. Taking care of him or her physically
    b. Bailing him or her out of legal or financial problems
    c. Allowing him or her to move into your home when drinking or drug use has created a crisis elsewhere
    d. Hiding alcohol or drug involvement from employers or other authority figures.
4. Providing financial or other support so that the addict doesn't have to shoulder the normal responsibilities of adulthood.
5. Seeking advice from friends and counselors, then failing to follow through with it.

Provoking. Behavior that directly encourages drinking or drug use by an addict.
1. Nagging, throwing out alcohol or drugs, picking useless arguments about alcohol or drug use.
2. Allowing yourself to believe in the promises the addict makes, then getting angry when you discover he or she doesn't keep them.
3. Punishing the addict for drug use—withholding sex, money, affection, etc.—rather than addressing the underlying issue of addiction.
4. Manipulating others against the alcoholic so as to isolate him or her and create a state of "war" within the family.
5 Precipitating an argument when the alcoholic is intoxicated, bringing on a conflict that results in actual abuse or in more drinking.
6. Drinking with an alcoholic. Using drugs with an addict.

How Do I Know When This Task Is Complete?
1. You can identify at least five examples of enabling or provoking behavior in your own past.

2. You can explain the effects of enabling and provoking to others who need the information.

Task Three

Stop these enabling and provoking behaviors.

If you haven't already done so, eliminate these activities.

This, however, should create a "vacuum." In other words, if you don't enable or provoke, then what do you do?

Let's say you assumed control of all the household finances, simply because your mate was too debilitated to remember to pay bills. That was enabling on your part. You had a very good reason, but then again, enablers always do.

Maybe you never really wanted this additional responsibility. On the other hand, at this point you're afraid to relinquish it. Suppose the alcoholic relapses as in the past? What if he or she turns out to be irresponsible or unreliable even without alcohol?

So now you have a problem. To insist on maintaining control will perpetuate conflict with the alcoholic. To give up control will make you anxious.

The typical enabler, given this choice, will opt to keep the checkbook. It's less scary.

"Let him prove himself first," the enabler thinks. "Show me he can be trusted. Then we'll talk about taking on some responsibility for money."

Our recommendation: come up with an alternative solution that both

1. gets you out of the position where you're attempting to "control" the addict's behavior, and
2. partially relieves your anxiety about not being in control.

There are a number of ways to accomplish this. For example:
1. You could take steps to separate your finances to an extent, so that your income and assets would be protected.
2. You could arrange to have routine financial matters handled through an outside party, such as your accountant.
3. You could divide financial responsibility equally, so that each of you would have a certain amount of control over your joint resources.

4. Or whatever other plan you can agree on.
The point is to avoid situations in which you are attempting to control the addict.

This is important for three reasons.

First, it's bad for your relationship. Marriages and families aren't meant to have one completely dominant partner. A lot of them do, but that's why they're in trouble. It becomes a chronic bone of contention that eats away at whatever affection and respect still exists.

Second, it's too much work. Taking responsibility for other people's behavior greatly reduces the time available for your own duties—let alone for relaxing and enjoying life.

Finally, it's an impossible task. Once people are past a certain age, you can't watch over them all the time. You have to let them succeed—or fail—through their own efforts. To attempt to control the behavior of another adult is to leave yourself wide open to frustration and failure.

So unless you have a compelling need to feel frustrated and helpless, we advise you to avoid situations like this. Even though it may temporarily relieve your anxiety, it will create more problems in the long run.

Or perhaps you find yourself in a different dilemma: your child has been through a treatment program and is now ostensibly drug free. She's attending groups and seems to be following directions. Yet you find yourself feeling suspicious that she's still drinking or using drugs. Sometimes you think you smell alcohol when you walk past her. At other times, you think she "looks funny" or is moodier than she should be. You worry that she's secretly relapsed. You find yourself obsessed with the possibility. What if she's keeping it hidden from the counselors? Are they getting regular drug screens? Could she be substituting somebody else's urine, or faking the test in some other way? Should you search her room? Challenge her directly? What if she simply denies it? How would you know if she was telling the truth?

You discuss the problem with your friends. Some urge you to be confrontive, others advise you to ignore your suspicions. The people you usually rely on for advice seem to be at a loss.

As you grow more and more anxious, you discover a powerful urge to confront her with your doubts. After all, you think, it isn't right that you should have to worry. She should be willing to provide you with some evidence that she's drug free. She should be willing to help you deal with your feelings as you helped her with her own.

Now you have a problem. If you confront her, she'll go on the defensive, accuse you of paranoia, deny everything. Worse yet, you still won't believe her.

If you don't confront her, you won't sleep at night.

This is an ideal situation for a return to *provoking* behavior. It's tempting to convince yourself that confronting her with your suspicions would be in her best interest. That she owes you the reassurance you crave.

There are two problems here. First: in your present state of emotional upset, your approach is bound to be aggressive. Your words may sound reasonable, but your manner will reflect your underlying frustration, mistrust, and resentment. Second: at this point, the only answer you'll accept is an admission of failure. You won't believe any other explanation.

Your daughter will react to this underlying reality rather than to your overt message. And suppose she really is drug free, despite your suspicions? She'll be deeply hurt, and of course angered, by your mistrust. She might even use it as a perfect excuse for a relapse.

It's ironic. In your efforts to "make sure" she's drug free, you'll have obtained exactly the opposite result.

Again, we recommend an alternative course. Something which both

1. helps to reduce your anxiety to a manageable level, while at the same time,
2. takes the addict out of the position of being responsible for *your* feelings.

Want some suggestions? How about:

1. Calling and making an appointment with your daughter's counselor, to discuss your fears and get recommendations from an expert?
2. Taking the issue to a self-help group, such as Alanon, and discussing it at the meeting or with individual members who've been through the same experience.

Why is this a better method? Because it avoids an unproductive conflict with the addict while at the same time providing the reassurance you need. Where your friends were at a loss, the professionals and the Alanon people won't be. They've been through this before. (You'll learn more about Alanon later in this chapter, and in Chapter 9.)

At first, you won't feel completely comfortable with this approach. But it works better than the old one. After a while, you'll be impressed with the results. Success reinforces itself.

But, you ask, *What if I was right?* What if she is using drugs and is managing to hide it from the counselors? Wouldn't it have been better to nip it in the bud?

When an addict returns to drug use, it's only a matter of time before that fact becomes obvious. Once it does, that's the appropriate time for action. Effective action should include everyone involved in the treatment process: family, counselor, and so forth. A return to *provoking* behavior on the part of one family member isn't going to help the situation.

How Do I Know When This Task Is Complete?

1. You can make a list of alternatives you plan to use in situations where you once fell into enabling or provoking.
2. You've reviewed this plan with knowledgable advisors who've given you feedback on whether or not they think it will work.
3. You've put some of these new behaviors into practice, and discussed the outcome with advisors.
4. You find yourself becoming more confident about your new approach.

Task Four

Examine your thinking for resentments and for defense mechanisms.

You've already identified enabling and provoking behavior. Now let's take a look at what causes them.

Enabling and provoking are partly the product of a misguided concept of addiction. You interpret your experience with the addict in the light of certain preconceptions and you react accordingly. After awhile these responses become set. In other words, you find yourself reacting in the same way to the same situation, over and over again. In turn, these reaction patterns— based as they are on an erroneous view of the disease— unwittingly protect and provoke the addictive behavior. You find yourself responding in a way that gets you the result you don't want.

Now: let's take a close look at your attitude toward addiction and toward the addict.

There are two things we're looking for in particular:

1. Resentments

A resentment is a little different than simply getting angry. Resentments are held over time and almost always have to do with a situation in which you believe you were:
1. treated unfairly,
2. prejudiced against, or
3. victimized.

Because of the way addiction affects others within the family— and because of the extended period over which it develops—it is rare to encounter a family that doesn't have a fair amount of resentment toward the addict, or toward those they believe to be in some way "responsible" for the problem.

For example: a woman we knew devoted ten years of her life to futile attempts to get her husband into treatment for his chronic alcoholism. During this period she suffered through numerous separations, physical abuse, financial insecurity and, of course, mental anguish. Through it all, she stuck by him. Despite all the evidence she persisted in the belief that he would eventually stop drinking.

When he did—because of a truly memorable case of pancreatitis—she initially felt vindicated and relieved. At long last they had a chance at a normal relationship.

He completed a treatment program and began attending AA. He made a lot of new friends and in general responded well to sobriety. He even went out of his way to make his wife comfortable and to do things that she liked to do.

Her friends commented on the marvelous change in her husband. Still, no matter what he did, she found herself getting angrier and angrier with him.

At first, she could control it. "I must be going through a phase," she told herself. "He's being an angel. Why is it I want to bite his head off for nothing?"

She visited a therapist, who helped her to realize that she was angry because she couldn't forgive her husband for what had happened during his active alcoholism. "I know it's wrong," she would explain to her counselor. "But I just can't make myself get over what he did to me. The neglect, the abuse. Whenever I see him, I start remembering it. I just don't see how I can be expected to let go of this."

As time passed, she lost the ability to suppress her anger. Any error on his part, no matter how small, brought about an explosion of temper. She began to carry her anger to her friends. They told her she was being overcritical, especially in light of having recently achieved her longtime goal. She couldn't accept that. There must be something he's doing wrong, she decided; if not, why did she feel so angry? Couldn't they see how perfectly awful he was, despite his superficial good behavior?

Her husband was at first puzzled, then discouraged by this response. He felt he had to make up for what he hadn't provided in the past and tried desperately to please his wife. But it seemed to him that the more he tried, the more he failed her expectations.

After about a year, he moved out of the house. His wife told her friends that she expected him to get drunk within a month. Instead, he met and married another woman, and has remained sober.

To his wife, this was further proof that he never really loved her in the first place. If he had, she reasoned, would he have deserted her, after she'd spent years sticking up for him through thick and thin?

In reality, she drove him away. Where drinking once interfered, now her longstanding resentments prevented a normal relationship.

This is a good example of a problem based primarily on the way someone views addiction, rather than on the disease itself. In essence, this woman saw her husband's alcoholism not as a disease but as irresponsible, abusive, inconsiderate behavior. Accordingly, she believed he had an obligation to make up to her for his past sins. But when he tried, she refused to accept his amends.

You can understand her feelings: how could anyone make up for ten years of anguish? But therein lies the problem:

No one can. It's not possible for one person, no matter how guilty he may feel, to undo that kind of pain.

Part of the beauty of the disease model is that it allows people to set aside many of their resentments about the addict's past behavior. If someone is toxic from the use of drugs—cycling between intoxication and withdrawal, memory fogged, mood fluctuating, ridden with defense mechanisms—it's unreasonable to expect them to be reliable, considerate, open, warm, or attentive in everyday life. Any opinions formed during that period are really opinions about the disease rather than the person. Once the drug is removed, and the addict has a chance to recover from its effects, the underlying personality can again emerge.

Resentments are to a significant extent the product of our moralistic view of alcoholism. Most people cling to the belief that alcoholics are irresponsible, undisciplined drinkers, simply because they have no compelling reason to change their perspective. But if you happen to be personally involved with a recovering addict, this attitude—and the resentment it breeds—can be the source of chronic unhappiness, even long after drug use itself has stopped.

2. Defense Mechanisms

Like addicts, family members often live with addiction for years before they recognize it. This is because *defense mechanisms* interfere with their perceptions. Though many of these defenses are stripped away before the alcoholic enters treatment, some remain. These can, if not addressed, also block you from identifying problems in recovery.

Start by taking a look at the defenses that prevented you from seeing the extent and severity of the problem. As with the addict, your defenses probably fell into four categories:

Denial: *Inability to recognize a problem despite evidence of its existence.*

Example: A father discussing his seventeen-year-old son: "We knew he had a lot of problems. He was pretty hard to live with. We also knew he was drinking a lot. Every day, actually. But *alcoholism* . . . I just didn't see how that was possible. I mean, the kid played football. How could you be a football player and an alcoholic at the same time?"

Rationalization: *Developing excuses for problems caused by drinking or drug use.*

Example: A forty-two-year-old woman discussing her husband's alcoholism: "I knew he was drinking more and more. But it seemed like it was worse when he was under stress at work, so I kept telling myself, maybe when this project's done, and the pressure is off, he'll cut down . . . and then that project would end, and another one would begin, and it just seemed to get worse and worse . . . "

Externalizing: *Blaming addictive behavior on forces outside the addict.*

Example: A thirty-six-year-old man describing his mother's drug use: "I knew she was taking a lot of pills. I could see her getting sicker. Sometimes, we'd go over to her house for dinner and she'd be so stoned she'd fall asleep at the table. But I figured a lot of it was my Dad's fault. He's a really cold, unemotional person. They don't get along. . . . Anyway, I thought the pills were just a symptom, and their marriage was really the problem. So I'm afraid we just did nothing."

Minimizing: *Making problems seem less important, and therefore not worthy of attention.*

Example: A forty-year-old woman discussing a recent incident between herself and her husband: "He came home really drunk—he'd been out celebrating somebody's promotion—and he decided he wanted to go back out. I hid the keys, so he couldn't drive. He came into the bedroom and threw me on the bed and grabbed me by the throat and started choking me. I think I blacked out. I was never so scared in my life. But now I think that maybe he didn't know I was choking, because there was only the one light on, and it was pretty dark, and maybe he couldn't see my face turning blue . . . and I couldn't tell him because he was pressing on my throat . . . so maybe it's not fair to say that he was trying to hurt me . . . "

How long did it take you to recognize that you were involved with an addict?

If it took quite a while—Why? What prevented you from seeing it? Did you simply lack knowledge of the signs and symptoms? Was it that your alcoholic was so good at hiding it from you? Was it solely because you were preoccupied with other matters? Or not around the addict long enough to see any of the signs?

Or was it because you didn't want to think of someone you care about as an alcoholic or drug addict?

If it's the latter, you're not alone. Living in the same house with addiction is a lot like living near an earthquake fault. You know it's there—but you'd rather not think about it.

The ability to "selectively ignore" certain unpleasant aspects of reality seems to have been hard-wired into the human brain. Everybody does it in one way or another. To some extent, denial is what allows us to function in the face of insoluble problems. Addictive disease nevertheless thrives in an atmosphere of neglect, and defense mechanisms foster this environment.

How to Identify Defense Mechanisms in Your Own History

1. Learn the definition of each of the four primary defenses.
2. Write out a list of examples from your own experience in which your defense mechanisms prevented you from seeing the extent or severity of an alcohol- or drug-related problem.
3. Correlate your use of defense mechanisms with **enabling.** Did your perception of alcoholism—filtered through *denial, externalizing, rationalizing, or minimizing*—contribute to enabling?
4. Correlate your use of defense mechanisms with **intervention.** How did your defenses interfere with your chances of getting the alcoholic into treatment?

And remember, defense mechanisms don't automatically disappear once the alcoholic stops drinking—in the alcoholic's thinking, or in the family's.

How Do I Know When This Task Is Complete?

1. You can explain the four primary defense mechanisms to someone who doesn't understand them.
2. You can give at least five examples of how defense mechanisms blinded you to the extent and severity of the problem.
3. You can list resentments you feel about the alcoholic's drinking and about events that occurred during the active alcoholism.
4. You have shared these resentments with a professional or with others at a self-help group and received feedback on how to handle them without interfering with the addict's recovery.

5. You have developed an *alternate plan* for dealing with:
   a. Residual resentments that you may not presently be aware of but that may appear during the initial months of the alcoholic's sobriety.
   b. Your own defense mechanisms. How will you insure that you are able to maintain a realistic perspective during the next few months? Who will you use for feedback for your ideas? Who will you go to when you have questions?

Task Five

Begin treating your own problems.

We've talked at length about the extent to which addictive disease adversely affects those around it. These effects don't automatically disappear when the alcoholic stops drinking. So we'd like to recommend that you involve yourself in some form of counseling and/or self-help group, aimed at improving your own psychological health.

First, the self-help groups:

Alanon

The oldest and best known of the support groups for families of alcoholics, Alanon was founded by Lois Wilson, wife of one of the men who began Alcoholics Anonymous. Its structure is virtually indistinguishable from that of AA, and it uses the Twelve Step model—however, rather than emphasizing the alcoholic's powerlessness over alcohol, it emphasizes that the Alanon member is powerless over the alcoholic.

Alanon meetings lean toward the small-group discussion format, though content and membership vary considerably. In some meetings, a topic is set forth, usually concerning one of the Steps. In others, discussion is pretty much open. Sometimes, a speaker will relate his or her story of involvement with an alcoholic (as at AA Speaker Meetings).

Alanon's value to the new member is primarily in two areas:
1. *Practical advice* about living with an alcoholic (either one who's still drinking or newly in recovery).
2. *Support* for the ups and downs that dominate this period.

Regarding the first, Alanon can be a fount of information for those who live with an alcoholic; there's probably not a question or problem you can think of that someone at the meeting has not already faced. They can tell you what works, and what doesn't, in response to any number of common situations. The average therapist—unless he or she is a specialist in addictions—simply can't provide this information.

Second, Alanon has a significant advantage over professional counseling in terms of providing support, largely because

1. it's free, and
2. it's convenient.

Because Alanon charges nothing, there are no forms to fill out, no insurance coverage to verify, no payment plans to deal with. You just go. When they pass the hat, you chip in whatever you can afford to pay for coffee and the room itself.

Because there are Alanon meetings every night in most urban areas, it's easy to find one close to your home. There are also meetings in the daytime, and some of the meetings provide child care. Call your local Alanon or AA Intergroup for a directory.

In most areas there are special meetings for teenagers (Alateen) and even preteens. There are meetings for gays, foreign-language meetings, women's meetings, and meetings aimed at parents or adult children of alcoholics.

There's a trick to Alanon, however, just as there is to AA. Information, advice, and support is waiting—but you have to ask for it. You can't just wander into a meeting, spend an hour sipping coffee, and expect the assembled membership to seek you out and start giving you the guidance you so desperately need. Alanon, like AA, works on a principal of attraction rather than promotion. Most members won't force themselves on you, or make a point of establishing a personal relationship—unless they get some kind of signal that this is what you want. There are exceptions, of course, but the best idea is to initiate contact yourself.

Listen to the discussion at several different meetings. If someone says something you like, approach them after the meeting and tell them so. Introduce yourself as a newcomer and give a bit of your own story. The reception is usually warm. These people know what you're talking about.

Some newcomers get turned off when they hear another member tell a story about spending years with an alcoholic who never stopped drinking. It's a painful thought—that somehow, despite the efforts of those who love them, some alcoholics die of alcoholism. Remember, though: that doesn't have to happen to you. In Alanon, it's the exception rather than the rule. Stick around long enough to learn more and you'll find that's true.

Or perhaps you'll encounter a meeting where the conversation is decidedly spiritual, filled with references to God and the power of prayer. If that's not your style, don't assume all meetings operate that way. As with AA, the tone of a group reflects not only the Alanon philosophy but also the needs of the people who attend it. Try out a number of meetings; you'll find one that feels comfortable.

Lastly, you may be surprised at how little time is devoted to discussion of the trials and tribulations of living with an alcoholic. Alanon's focus is on the attitudes and behavior of its own members. They want to hear about you, not your addict.

There are similar groups geared to persons involved with narcotics and cocaine addicts. Whichever is the case, we recommend taking advantage of this resource.

Professional Counseling

Enabling and provoking behaviors are found in every addictive situation. They're common enough to be regarded as a "normal," or at least routine, byproduct of the disease. They need to be identified and changed, of course; but, in most cases, this presents few problems.

Sometimes, though, a family member's involvement goes way beyond simple enabling and provoking. They become what some psychologists like to call co-dependents, co-alcoholics, or co-addicts. In a purely psychological sense, they may become as "sick" as the alcoholic.

They don't get liver cirrhosis, of course. But they're likely to be every bit as miserable—and their behavior is as self-defeating.

Not everyone involved with an alcoholic or drug addict needs professional counseling. But this group generally does.

How do you determine whether or not you fit in this category?

Through yet another process of self-diagnosis. You examine your own experience (or that of others in your family) in light of certain signs and symptoms.

Let's look at this syndrome in some detail.

Co-Dependency: Love as a Disease

It should come as no surprise that love—that most admired of emotions—can sometimes be perverted into something quite destructive. Nowhere is this more obvious than in some instances of addictive disease.

We've discussed enabling and provoking as normal if unhelpful responses to undiagnosed addiction. Some persons, however, go far beyond the limits of ordinary enabling to develop a behavioral and psychological syndrome called co-dependency.

There are a number of definitions. Our favorite: *ongoing mutually destructive involvement with the sick, especially in the face of mounting negative consequences stemming from this involvement.*

Co-dependency isn't physiological in origin, like alcoholism. It develops from long-term exposure to chronic, progressively debilitating disease. It's most likely to appear where the disease is characterized by escalating levels of unpredictable behavior. It's also apt to appear when persons around the sick individual do not understand the causes of his or her behavior, and relate them to moral, psychological, or social difficulties rather than to an identifiable pathology.

Thus this syndrome is in a sense a byproduct of stigma associated with certain diseases. It develops more readily (although far from exclusively) in families of patients with stigmatized illnesses—alcoholism, narcotics addiction, schizophrenia—than in situations where the physical etiology of the disease is widely accepted.

What are its symptoms?

Obsession with the Behavior of the Addicted Person. Co-dependents frequently have difficulty devoting time and energy to anything other than the addict's behavior. This obsessive involvement represents a vain attempt to control or forestall certain negative aspects of addiction, and it continues in the face of repeated failures. When the alcoholic finally does stop drinking, the co-dependent may be unable to relax his or her vigilance, convinced that drinking will resume any minute.

Repeated Involvement in Relationships with Addicted Persons. This may be accompanied by an absence of interest in persons who aren't addicted. Notice the important difference between "addicted" and "recovering." The co-dependent will find persons with stable recovery much less fascinating than those still actively drinking or using drugs—or on the verge of relapse.

Immobilization in the Face of Active Addiction. Though co-dependents are often vocal in their complaints about drinking or drug use and may seek advice from a wide variety of friends and experts, they balk at taking positive action. Just as addicts routinely require external motivation to accept treatment, so do co-dependents resist help except when faced with a crisis.

Once the crisis is resolved, however, the co-dependent (again like the addict) is quick to resume a passive posture, falling back into an enabling and provoking role until the next crisis.

Inability to Avoid Provoking Behavior. Co-dependents regularly practice behaviors that they know from experience produce negative results, or even painful consequences. One lady we know is terrified to mention drinking to her husband when he's sober, yet never fails to angrily accuse him of being a drunken sot when he's dangerously intoxicated. This almost guarantees a verbal or even physical assault. Ironically, she lists "fear of his temper" as a reason she can't approach him about his drinking under normal circumstances.

Emotional Decompensation When the Addict is Recovering. Co-dependents, who may appear towers of strength during the worst of addiction, often become depressed, anxious, or openly hostile once the alcoholic is in treatment. They may even go so far as to unconsciously undermine the course of treatment.

In simpler terms: as the alcoholic gets better, the co-dependent sometimes falls apart.

What's the explanation for this behavior?

Just as it's impossible to blame alcoholism on a single physical adaptation, so too is it difficult to find one "cause" for this complex syndrome. We'd have to call it an adaptation to a "toxic" situation. It's deeply ingrained by the two best teachers of all—repetition and reward—though its existence is often overlooked in the general turmoil surrounding the alcoholic.

Like addicts, co-dependents defend their behavior with defense mechanisms. They prevent themselves from becoming fully aware of the negative outcome of their actions. They gather information and advice, then ignore it; they make the same mistakes, over and over again.

As a result, co-dependents must undergo a process of self-diagnosis in order to find motivation for lasting change. They have to learn to see themselves as part of the problem, and to seek help for their own behavior, rather than the addict's.

Family members other than the active co-dependent may be most helpful in enlisting him or her into treatment. Since not everyone develops co-dependency—even many primary enablers manage to avoid it—there are usually others on the scene capable of intervening with the resistant co-dependent.

The important point is that co-dependency can be viewed as a disorder in its own right. Co-dependency in childhood and adolescence—grown in response to parental addiction—can indeed affect adult relationships. A co-dependent spouse who angrily divorces one alcoholic may quickly marry a second.

It's helpful to think of co-dependency as more than a "role" adopted by someone within an imaginary "family system." It may have begun that way—but it grows into a behavioral disorder of remarkable persistence.

Here are two examples of co-dependency in action. Both are fairly extreme, selected because they illustrate the syndrome dramatically. The behaviors they portray, however, are found to a lesser extent in many families.

Case One

Mr. D. was married to a woman afflicted with alcoholism and severe psychiatric illness. During her drinking episodes, she could become threatening, even assaultive. One night he awakened from a sound sleep to find her standing over him, butcher knife in hand. She appeared unable to recognize him. Despite urging from family and friends to seek psychiatric help, he resisted this on the grounds that it would be of no use to his wife. When he finally did seek counseling, he refused to follow the doctor's recommendations. Eventually, fear for his own safety and that of his children forced him to move to a different house, but he continued to pay all his wife's bills and to provide money and food while she drank. When she set the house afire, he initiated proceedings for divorce, but quickly dropped them and lapsed back into passivity. His wife's condition continues to deteriorate. He "looks in on her" daily.

Case Two
Ms. E. is a twenty-five-year-old woman who lives with a PCP addict. Her lover refuses to seek treatment despite increasingly psychotic behavior, including paranoia and episodes of assault on friends and family. Despite the obvious danger to herself, she refuses to separate, insisting that she "couldn't live with the guilt" if something happened to him after her "desertion." Though she complains constantly about the money he spends on drugs, she has loaned him thousands of dollars and took up a collection from the neighbors to "tide him over" the last time he was fired from his job.

Note how clearly the co-dependent's actions contribute to the very problems he or she ostensibly seeks to avoid.

Co-dependents seldom get better without outside help, either through Alanon or through some type of professional treatment. Structured counseling may produce quicker results and is better for altering specific behaviors than the more gradual change experienced within the self-help fellowship.

The best way to obtain professional counseling for this syndrome is to contact your local addiction treatment center and ask for a referral to a counselor who specializes in this area.

How Do I Know When This Task Is Complete?
1. You've visited at least five Alanon meetings and introduced yourself to one person at each, telling some of your story and listening to theirs.
2. You've read some of the Alanon literature and discussed the benefits to be obtained with one or more members.
3. You've selected one meeting group—the one you like best— and made it your "home group," where you can go in the future.
4. You've compared your own experience with the description of the co-dependent syndrome.
5. If you feel you may qualify as a co-dependent: you've taken steps to enter treatment, either formally or through an organization such as Alanon or a similar self-help group for families of alcoholics.

Task Six

Set reasonable expectations for the immediate future.

Sit down and write out, in outline form, what you would like to have happen during the next three- to six-month period. In other words, if everything went according to your expectations, what would occur during that span?

Done? Read it over. Make additions if you forgot something. Then set it aside for a minute.

Now, take a second piece of paper and make the same kind of outline. Except in this case, list the things you're afraid will happen over the next three to six months.

When you're finished, review it, making additions and corrections if needed. This is your "worst-case scenario."

Set it alongside the first list. Compare and contrast the two, if you want. Then wad both up in little balls and throw them in the wastebasket. Neither one is going to come true, anyway, so let's not waste any more time on them.

Instead, let's talk about reality.

Which we define as: *what actually happens, whether or not you were expecting it.*

We have a friend who's an important executive in a large business. His budget is in the millions and the scope of his responsibility is impressive. Every year or two, he, along with every other executive in that firm, devotes several weeks to developing, revising, and updating a "five-year business plan."

"It's quite a production," he tells us. "The company brings in consultants. We go on retreats in the country to lodges that don't have enough heat, and hold meetings late into the night when we'd all rather be watching television. But the most amazing part is that in all the time I've been doing this, hardly any of the things in the five-year plan have actually come true."

"So why do you do it?" we ask.

He shrugs. "Beats me. They pay me a salary, so I figure I'll do what they tell me."

Actually, addictive disease does permit us to predict the future to a certain extent. If drinking and drug use continue, we can anticipate what will happen as a result of it—although we have trouble predicting when these catastrophes will occur. On the other hand, if drinking stops, we can make the assumption that certain things probably won't happen—such as death by liver cirrhosis.

What we can't predict is the rate of recovery. We know that when an alcoholic stops drinking, his emotions become easier to control, his moods fluctuate less, his judgment improves, and his relationships benefit.

We also don't know whether or not this will happen as fast as the people around him want it to.

It's an important variable: What does the family expect from the alcoholic's recovery? And are these expectations—perhaps based on some hidden five-year plan of their own—reasonable in light of the nature of this disease?

There are traps in this area. Here are two common ones.

Error: *Assuming that everything will be OK now that the addict is off drugs.*

You can safely assume that most things will be better. But every aspect of existence? No way. And that you'll be satisfied in all the ways you were previously unsatisfied? Highly unlikely.

For some reason, people seem to expect a lot more out of recovery from alcoholism than from other diseases. As though eliminating drugs were a panacea for every problem that exists.

When was the last time you heard someone say, "Oh boy, am I ever glad your *cancer* is in remission. That should definitely improve our interpersonal communication"?

Of course, lots of recovering alcoholics and addicts go on to new heights of achievement and of mental and spiritual health. They reach a point that one noted psychiatrist describes as being "weller than well."

But that's pretty far down the road, and there are a lot of bumps along the way. The main benefits of initial sobriety have to do with avoiding what we refer to as being "sicker than sick."

It's the same way with smoking. We have a friend who gave up cigarettes a while ago. People ask him: "What's the best thing about not smoking? Feeling good in the morning? Having your food taste better? Saving the money you used to spend on tobacco?"

"Nope," he tells them. "The best thing about not smoking is not getting lung cancer."

Alcoholism is the same way. The main motivation for traveling the bumpy road of sobriety is fear of the alternative. The best part of early recovery is what doesn't happen to you.

But for some reason, both addicts and their families tend to forget this. As time passes and they begin to enjoy a little success, their expectations rise—often too rapidly for reality to keep up.

A young wife called us to complain that her husband was going to too many AA meetings. "He's out almost every night," she says. "Even now that he's been sober for *six weeks*. And the only thing he talks about is staying sober and what his sponsor told him and all that stuff. It's worse than when he was drinking. Sure, he was drunk, but at least he was drunk at home."

Just a few short months before, this same woman would have given her right arm just to get him to attend an AA meeting. How quickly things change.

Error: *"Now it's the addict's turn to prove himself."*

The second major mistake—closely linked to the resentments we discussed in Task Four—is to put the addict "on probation" during early sobriety.

That's a procedure that the courts, and some employers, use to considerable advantage. It doesn't work as well within the family.

One wife agreed to let her husband return home after completing a treatment program. But she made a silent pact with herself: if he didn't meet her expectations, she was going to divorce him. "This is his last chance," she told herself. "Either he shapes up, or he's out on his ear."

This put her in the role of judge and jury rather than mate and lover. And sure enough, even though her husband remained abstinent, their marriage continued to deteriorate. He was frequently depressed. "You never want to go out or do anything together," she'd complain, "and I told you, I'm not putting up with that anymore." He began to work late to avoid having to listen to her criticism. Their sex life was worse than ever. "And I'm not putting up with that, either," she yelled one night. "You either perform as a husband, or you're through." As you can imagine, he wasn't able to meet this demand.

After six months he left her. Married someone else, of course.

This business of living up to other people's expectations—and expecting them to live up to yours—is always tricky. Especially when there's a disease involved. Because chronic diseases make "demands" of their own. And if you don't meet them, you're in big trouble.

We think it harkens back to that old-fashioned, moralistic view of addiction. In which the family operates under the assumption that the alcoholic is wrong rather than sick, undisciplined instead of powerless, irresponsible rather than toxic. It comes from the part of them that still believes the addict was deliberately trying to hurt or shame the family through addictive behavior.

What is a reasonable expectation for the first months of abstinence?

That the alcoholic or addict will abstain from drugs. Or if relapse does occur, will immediately accept intervention.

That he or she—and therefore, you—will experience improvement in a number of the major areas of life.

That his or her behavior—barring interference from other illnesses—will be more predictable, more reliable, more appropriate than when under the influence.

That many of the things you've been afraid of—from the months or years of active addiction—will not come true.

That you will be asked to adjust to things you did not anticipate (as will the alcoholic).

How Do I Know When This Task Is Complete?
1. When you've made a list of your expectations for the initial three to six months and have discussed it with people familiar with recovery.
2. When (depending on their feedback) you've revised your expectations to make them more *realistic*.
3. When you believe you are ready to accept what happens over the next few months, whether or not you planned for it.

Task Seven

De-emphasize the alcoholic or addict in your daily life.

During the active addiction you most likely devoted a great deal of time and energy—even if only in your head—to worrying about the addict and trying to get him or her into treatment.

Addiction makes that unavoidable. It's so unpredictable that people who live with it get in the habit of thinking about it most of the time, in a vain effort to prepare themselves for the next crisis. It's often the first thing they think about when they get up in the morning and the last thing they think about when they go to bed at night—provided they were able to stop thinking about it long enough to go to sleep.

The worse it gets, the more it intrudes on other areas of life. It isn't difficult to become obsessed with someone else's drug problem. You lose track of your own interests, dreams, aspirations, problems. Your moods begin to fluctuate along with the alcoholic's. When the addict has a good day, you have a good day—and when the addict has a bad day, you suffer.

It's as though you took the other seat on the alcoholic's emotional roller coaster. And after you've been going around for awhile, something funny happens. You find that it's difficult to get off. The constant ups and downs seem normal to you.

It may actually seem odd to focus attention on yourself. To wake up wondering what you, instead of the addict, are going to do.

Your first impulse may be to refocus your attention on the alcoholic. "That's where the problem is," you tell yourself. "I have to remain vigilant. See if there's anything I can do to keep him [or her] on track."

We suggest the opposite. _Reduce your focus on the addict._ Let him or her out of the spotlight for awhile. Pay attention to your own needs—or to those of others that you may have neglected because of your preoccupation with the drinker.

There's another angle to this. Remember that in many instances, the family gradually rearranges itself around the addict, so as to minimize the impact of his or her dysfunction. This "reorganization" of the family unit can lead to problems when the addict gets off drugs.

To explain, we'll employ one of our favorite illustrations. We call it the "Leave It to Beaver Model of Family Dynamics."

Take your typical American nuclear family as portrayed on TV in the 1960s. You've got a minimum of four components.

FATHER (Ward):
Principal Role: provide the bulk of the family's money, as primary breadwinner. Give patient, fatherly advice to less-than-gifted sons.

MOTHER (June):
Principal Role: manage the household, including care and feeding of sons; make sure bills are paid, budget kept. Be nurturing.

ELDEST SON (Wally):
Principal Role: be a teenager, involved in typical teenage activities like glee club and long-distance crew; have typical teenage problems like asking girls to the prom and worrying about acne, that provide Ward with opportunity to dispense patient, fatherly advice.

BABY (Beaver):
Principal Role: be a typical elementary school–age kid, having typical elementary school–age problems, usually through following bad advice of brother. Provide opportunity for June to express motherly concern and Ward to dispense patient, fatherly advice.

Got the picture? Now, let's suppose that *Ward* is secretly a chronic alcoholic. Gradually, he worsens to the point where he gets fired from his job. Instead of looking for alternative employment, he decides to take some time off to "consider a midlife career change."

Translation: sit in the den drinking beer, smoking cigarettes, and watching game shows and football on the tube.

Now: the rest of the family has a problem. The breadwinner is no longer winning bread. Which means that burden falls to the only other candidate: *June.*

Suppose she goes out and gets a typical housewife–returning –to–the–workplace–after–fifteen–years–raising–her–family job —passing out cheese samples in the grocery store for a dollar-an-hour over minimum wage. She has to work double-time just to make ends meet.

That means that her traditional role—household manager— falls to the only other possible candidate: *Wally.*

Now it becomes his responsibility to make sure that the Beav gets to school on time every morning and doesn't forget his peanut butter sandwich or his baseball cap. And he's the one who has to meet the kid after school to make sure he doesn't get into even more incredible scrapes than before.

Which means Wally has to give up glee club and long-distance crew, as well as girls. He doesn't have time to be a normal teenager.

Beaver, on the other hand, will be raised by Wally instead of his mother and father. Those of you who were raised by their older brothers know what this means. They all tend to adhere to the school of parenting known as "Do what I tell you or I'll hit you in the head."

The Beav, in turn, begins to act older than the other kids. You often hear that about children of alcoholics: "He seems so mature." He'd better be.

Meanwhile, who's the baby in this family? Right. It's Dad.

Now suppose that Ward gets bleeding ulcers from the "stress" of being unemployed (it couldn't be the beer, could it?) and checks into the local detox unit. He discovers the joys of not drinking and returns home committed to sobriety. Does the family welcome him with open arms? Do they immediately restore to him all the rights and privileges he once enjoyed?

Probably not. They're not sure they can depend on him. After all—for all they know, he could be drunk by five o'clock that evening.

They cling to the organizational system that developed around the active alcoholism. Unfortunately, there's no room for a sober alcoholic in this system. It must change.

The best way to initiate this is for each family member to give back some of the responsibility that was assumed because of the disease. To ask himself (or herself) the question: Why am I doing this? Is this really my job? If not, then what is?

Adjust roles within the family so that instead of this:

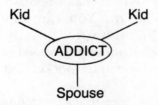

they look more like this:

and you'll find things "work" better.

How Do I Know When This Task Is Complete?

1. Make a list of things you do and responsibilities you have within the family that you suspect are not rightly yours. Share this list with a counselor or other person knowledgable about alcoholism. Get feedback from them. Make changes based on their recommendations, if necessary.
2. Give back some of these responsibilities, a little at a time.
3. Make a list of things you would like to do, independent of the addict. Include things you once enjoyed doing but gave up as part of your struggle with addiction. Set aside at least a few hours weekly for those activities.
4. Develop a practical method for stopping yourself if you begin thinking obsessively. Get suggestions from counselors, books, or self-help groups.

Task Eight

Consider the possibility of relapse.

Of course, you've been considering this all along. But by now, we hope you're ready to consider it rationally.

The first rule of dealing with relapse is: if it's going to happen, you can't prevent it.

The addict can, of course. But *you* can't.

Oh sure, you can help to make relapse less likely. You can avoid provoking behavior. You can support the alcoholic's efforts at recovery. You can strive to get well yourself.

But ultimately, the alcoholic is responsible for his own recovery. You can't ride around in his pocket and pop out whenever a reminder is needed.

We know from experience that a certain number of addicts will relapse following treatment. What we can't say for sure is which ones, and when.

It's a little like predicting certain types of accidents, an activity to which insurance companies devote considerable time and attention.

Take an apparently "unpredictable" event, like somebody being killed by a falling roof. Who would expect it to happen to them?

Yet the fact is, it happens to a certain number of people every year. That number has remained remarkably stable. It's so predictable that insurers can set rates for protection against death by falling roof. They don't know when or where it will occur, but they do know it will happen about the same number of times every year.

Relapse is the same way. Take a few hundred thousand alcoholics and send them through treatment programs. A certain percentage will relapse.

When we ask why, all we get are theories. Turn to Chapter 8 on relapse to read about our own theories. But the only thing we can say with absolute certainty is: it happens.

Of course, it could happen to your alcoholic. Then again, maybe it won't. It's no use worrying about it. The only rational course is to do whatever you can to make your environment conducive to reality—and think of a plan to put into effect in case relapse occurs anyway.

The best plans feature provisions for a second intervention, using many of the same techniques involved in an initial intervention. To refresh your memory on how intervention works, read Chapter 3 again, on how to get someone into treatment.

How Do I Know When This Task Is Complete?

1. You are able to get through the day without worrying about the possibility of relapse.
2. You've made a plan—in the form of a written outline—of what steps you can take to get the addict back into treatment should relapse occur.
3. You've discussed this eventuality with a counselor or other knowledgable person, and received feedback and suggestions for action.

Task Nine

Learn to control your own emotions.

Emotions are great. To a certain extent they're what make life worth living. To experience the full range of human feeling—this is terrific stuff.

As one of our friends likes to say: "There are four great emotions everyone should experience in life—joy, love, hope, and pizza."

Still, you've got to admit that rampant emotionalism doesn't take us very far in recovering from addictive disease. In fact, that's what hooked us in the first place. We responded to the addict's difficulties *emotionally*—and the disease used our own feelings against us.

In order to survive, we had to learn to distance ourselves from some of our fear and anger. To break the cycle of unproductive emotional response. To seek outside guidance from uninvolved persons. We learned to act rationally rather than react emotionally.

We still felt the same feelings. But we didn't allow them to dominate our lives.

At least, not as much as they once did.

We're not pretending to have achieved emotional serenity, or to always obey logic rather than impulse. We're borrowing the old AA slogan: "Progress, not perfection."

The best way to learn to control your feelings is by learning to monitor and alter your own thinking processes. There's nothing original about that—it's the basis of most forms of "cognitive therapy," including Albert Ellis' Rational Emotive Therapy and William Glasser's Reality Therapy.

Psychoanalysts like to say that people can't change the way they feel about something. And in one respect that's true. It's tough to say to yourself: "Self, don't feel that way." It might actually make the feeling stronger.

A better approach is to deal with your thinking. In other words, examine the train of ideas that led you to that unpleasant feeling.

For instance, women who live with cocaine addicts are almost always anxious. Why? Because they're thinking about what's going to happen next. And about what they should be doing to forestall it.

This is understandable. Anyone would feel this way in a similar situation. Still, anxiety makes things worse.

Now, instead of having one crazy person to deal with, we've got *two*. We've got the addict. And we've got the panicky spouse.

The logical course would be for this spouse—who after all is not under the influence of drugs—to devise a plan to get the addict into a treatment program. But often she can't. Why not?

Because she's too busy dealing with her own anxiety.

She literally can't find the time to think about a solution. All she can think about is the problem. And that makes her even more anxious.

This goes on for months. Finally, some crisis occurs that drives her to a counselor. There she sits, asking for help, but at the same time she's strangely incapable of listening. The most she can do is talk about how horrible her life has become. And recite a catalogue of failed attempts to remedy her situation.

The counselor soon realizes that as long as she's in the grip of this anxiety, she'll never be able to take productive action. She'll just go around in circles. So his first act is to interrupt her train of thought.

Maybe he'll ask her for a detailed history, featuring plenty of peripheral data. He doesn't really need all this information—in terms of the addiction itself, he's able to guess most of it. The underlying purpose of his questions is to slow down her thought process. To help her put events into some sort of logical perspective. To allow her the time and space to consider her situation with some degree of objectivity.

Pretty soon she's calmer. If asked, she'd probably say the counselor "made" her feel better, through reassurance and emotional support.

But in fact, counselors usually provide little in the way of direct support. What he did so skillfully was simply to interrupt the thought process that was making her anxious.

In a sense, he helped her change the way she was *feeling* by getting her to change the way she was *thinking*.

When she goes home—actually, it will start in the car on the way back from his office—she'll return to her familiar patterns of thinking. Within a few hours, she'll feel anxious again. No doubt she will blame that on the uncertainty of her situation. But it's due as much to the way she thinks about her situation as to the situation itself.

If she continues seeing the counselor, her anxiety will probably begin to lessen. The periods wherein she finds herself able to step back from her situation and consider it objectively will lengthen. And the clearer her thinking becomes, the closer she will be to taking positive action. Sooner or later, she'll actually do something about her husband's addiction—and her life will suddenly improve as a result.

Of course, she might be unlucky enough to stumble on a

counselor who believes the solution to her current problem lies in an in-depth exploration of her hidden feelings. In this event, she could very well get worse. This is neither the time nor the place for that kind of self-discovery.

Our point is simple: you can learn to do this for yourself. Become your own therapist, as it were. That way, you can adjust your thinking as a way of altering your emotional state. You can call some of the shots, instead of simply reacting to the disease.

How Do I Know When This Task Is Complete?
1. Make a list of your three most bothersome emotional states—depression, anxiety, fear, anger, impatience, and so on.
2. Link them up with thinking patterns. In other words, do these states usually appear when you're thinking about a certain thing, or in a certain way?
3. Once you've identified any thinking patterns, examine them objectively, in light of the emotional state they produce. Are there alternative ways of viewing these situations?
4. Make a plan for dealing with your own negative emotional states. What can you do to make them go away or to interrupt them at an early stage?
5. Share this plan with your counselor or other knowledgable persons. Get their feedback.

Task Ten

Learn to look for progress instead of perfection.

Life is full of imperfection. There's no better illustration than the existence of disease.

Still, people forget this. All of us indulge to one degree or another in the bad habit of perfectionism. We like to justify it by claiming that lofty expectations motivate high achievement. In reality, expecting a great deal from someone recovering from a powerful, life-endangering disease is more likely to motivate failure. If the standards are too high, people tend to give up.

Think of an athlete recovering from a career-threatening knee injury. He looks at his wrecked cartilage, remembers his former ability, and decides, *No way I'll ever be able to run or jump like I once did*. On the heels of that thought comes another: *Then why bother trying?*

If the same athlete looks at the knee and thinks, *I may not be as strong as before, but I can play again*—he'll begin the process of rehabilitation, and find the motivation to continue. He knows it's just a matter of time until he's successful.

It's the difference between thinking about what you can't do and concentrating on what you can. The first approach is discouraging. The second is motivating.

Abandon perfectionism when you're dealing with an incurable disease. Abandon it as well when judging your own progress. Instead of asking, "Am I well?" ask, "Am I better?"

How Do I Know When This Task Is Complete?

It never is. This one you work on *forever*. But then, you're only required to make progress, right?

Chapter Six

The Ten Tasks—
for the
Alcoholic or Addict

As you know from the last chapter, we strongly urge family members to take part in their own "ten task" recovery program. But regardless of whether or not you choose to follow such a program yourself, the recovering alcoholic or drug addict *must*. Relapse is just too predictable a danger in the early months of recovery without the focused support of such a plan. Of course, this doesn't mean it has to be our specific ten tasks presented here (there are other good approaches), just as long as the program the addict adopts is a strongly task-centered one.

We've written the ten tasks presented in this chapter as if we were speaking directly to recovering addicts themselves. As you read, imagine you are an alcoholic or drug addict. This is what we would advise you to do.

Task One

Stop drinking and taking drugs.

Some therapists think you (the addict) ought to work up to this one. We don't. We think this is where you start.

Drugs alter the way you think, feel, and act. Nowhere is this more obvious than in persons with addictive disease. Drugs not only change the addict's consciousness—*they activate and sustain the disease process itself.*

They're the "trigger mechanism" for addiction. And when they're removed for any extended period, the alcoholic invariably improves.

So this becomes the initial task of recovery: to cleanse the brain and body of toxic chemicals, and to break the cycle of intoxication and withdrawal.

How do you know when you're addicted to a drug? You feel bad when you don't have it. Withdrawal syndromes vary, depending on some or all of the following factors:
1. The drug or drugs used.
2. Quality of the drug, or amount, frequency, or duration of use.
3. Differences in individual health or constitution.
4. Stage of the disease.
In other words, the extent and severity of symptoms experienced during an attempt at withdrawal is somewhat unpredictable. Many addicts will feel quite sick; others won't. Some will find that the worst is over quickly, while others will suffer for a considerable period. Some will be able to continue functioning in everyday life, while others will have to be hospitalized.

Don't underestimate withdrawal. Even if you (the addict) have quit before with few difficulties, that doesn't guarantee a repeat of the same experience. The nature of the disease is to grow worse.

So we recommend that any attempt at detoxification be under medical supervision. The resources are there; it's stupid to ignore them.

You can go to a treatment center, of course. For our suggestions on selecting one, turn to Chapter 4 on getting treatment.

Perhaps you want to find the right doctor before you commit to treatment. You can't always rely on your family physician—treating addictions is something of a specialized field. If your doctor can't recommend someone, the treatment center can. Make an appointment and go see the physician.

Really, this is very straightforward. You've come to realize you have a drug problem. The first step in remedying it is to get off drugs and alcohol.

We're always surprised when people manage to complicate this task. Nevertheless, they do.

Here are some common errors:
1. *Cutting back* on consumption

2. *Switching to* a "lesser" drug

3. *Giving up* some drugs and not others.

Simply acknowledging the existence of a "drug problem" doesn't automatically mean you've decided to abstain altogether from drug use. It's always tempting to think that you can get away with changing the way you use drugs.

You might convince yourself that your problems stem from using too much of a given drug, or from using it too often. Or perhaps you decide you got into trouble because you used too many different drugs, or you used them at the wrong times or in the wrong places. Or maybe you think your mistake lay in choosing the wrong drug, or in using it in the wrong way.

To the addict or alcoholic, drugs and alcohol seem intrinsically good. They make you feel better. They remove various aches and pains, both physical and psychological. They make time pass more quickly, or at least in a more entertaining fashion.

So addicts initially approach the problem in terms of changing their pattern of use rather than practicing abstinence.

In other words, "quitting" may actually refer to "cutting back" on consumption, or to switching to "lesser" substances. The addict's goal is to learn to use the drug differently so as to minimize the problems he or she is currently experiencing.

We routinely ask new patients whether or not they've ever put together an extended period of abstinence, with or without treatment.

"Absolutely," one man affirmed. "I was sober for eleven months, until January of this year. I made a stupid mistake and had a glass of wine on New Year's Eve. After that, I lost my resolve and started slipping back into drinking, and that's how I ended up in Detox."

"So you were completely abstinent for eleven months."

"Completely."

"No alcohol at all."

"Absolutely none. No liquor in any form."

"No beer, either?"

He looked blank.

"*Beer?* What's wrong with *beer?* I never had any problem with beer."

Turned out this gentleman consumed six to twelve beers daily throughout his entire period of "total abstinence." Not only that: he'd forgotten to count a few "celebratory occasions" when he'd indulged his taste for fine wines, and several business lunches where he'd tossed back a couple of drinks "just to be sociable."

"But I didn't get in trouble," he insisted. "I stopped myself each time. Most of the time, my wife couldn't even tell I'd been drinking, for God's sake. I don't see how you could consider that a problem."

To him, total abstinence was defined as: an extended period without any alcohol-related problems severe enough to bring down the wrath of his wife.

Another man—accustomed to consuming prodigious amounts of alcohol—claimed to have stopped on his own prior to coming to see us.

"I'm off the booze already," he explained. "Haven't touched a drop in three weeks. Had hardly any withdrawal at all. You guys made it sound much worse than it was. Oh, I'm a little irritable," he went on, "but the pills take care of that."

He'd gone to a physician and obtained a three-month supply of tranquilizers—which, not surprisingly, he'd used up in less than three weeks. He'd come to us in hopes of a refill. "Those little pills are great," he said. "Fix you right up."

"Being sober isn't as bad as I thought it would be," he concluded.

Stopping and Starting Again

There are other people who are more than willing to stop but have great difficulty staying sober long enough to experience much benefit.

"Sure, I can give up alcohol," they'll tell you. "I've done it hundreds of times."

It's *extended abstinence* that brings health. Climbing on and off the wagon produces some improvement, but no lasting change. Using alcohol or drugs after a short interval of sobriety is a little like exposing yourself to the flu virus just as you're beginning to get over the mumps.

You're never really "well"—you just have periods where you're "less sick."

We see the same phenomenon with fad diets. Once the diet is technically "over," most people quickly regain the lost weight— plus extra poundage as a result of a rebound effect. That's why many experts discourage quick weight-loss plans in favor of measured, extended behavioral change.

Fortunately, alcohol and drugs aren't like food—you can give them up entirely instead of being forced to control your consumption. Take advantage of this.

How Do I Know When This Task Is Complete?
1. You've completed a program of inpatient or outpatient detoxification, under a physician's supervision.

Task Two

Learn about your disease.

Sure, you already know a lot about drinking or drug use. But that doesn't mean you know very much about the disease that causes it.

The typical alcoholic entering treatment may know everything there is to know about being sick, but has very little information about getting well.

In fact, much of what he or she believes to be "true" about recovery is most likely false. It's the product of unfounded rumor, half-understood magazine articles, bad "Phil Donahue" shows, and amateurish attempts by well-meaning friends to "motivate" recovery. Mix this with the addict's natural anxieties and it's a prescription for falling flat on his face.

Recovering alcoholics and drug addicts need hard, reliable facts in order to learn about their disease. In this book, we don't expect to provide all the information they require to answer their questions. Accordingly, we've included a list of recommended reading at the back.

The reason for our emphasis on education is simple. Where we have no cure for a disease—addiction being such an instance— we have to rely on the patient's ability to follow a regimen of treatment. In a very real sense, the patient is forced to take on many of the responsibilities normally given over to the doctor. Success or failure of treatment depends on the patient's willingness to cooperate.

In the case of addictive disease, success or failure is often synonymous with life or death.

Therefore, it's only good sense to teach the alcoholic as much as possible about his disease. Given the fact that he is the one who'll have to treat it.

That's your task: learn. Become something of an expert in the treatment of addiction.

Who could possibly benefit more than you?

How Do I Know When This Task Is Complete?

1. You've read Chapter 1 and the Guide to Addictive Disease and have identified your addictive pattern.
2. You can define the following terms and give examples of each:
   tolerance
   dependence
   organ deterioration
   loss of control over amount, time or place, duration of episode
   blackouts
   continued use despite adverse consequences.
3. You have reviewed your understanding of addictive disease in detail with at least two knowledgable persons and been told you seem to have a good initial understanding of addiction.
4. You can explain the above terms and the dynamics of addiction correctly to someone who knows less than you do.

Task Three

Use this information to self-diagnose.

Now that you've replaced bad information with good, use this knowledge to diagnose your disease.

In other words, go over your own experience with alcohol or drugs, in detail. Identify the symptoms of addiction you find there.

Why? Because this is the source of your motivation for recovery. Without self-diagnosis your chances of lasting sobriety reduce to two likelihoods, slim and none.

Recall that most people enter treatment due to some kind of crisis. It can be in the area of health, finances, relationships, legal problems—whatever. That's the motivating factor. Without that gentle prod you might still be out there drinking, trying to "lick" the disease on your own.

It served its purpose. You're on the road to recovery. But the longer you're sober, the better you'll feel, and the more remote this crisis will seem. Soon enough, it will disappear from your thinking altogether.

And if that crisis was all that was keeping you sober, your sobriety will disappear with it. If this happens, it's only a matter of time before you encounter another crisis, worse than the first.

How do you avoid this? By using the "window" provided by the crisis to motivate yourself for further recovery.

By coming to understand that your crisis was the result of a chronic, progressive, and potentially fatal disease—which if left untreated will produce still more crises, up to and including a final, fatal one.

Self-diagnosis is perhaps the most important task of treatment because it motivates recovery itself. It's one thing to feel you've been "overdrinking lately" or have become "a little too fond of cocaine." It's quite another to believe you suffer from a disease that may very well kill you if you don't do something about it.

What stands in the way of self-diagnosis? Two things.

"Comparing Out"

Alcoholics operate under the misconception that you need all the symptoms of alcoholism in order to diagnose the disease. That isn't true.

Like all progressive disorders, addictive disease develops over time. Very few persons start out with *all* the symptoms. As the disease progresses, additional ones appear.

The alcoholic may fail to notice them, however, because he or she is paying attention to the symptoms that have not yet arrived. This is called "comparing out."

To illustrate: we interviewed a forty-three-year-old executive in an engineering firm who believed he had been unfairly accused of alcoholism.

"In the first place," he insisted, "I drink less than most of my friends. The men, at least. At any party, there are half a dozen people who drink more than I do—and nobody calls them alcoholics.

"Secondly, you can't say drinking interferes with my job. I work ten hours a day, six days a week. I just got a promotion. I make a good salary. I support my family.

"I had a physical not six months ago. The doctor told me I was in good shape. My kids are making A's in school. My wife and I don't argue. My house is paid for. You can't convince me I could have done all that if I was an alcoholic."

On the surface, a convincing argument. But closer examination reveals a few holes in this man's account of his current lifestyle.

For one: he has two DWI's. His wife swears that's entirely a matter of luck—it could easily have been a hundred. For another: she doesn't argue with him because "it doesn't do a bit of good, and I was tired of getting yelled at." She claims she would divorce him if she could afford it. His perfect children are having emotional problems, and one dropped from A's to D's last semester—possibly because of drug use. The doctor who administered his physical didn't bother to perform liver function studies—which would have revealed an enlarged liver.

His promotion was really an attempt by management to "kick him upstairs" before his staff—who had complained for months about his unpredictable, overbearing, irrational behavior—quit en masse. And his heavy drinking friends, with whom he compares favorably, are in fact alcoholics themselves. Two have already lost their driver's licenses for alcohol-related offenses.

Given the nature of chronic disease, this process of "selective thinking" is terribly destructive. Imagine the same line of reasoning on the part of a heart patient:

"The doc says I could have a heart attack," he reflects, "but I don't understand how. I feel good. I'm only about ten pounds overweight. I cut way back on the red meat, and I hardly ever have eggs for breakfast. I'm in better shape than a lot of guys my age."

Look closer, however, and we discover that this man has a strong family history of heart disease, is already hypertensive, and works ten to twelve hours daily. In fact, he's a prime candidate for a heart attack.

In the same way, alcoholics and drug addicts fail to recognize addictive disease until it's well advanced, because they fall into the trap of concentrating on the symptoms they don't have, instead of on the ones they do.

Defense Mechanisms

Perhaps the greatest obstacle to self-diagnosis are the defense mechanisms that blind the addict to the extent and severity of the disease.

There are five which produce most of the difficulty.

Denial: *Inability to recognize a problem despite evidence of its existence.*

Example: from an interview with a thirty-six-year-old man admitted for cocaine addiction of six years standing:

ADDICT: I really don't belong here, man. Sure, I've used coke. I admit that. I'm not ashamed of it. But I haven't touched the stuff in over a month.

COUNSELOR: Your wife says you freebased all last weekend.

ADDICT: She's confused. I remember when it was, and it was a month ago. Or three weeks, at least. Can't have been less than that.

COUNSELOR: She says you're stealing from the family to pay for it, and she thinks you took a thousand dollars from your joint account a week ago.

ADDICT: No way. I took some money out, but I spent it on other stuff.

COUNSELOR: What?

ADDICT: Clothes and stuff. I don't really remember. But it didn't all go for drugs. Some of it, maybe. But no way I would ever have blown a thousand on cocaine.

COUNSELOR: You also turned up positive for cocaine on the urine test.

ADDICT: I told you I used it a month ago, man. Must still have been some in my system.

COUNSELOR: Not likely.

ADDICT: Well, those tests can be wrong, man. I read about it. You got a wrong result, is all.

If we were to administer a lie detector test, this fellow would probably pass. A friend of ours says: "That's why alcoholics are so convincing. They actually believe these stories they tell you."

Rationalization: Providing excuses for problems caused by alcohol or drug use.

Example: from a fifty-one-year-old alcoholic mother of six who is also a practicing attorney, discussing (with her married daughter) her behavior at a recent holiday party:

ADDICT: "Look, I know you're mad about what I did at Christmas. And I don't blame you—I really went too far, I know it. But you have to understand the circumstances. You know that case I was working on? The client called me up that very morning—Christmas morning, if you can believe that—and fired me from the case! Talk about ingratitude! I was so upset—I shouldn't have let it get to me, I know. But I didn't want to tell you about it and ruin your holiday. So I kept it inside, and I guess I just got a little carried away with the wine. . . . What? I never said that. Did I? Oh, yes, of course I remember. It just slipped my mind. Well, I didn't mean it. I was just a little ticked off at your sister, is all. She was supposed to bring the dessert, and she didn't even call . . . "

The rationalizer views all problems in terms of the circumstances in which they occur. There's a "reason" for everything, but that reason must never be alcoholism or drug dependency. Problems can be attributed to misunderstandings, communication breakdowns, stress, carelessness, exhaustion, or simple forgetfulness. Drinking and drug use have to be seen as the *response* to problems—not as problems themselves.

In the mind of the rationalizer, every crisis stands completely separate from all others. This makes it virtually impossible to see the larger, dominant pattern of addictive disease—the "forest" that is hiding behind the trees.

Externalization: Blaming drinking or drug use on forces or circumstances outside yourself.

Example: from a twenty-two-year-old cocaine addict, a young woman:

ADDICT: "In the first place, I don't really crave cocaine. The only reason I do it is because somebody else around me is doing it. Well, I might do a little by myself, but I mainly just go along with the crowd. All my friends are into coke, you see.

"Actually, the biggest reason I have for doing coke is my boyfriend. He doesn't like to do coke alone, so I keep him company. But if he wasn't there, I probably wouldn't do it at all. I certainly wouldn't pay money for it. It's free, you see. He deals a little. I never use it unless he does, though. Unless I'm having a bad day, and I need a little boost. But otherwise, never.

"So I think, really, the solution to my problems is to get another boyfriend. You want to know a coincidence? My last three boyfriends have been coke dealers. I don't know what it is about them that I like."

We do. They have cocaine.

To the externalizer, drug use is the result of "outside motivators." But a pattern emerges: when one external motivator disappears, they seek out another.

This young woman was able to find another cocaine-dealing boyfriend with virtually no interruption in her supply.

It's like the old story about the alcoholic who insisted he drank because of his arguments with his wife. When she left town for an extended visit with her mother, he found himself with no reason to drink. After a few hours, he called her on the phone and picked a fight, just to have something to drink over.

Most addicts who externalize manage to hook up with a provoker: someone whose behavior—usually nagging, criticizing, or outright attacks—provides unlimited excuses for drug use. The alcoholic can devote all his attention to the provoker, and therefore doesn't have to examine his own behavior.

This is the pattern of those who drink "at" people, or "because of" tragic events.

"She had no right to talk to me like that," the alcoholic insists, as he stumbles, sick and miserable, into the hospital. "Anybody would have gotten drunk after something like that."

He really showed her, didn't he?

Or there are alcoholics who attribute their drinking to various tragic events of the dim past.

"It was after we broke up," you'll hear. "The drinking really started around that time."

In reality, drinking may have been one of the reasons that particular relationship failed. Besides, it ended years ago—which makes it a dubious excuse for today's drinking.

Of course, there's no statute of limitations in the mind of the externalizer.

Minimizing: Making problems seem less important than they are, and therefore not a subject of concern.

Example: from a fifty-one-year-old alcoholic man with multiple DWI arrests:

ADDICT: "I think there's entirely too much made of this DWI thing. I've had two of them. I know that's wrong. But I'm fully capable of handling it myself. When you start bringing up treatment, that's where I draw the line. I think you're making things out to be worse than they are. I've got a good job, I have a family that loves me, I'm a good citizen. Okay, so I've broken the law, take away my license. I'll suffer but I think that's fair. But to drag me into some treatment program, with all those alcoholics . . . I don't think I've done anything that merits that kind of punishment."

The *minimizer* convinces himself that people are overreacting to problems caused by drinking or drug use. His motto: "It's no big deal. Nothing to get all concerned about." And of course, for awhile, this seems to work. Storms blow over; people forget events. But the best way to turn little crises into big ones is to pay no attention to them. Sooner or later, a major crisis hits, and no one is more surprised than the addict.

"What do you mean, divorce?" the minimizer shouts, as his wife is preparing to leave. "Things can't be that bad. Where's your sense of loyalty?"

Or to his boss: "Fire me? You can't fire me! If you felt that strongly, why didn't you say anything about it . . . ? Well, you didn't say it forcefully enough! How was I to know you really meant it?"

Projection: Projecting your thoughts, beliefs, and feelings onto those around you.

We've discussed the extent to which addictive disease distorts the way you think, feel, and act. By affecting brain activity, it alters your perception of reality in an amazing variety of ways— ranging from obvious hallucinations and paranoid delusion, to more subtle distortions of emotion, memory, judgment, and intellect.

But alcoholics aren't aware of this. Like most people—

accustomed to depending on their own perceptions—they operate on the assumption that everyone else feels pretty much the same as they do.

This, of course, is often not the case at all. And as the disease progresses, the addict's assessments of others become more and more inaccurate.

After all, it's an assumption, not an objective evaluation. Yet for all practical purposes, it becomes reality, because the alcoholic bases his actions on it.

Example: from an interview with a young woman, a cocaine user at odds with her family.

ADDICT: They don't really care about my welfare. They hate me. They're just trying to get rid of me.

COUNSELOR: Why would they do that?

ADDICT: (looks blank) I don't understand the question.

COUNSELOR: Why would they be trying to get rid of you?

ADDICT: I don't know. You'd have to ask them.

COUNSELOR: Well, think about it from their perspective. What would they gain from getting rid of you? Why would they bother with it?

ADDICT: (puzzled) I don't know.

COUNSELOR: So how do you know that's what they're trying to do?

ADDICT: (hesitates) I just feel sure that's what they're up to. It's no one thing you can point to.

The addict projects her own anger onto her family—largely the result of her toxic mental state. And pretty soon, with considerable provoking on her part, her family really will get angry with her.

Thus addicts are fully capable of interpreting the most innocent interactions as insults and personal attacks—and of using these resentments to fuel further drinking or drug use.

Defense mechanisms are a normal human response to an uncomfortable reality. If there's something we don't like about our situation—such as the possibility of nuclear war, or intimations that we suffer from a chronic, progressive, potentially fatal disease—we create an alternate reality that explains away (or simply fails to include) the unpleasant part.

Which doesn't make it any less dangerous. It just makes it that much harder for us to survive it.

How Do I Know When This Task Is Complete?

1. You have reviewed your history of involvement with alcohol and drugs and have identified symptoms of addictive disease.
2. You have discussed these symptoms with at least one knowledgable person and gotten their feedback.
3. You have written out the definitions of the various defense mechanisms, as well as one example of each from your own experience.
4. You have reviewed this list with at least one knowledgable person.
5. You have written out a statement explaining why you now believe you have a chronic, progressive, and potentially fatal disease, and what you plan to do to treat it.
6. You have reviewed this statement with at least one knowledgable person.

Task Four

Reduce your frame of reference to a single day.

Sounds simple. But believe it or not, this is very difficult for most newly sober people.

That's because your natural inclination is to explore the past in an attempt to "explain" your difficulties, and to look toward the future in an effort to prevent new ones. It's human nature, and it makes perfect sense—until you realize what it will do to your emotional state.

Everyone's past holds a certain amount of pain and disappointment. This is especially true if you've spent a good portion of your life under the influence of addictive disease—your own or someone else's. Of course, there's nothing intrinsically wrong with exploring your feelings about the past. This is not the time for it, however—for two good reasons.

Problem 1: Your nervous system is still adjusting to life without chemicals. It's in something of an uproar. During this period you're especially likely to overreact to stress.

The stress itself may be normal, but your reaction isn't. Instead of getting anxious, you might find yourself experiencing a panic attack. Rather than feeling frustrated, you might explode in a fit of temper.

So looking back on life's tragedies doesn't necessarily lead to the emotional catharsis or resolution you seek.

You may sink into depression. Or find yourself bitterly angry about something that happened years before. Or feel hopeless about ever making things right again.

Think about it: will any of this make it easier to stay sober?

Of course not. It makes it harder.

It's a little like walking backward. You get a better view of where you've been, but it interferes with your ability to go where you want to go.

Problem 2: What's the point of dwelling on the distant past? After all, there isn't anything you can do about what already happened.

By definition, it's too late.

It's the present that requires your attention.

Your most crucial problems—and their solutions—are locked into your day-to-day existence. You need to examine your behavior and make changes in it. If you're thinking about and reacting to something that happened months or years ago, when do you plan to think about and react to what's going on today?

Years from now? Sorry, that won't work.

It's equally destructive to let your mind drift too far into the future. Sure, it's full of uncertainty. But is that remedied by obsessive worry on your part?

Worrying becomes a habit. People do it because they believe, on some level of magical thinking, that it protects them against greater harm. But of course, it doesn't.

Taking precautions protects you from harm. Once you've taken them, there's no point in worrying about the outcome.

An example: no business is more uncertain than the restaurant trade. Yet when one man who owned a chain of eateries was asked how he handled the stress of potential failure, he answered:

"To be honest, I used to worry all the time. Then I realized how useless that was. What does worrying accomplish? Did I really think the customers would say to themselves: 'Gosh, that owner sure is worried. I better go over and eat at his restaurant?' It was just a total waste of mental energy.

"Now, I take the approach that if I've done what I can to make something work, and it still doesn't, then it wasn't meant to."

Of course you have to plan for the future. But you have a choice: you can make time work for you or against you.

To make time work for you, assess each problem in terms of what you can do about it today—and if the answer is *nothing*, move on to some other item.

Preferably something you can change for the better.

How Do I Know When This Task Is Complete?

1. Begin planning your days. Schedule where you'll be, and when. Include activities that support your sobriety—such as attending groups—and as far as possible, do not alter them.
2. When you think about something that happened in the dim past or is coming up in the future, ask yourself: Is there anything I can do about that today? If the answer is *yes*, schedule time to do it. If it's *no*, don't dwell on it.
3. Go over your schedule with a counselor or some other knowledgable person. Ask them if your plans seem realistic. Are you trying to squeeze in too much? Are you leaving yourself too much slack time?
4. If you find yourself unable to concentrate on the present— you're interrupted by thoughts of bad events that occurred in the past or worry about the future—schedule in time for meeting and discussing these with a counselor or a knowledgable friend. Make this a regular part of your routine.
5. If intrusive thoughts about past or future continue, tell yourself you'll talk about them during your scheduled time—and postpone it until then.

Task Five

Rearrange your activities to support recovery.

Like most things in life, recovery is largely a matter of priorities. As long as it occupies an important place on your list of things to do, you'll probably be able to maintain it.

If you put other activities before sobriety, however—especially during these all-important initial months—you could easily fall flat on your face.

In fact, you'll find a sign posted in many treatment centers:

Sobriety
  Loses
    Its
      Priority

The meaning should be clear. Letting abstinence slip from its place of importance is a direct precipitant of relapse.

Given the extent to which addiction dominates the addict's lifestyle, it's amazing how many things alcoholics come to regard as "more important" than treatment.

Here's a man planning his participation in an aftercare program following discharge from a treatment center:

ADDICT: Boy, I'm glad to be going home. But this has really been a great experience. I didn't want to come in, but I'm happy I did. I was this close to losing my job, you know. But they're going to give me another chance—provided I don't blow it with alcohol. So I'm going to do whatever you people tell me.

Now, the same fellow, six weeks later, calling up to excuse himself from an aftercare session:

ADDICT: I have to work late tonight. Sorry. It's unavoidable.

COUNSELOR: It's the third session in a row. I think you ought to come.

ADDICT: I can't, I told you. It's work.

COUNSELOR: Did you tell your boss you had to go to Aftercare?

ADDICT: No, I did not. I don't see what business it is of his.

COUNSELOR: Does he know you were in treatment for alcoholism?

ADDICT: (hesitates) Yes. He was the one who sent me.

COUNSELOR: So why don't you tell him you have to go to the Aftercare session? He already knows about it.

ADDICT: (angry) I am not going to tell him any such thing. Look, I'm in enough trouble at work already, because of this damned alcohol thing. I need to do everything I can to get back in their good graces. Otherwise, they may just decide to replace me.

COUNSELOR: Just one more question. Did your boss ask you to work late?

ADDICT: Yes. He said we had a lot of work to do, and wanted to know if anybody wanted to stay after and help.

COUNSELOR: I get it. You volunteered.

ADDICT: So what of it? It's an opportunity. I'm short of money. I missed a lot of work while I was in that program.

Look how this man's priorities have changed. He's actually volunteering to miss treatment, though he blames it on "having to work overtime."

Another common mistake is to hang around "slippery" people or places—defined as *environments conducive to relapse rather than sobriety.*

Another example, from a young woman recently readmitted to a hospital after relapsing with cocaine:

COUNSELOR: Why did you start using again?

ADDICT: Somebody offered me coke. I should have turned it down, I know. But for some reason—I guess I was having a bad day—I didn't. And then I just kept on going.

COUNSELOR: Who offered you drugs?

ADDICT: Some guy I know. An acquaintance.

COUNSELOR: Where were you at the time?

ADDICT: With friends. Talking.

COUNSELOR: Where, though? At your apartment?

ADDICT: In a bar.

COUNSELOR: A bar? You were hanging out in a bar, when you'd only been out of the hospital for three weeks?

ADDICT: I wasn't drinking, if that's what you mean. I was just there with a couple of my friends.

COUNSELOR: Were your friends drinking?

ADDICT: Sure. I mean, just because I don't drink, doesn't mean my friends can't.

COUNSELOR: Were these by any chance friends you used to do cocaine with?

ADDICT: Sometimes. One of them is a pretty heavy coke user. The other just drinks, mostly.

COUNSELOR: And what about the guy who offered you the coke? Who was he?

ADDICT: A guy. I used to know him. I used to score from him, actually. We kind of lived together for a while. I moved out because he was dealing too much dope, and I was afraid of getting busted.

COUNSELOR: And when he offered you the dope—what exactly did he say?

ADDICT: Nothing in particular. Just that he had some good blow, and did anybody want to do a few lines?

COUNSELOR: I get the picture. You went out and managed to find some people you used to do drugs with, and they took you with them to a bar where people can get cocaine. Sure enough, your old boyfriend the drug dealer was there, and he of course asked if anybody wanted some blow, and you said yes.

ADDICT: You make it sound like I set the whole thing up.

COUNSELOR: You did.

The rule: stay away from slippery people and places until your sobriety is strong enough to withstand them.

But if that's too complex, think of it this way: at this early stage the principal slippery person is you. And the slippery place is wherever you happen to be. So if you need to socialize, try hanging around with people who present absolutely no danger to your own recovery.

How Do I Know When This Task Is Complete?
1. Each day, make a list of priorities for that day. Put "sobriety" at the top.
2. Make sure you don't bump recovery-related activities for other "more important" functions.
3. Go over your priorities with a counselor or other knowledgable person. Get their feedback.

Task Six

Make abstinence unconditional.

Human beings hate to feel trapped by their own decisions. We like to leave ourselves an "escape clause"—something that lets us feel we have a way out if things don't turn out as we planned.

When you make the decision to abstain from alcohol and other drugs, it's tempting to build in various conditions under which you can change your mind. These conditions usually have to do with circumstances.

So when many alcoholics express an intent to remain sober, what they're really thinking is: "I'll stay away from drugs, unless—

    ... I lose my job."
    ... I have trouble getting along with my wife."
    ... the judge is going to send me to jail for those DWI's anyway."
    ... my teacher is too critical."
    ... I find out my boyfriend is cheating."
    ... my parents keep nagging me."
    ... I get a real bad craving."
    ... I can't sleep."

    . . . I get depressed."
    . . . I'm with a bunch of people who are drinking and I don't
        want to seem weird."
    . . . somebody offers me some."
    . . . it's Christmas."
    . . . my boss makes me work overtime."
    . . . I get passed over for a promotion."
    . . . my ex-wife sues me for nonsupport."
    . . . I have anxiety attacks."
    . . . I get bored."
    . . . I discover I'm still not happy."
And so on and so forth.

This makes sobriety dependent on other people and outside events. "I'll try," the alcoholic tells himself. "As long as I get some cooperation. But if things don't go right, I won't promise anything . . . "

It's understandable. After all, it's tough to stay sober in the face of problems. Nevertheless, that's exactly what you have to do.

And remember: it's not because your counselors or doctors insist on it. They of all people understand how tough it can get. It's hard not to think about a drink when you have trouble sleeping, or when your friends don't understand you, or when you see them drinking or using drugs and getting away with it.

We want you to know that we understand—and sympathize with—the various reasons for going back to alcohol or drugs.

Unfortunately, your disease doesn't.

Individual nerve cells aren't terribly concerned with your motivation for relapse. They react to the presence or absence of a chemical. If it's there, they respond. If it isn't, they don't.

Suppose you've been clean for awhile. Then something awful happens—something legitimately tragic, like a death in the family—and you decide you can't handle it. So you go out and get yourself some cocaine. You smoke a lot of it—after all, you're really depressed. You need more, just to forget.

And you're sitting there, smoking pipe after pipe, and all of a sudden, something funny happens in your chest. There's an odd feeling—as though your heart isn't beating right—sometimes too fast, sometimes out of rhythm. You feel a burning sensation, and you begin to panic. "Oh, no," you scream inside your head. "Not this! . . . "

What are you going to do? Explain to your heart that you had a very good reason for using drugs? That you were in legitimate emotional pain? That you'll never touch cocaine again? That this was just a one-time thing? A lousy slip, for God's sake?

Good luck. Hey, maybe it will work. We'd like to see what odds you get in Las Vegas.

We can see the headlines: "Man Halts Own Heart Attack with Excuses."

This is no joke. It happens all the time. Alcoholics go on binges, thinking the worst that can happen is they'll wind up back in detox . . . and instead, they die. In a car wreck, or a fire, or from some unforeseen medical complication. We knew one fellow who, after three years sobriety, decided to indulge in a monumental drunk following the desertion of his wife. We're sure he saw it as a chance to "let it all hang out" emotionally. Unfortunately, his liver collapsed. He was taken to the hospital and died a week later.

Think about it: can you really afford to make your sobriety—and therefore, your prospects of long-term survival—dependent on circumstances?

Can you afford to get drunk if somebody hurts your feelings, or fails to meet your expectations? If that's your plan, you might as well go out and buy the bottle now. Because it's probably going to occur in the next twenty-four hours.

We see life as a series of events, both good and bad—some predictable, some a complete surprise. If we permit ourselves to fall apart when something bad happens, we may not be around for the good stuff that is yet to come.

We justify relapse by attributing it to outside forces or events. It's really a form of externalization that lingers into sobriety.

The silliest example would be the alcoholic who drinks to get back at someone. "I'll show you," he thinks. "If you're not going to treat me right, I'll just get drunk again."

One man returned to work after completing a treatment program, only to discover his boss still disliked him. "I want you to know I'm not altogether convinced you're off drugs for good," the boss told him. "If it was up to me, I'd fire you. But the company says I have to give you another chance. You better do a good job. And if I see any signs you're back on drugs, I'll get rid of you."

The addict complained to the company employee-assistance counselor, who advised the employee to apply for a transfer. "It'll probably take a few months, though," she said. "Just go to your meetings and try to avoid your supervisor as much as possible.

He can't do anything to you as long as you're sober and still in treatment. He's powerless."

The boss was careful not to say anything more to the employee, but the damage was already done. The addict couldn't forget the insult. The more he thought about it, the angrier he got. "He has no right to talk to me that way," he thought. "I don't have to put up with this kind of harassment."

Everyone around him—counselors, co-workers, friends—advised him to keep cool and wait for the transfer. But one night, he got so angry he had to have a few beers "just to calm down." On the way home from the bar, he was arrested for drunk driving. His name was printed in the newspaper, for everyone to see. The treatment program discharged him for noncompliance. The court pulled his driver's license. The company fired him, as they'd said they would.

The boss felt vindicated. "I told you people this would happen," he smirked. "But you wouldn't listen."

It's not unlike the old joke about the man who finds his wife in bed with his best friend, gets out his gun, and points it at his own head. When the startled lovers begin laughing, he snarls: "What's so funny? You're next."

It's the nature of life to produce a certain number of unpleasant occurrences. It's essential therefore, to avoid making something as important as your sobriety contingent upon uncertainties (such as whether or not you feel depressed at that particular moment, are getting along with your mate, feel satisfied with your career, or have enough money in your bank account).

Those things fluctuate. If you maintain sobriety, you'll be able to solve problems like these—or at the very least, wait it out while they solve themselves.

How Do I Know When This Task Is Complete?

1. Unearth any conditions you've put on your sobriety by listing situations in which you feel relapse might be *understandable*.
2. Then, play each situation through in your mind. Suppose you did relapse? What would be the outcome? Would it solve any particular problem? Would it improve your situation in any tangible way? Would your mental and emotional state benefit in any lasting sense from more drug use?
3. Then, make a list of the *worst possible* outcomes for each of

those situations, presuming you did use alcohol or drugs. What new problems could it lead to? Might any of those problems be worse than the ones you have now? Could anything happen during your "slip" which might be impossible to correct?

Task Seven

Inform significant others of your recovery plan.

Up to now we've asked you to do a fair amount of communicating with other people—but we've been careful to specify that they be knowledgable about addictive disease and the process of recovery. Now, it's time for you to discuss the very major changes you are going to make with people who may not be very knowledgable—and with whom, more importantly, you have a much different kind of relationship.

These people qualify as your "significant others." Your family, of course. Your friends. Maybe your employers or your physicians.

We talk about the importance of changing your lifestyle to support your recovery. In a very real sense, these people are your lifestyle. You depend on them, and they on you.

Yet there's a good chance that not one of them is an expert on addiction. Like you, they have a lot to learn—and again like you, they have other things to worry about. So you can't simply expect them to demonstrate automatic support and understanding for what you have to do. Thus, the first part of the communication problem: *If you want them to understand, you'll have to learn to explain your actions*.

Some recovering addicts resent this. "I'm doing what they wanted," they think. "Why can't they appreciate it more? Can't they see how hard I'm working?"

The answer is: probably not. What's their frame of reference? The average nonalcoholic is able to quit drinking with few problems. Many have never even tried drugs like cocaine or narcotics. How could they understand what it's like for someone who's been addicted?

They can't—any more than a nondiabetic can imagine what it's like to have a diabetic crisis. Or someone with a healthy heart can understand how it feels to have had a heart attack.

Addiction is the same way. We used to have a friend who smoked no more than two or three cigarettes a week. To us—heavy smokers at the time—this was incomprehensible.

"How can you stop after two or three?" we'd ask.

"How can you bring yourself to smoke more than two or three?" she'd respond, equally puzzled. Our behavior—and its motivation—wasn't in her realm of experience. As hers was foreign to us.

So if you expect a degree of understanding that others don't possess, you'll be sorely disappointed. Better to explain what you're doing as you go along.

Here's an example: a man graduates from a treatment program. He returns home to his family and begins attending AA nightly. They know this is good—after all, he's not drinking—but they have all sorts of questions about his behavior.

"Does he have to go out every night?" his wife asks. "That's what he did while he was drinking. Isn't he supposed to spend time with his family?"

"He's better, but you still can't talk about your problems with him," says his teenage daughter. "I feel like I can't bring up anything without him getting uptight. I think he should have to listen to our feelings, just like we have to listen to his."

"Why do we have to start going to church every Sunday?" his ten-year-old son wants to know. "I don't like it. We never had to go before."

"Every time you try to talk to him," his mother adds, "he just says we don't understand, and that this is a selfish program. Well, I don't think it's right to tell people they should be completely selfish. AA shouldn't do that."

First of all, this is a classic communication problem. The explanations they seek are readily available. The problem is that the alcoholic refuses to provide them.

We asked him why.

"I'm doing the whole thing for their sake," he complained. "You'd think they'd appreciate it. It's hard enough dealing with my own problems, let alone worrying about theirs. I thought all they wanted was for me to stop drinking. Now I've done it, and it isn't good enough."

"You quit drinking for their sake?" we asked. "If it wasn't for them, you'd go back to booze right now?"

"Well, I'm not saying that, exactly. I knew I had to quit for myself. I know I have a disease. But they're so impatient. They have to understand that I'm not completely well yet. That I don't really know what's going to happen. I'm just hoping to stay sober a day at a time."

"Why don't you tell them that?" we suggested. "And stop telling yourself that you're staying clean for their sake. If that was the case, you'd already be drunk. Besides, it just makes you resent them. Stay sober because of your disease. That's your opponent. Not your family."

Now for the second part of the problem: *dealing with their reaction to your program of recovery.*

In the earlier example, we see a good illustration of some of the ways people around addicts interpret the behaviors associated with recovery.

The alcoholic's mother protests the "selfishness" of the AA program. She doesn't understand that part of the reason is to combat the alcoholic's natural tendency to focus on outside problems and the behavior of others rather than on himself. She doesn't realize that recovery must assume a preeminent place in the sober person's life, until it's firmly established.

Otherwise, it might not ever get firmly established at all.

She interprets "selfishness" in the light of her own experience—and naturally considers it a "bad" quality. It's only when viewed in the context of the disease that its role becomes understandable. Somehow, this has to be explained to her.

Or take his teenage daughter's complaint that her father won't listen to her opinions. It turned out that what she wanted to express was her intense dissatisfaction with the way he treated her when he was drinking—she felt he'd been overbearing and insensitive, and a poor excuse for a father.

Of course, that was probably true. Nevertheless, it wasn't difficult to see why he became "tense" and refused to listen when she tried to "share" these sentiments. His augmented nervous system (see Chapter 7) began to jangle, and his principal desire was to get out of the house.

Yet when he stormed away without comment and later refused to discuss his reaction, he chose the one course of action that virtually guaranteed a recurrence of the conflict. Sooner or later, his daughter's resentments would resurface, and the fight would begin anew.

What else could he have done? He might have gotten her to a counselor, or to Alanon, where she would have received some practical advice on how to deal with her own resentments.

He might have taken the time to explain to his wife the importance of attending meetings nightly during the first months of sobriety—or offered to take her along to Alanon, where she'd hear the same information. And he might have discussed his sudden return to church attendance with his son, rather than just dragging the kid off to a sermon every Sunday.

Each of these solutions would have reduced the likelihood of future conflict in these same areas, because his family would gain more knowledge about recovery. Their expectations—which he found so burdensome—would become more realistic. Hopefully, his family would eventually become allies in recovery—rather than obstacles to it.

And that raises the third part of the problem: *What if they're still angry about what happened in the past?*

Well, it would be easy to understand, wouldn't it? For most of the period of active addiction, they—like you—failed to understand the role this disease played in your behavior. They took it personally. Got involved emotionally. Felt hurt, resentful, and suspicious.

These things don't go away overnight. It takes time and education. And more help than you can provide them.

So wherever you can, encourage your family to participate in counseling and to join self-help groups. Don't start worrying about what they'll say about you behind your back. Don't convince yourself it's entirely your problem. The people you're involved with need advice and assistance as well. The closer they are to you, the more help they'll probably need.

And paradoxically: the better they get, the more you'll benefit.

How Do I Know When This Task Is Complete?

1. Go over your recovery plan—the things you're going to do or change in order to facilitate recovery—with your counselor or sponsor. Discuss the reaction you think you'll get when you put it into effect.
2. Get the counselor's feedback on the way you present it. Make changes in your presentation to make it more likely you'll get a *positive response* from your significant others.

3. Discuss what you're going to do with each significant other. Let them ask questions. Try not to get mad if you feel they don't trust you, or haven't forgiven you for the past. Discuss that later with your counselor.
4. Make it clear to your family that you think it's a great idea to participate in counseling or a self-help group.

Task Eight

Examine factors that might contribute to relapse in the initial stage of recovery.

The first seven tasks were designed to motivate you for ongoing treatment and then to get you "up and running" in a program for recovery. The next two tasks are specifically oriented toward preventing relapse.

Remember that addiction is chronic. It's a challenge not only to get well but to stay that way.

Since we've already discussed the wisdom of making abstinence unconditional, let's see if we can't figure out how to make that as easy as possible. The way to do that is to take a look at the things which make recovery difficult.

These fall into two categories: *external* and *internal*.

External Factors

We're referring to situations in which you're most likely to—if we may be indelicate—fall flat on your behind. Some examples:

Drinking Occasions. Parties where alcohol is served can be particularly difficult for the newly sober. In the first place, people actually offer you drinks, which means you have to think of a reason to turn them down. Since most folks are reluctant to say, "Actually, I'm an alcoholic, currently involved in treatment," they have to think of some silly lie which generates still more stupid discussion. If you say something like, "I'm currently under a physician's care, and he's recommended I abstain," you might get more inquiries about the nature of your illness— which requires you to concoct yet another lie.

Of course, you could say that you'd rather not discuss the exact nature of your condition. But then you have to spend the rest of the party wondering whether or not this bozo is telling everyone you've got AIDS.

Chronic Conflicts. Nearly every addict is involved in at least one relationship that is characterized by a degree of chronic conflict. Such relationships provide unlimited excuses for relapse.

For example, suppose you and your father haven't been able to spend twenty minutes in conversation without an argument since you were eleven years old. Suppose also that your traditional response to these arguments is to go to a bar and get progressively drunker while replaying the latest round over and over in your head. This is probably not going to change simply because you've quit drinking. It's highly likely there will be more arguments—and more opportunities for relapse—in the future.

Predictable Crises. These would be the problems stemming from your active addiction, left unresolved, which come back to haunt you when sober.

Bill collectors and bounced checks. Upcoming trial dates or sentencing for convictions. Your car may be repossessed. You're in line to get laid off. You think you'll get involved in a child custody fight.

A number of them won't happen simply because you're no longer putting yourself at risk through alcohol or drug use. But which are the areas where problems are likely to occur in the near future?

Other Drug-Using Friends: Are you actively involved in a relationship with somebody who has a drug or alcohol problem? And planning to maintain that contact, even though that person will probably continue to use drugs?

Internal Factors

There are a number of attitudes commonly found among the newly sober which breed discontent and therefore make recovery more difficult than it would otherwise be. Here are five examples; there are many more.

"This is not fair." As in: "All my friends drink as much as I do. I have to quit, and they don't?" Or: "I don't think it's fair to expect me to devote so much time to staying off drugs. When am I supposed to do anything else?"

"But I'm not like these people." Example: "I listened to those stories in the group, and none of that stuff ever happened to me." Or: "I feel lucky to have caught my problem early. It won't be difficult to beat." Or: "Listen, I don't mean to sound like a snob, but some of those people in that treatment center have been arrested."

"Sobriety is boring." As in: "What am I supposed to do for fun? Stay home and watch TV?" Or: "These meetings are dull. Why don't they get some better speakers?"

"I'll never be able to get over that." To wit: "Even if I quit drinking, how will I live with the memories . . . ?" Or: "Drugs were my way of coping with the pain of my divorce. What will replace them when I feel depressed?"

"You people have to make some changes too." For example: "I'll try to stay away from drugs, but if my friends start coming around again . . . " Or: "Look, if you want me to quit drinking, you're going to have be an easier person to live with . . . "

We go along with Abe Lincoln in the belief that people are about as happy as they make up their minds to be. Our opinion is that the above attitudes (and others like them)—each of which is perfectly defensible in normal situations—nevertheless contribute mightily to unhappiness in persons who are trying to recover from addictive disease. Why? Simply because they foster unrealistic expectations that are likely to disappointment, and thus lead to relapse.

How Do I Know When This Task Is Complete?

1. You've made a list of both external and internal factors that might make sobriety difficult and contribute to relapse.
2. You've gone over this list with a counselor or other knowledgable person and gotten their feedback.
3. You've revised your list where appropriate to include their suggestions and comments.

Task Nine

Develop a plan to prevent relapse.

Now, use the list you made in the previous task to develop specific strategies to avoid relapse. Here are some suggestions, based on the hints we gave.

How to Deal with Drinking Occasions

As far as possible, avoid social gatherings where liquor will be served during the early months of sobriety. If you have to attend, go with someone who's also going to refuse offers of alcohol. If you think it might be wise, use Antabuse for those occasions.

How to Deal with Chronic Conflicts

Sit down with your counselor or sponsor and analyze the nature of these conflicts. Ask yourself:

   . . . What do I argue about?

   . . . Can these topics be avoided?

   . . . Is it possible to avoid this person entirely for a period? If not, how can interactions be controlled so that conflict is minimized?

   . . . Who usually fires the first salvo? How could arguments be derailed before they get a chance to gain momentum?

Devise a plan of action for dealing with each such relationship. Don't allow yourself the luxury of simply *reacting* to situations that occur.

How to Deal with Predictable Crises

Make a list of these crises. Then write out two options for dealing with each. Discuss it with another knowledgeable person. Decide what alternative will be your first choice should the crisis occur tomorrow. When you're satisfied you have the best solution possible—it won't be perfect—forget about the problem and get on with your daily program.

How to Deal with Drug-Using "Friends"

Stay away from them. No, it is not feasible for you to move back in with your cocaine dealer in order to encourage him to get into treatment.

Make new friends. In fact, make a plan for making new friends. Where can you meet them? What kind of people are you looking for? Go over this plan with another knowledgable person. Where are its weaknesses?

How to Deal with Your Own Unhelpful Attitudes

There are as many ways to deal with these as there are unhelpful attitudes. Discuss this with your counselor or group. How do they deal with their negative attitudes?

Here are our suggestions for the examples we gave:

"This isn't fair." Right. There's very little about addictive disease—or most diseases, for that matter—that is fair. As a matter of fact, there's very little about life in general that is fair. People develop elaborate schemes in an attempt to provide a modicum of fairness and equity in the world—the law would be an example—and things are still unfair a good percentage of the time.

Fairness is a human doctrine. Nature clearly doesn't understand it. It continues to present you with difficult choices—such as "treat this disease or suffer"—and completely ignores your protests.

So it seems you have still another choice. You can rail against the disease and against what you have to do to survive it. Or you can get on with recovery and adjust to the reality of your situation.

Which do you think will be the smoother course?

"But I'm not like these people." Untrue. You're not *exactly* like these people. Each person is unique. Nevertheless, you do have the same disease.

One of the really miraculous things about addiction is that it takes persons from all backgrounds, education, ability, and circumstances and makes them act pretty much the same. Self-help groups are built on that commonality. If it didn't exist, there wouldn't be any self-help movement.

So you have another choice. You can dwell on the differences between you and those other folks. That will leave you pretty much on your own. Your willpower versus your disease.

Or you can note the similarities and make use of other sufferers as a support for recovery.

It's up to you. Which alternative is most likely to increase your chances for success?

"Sobriety is boring." Sure it is, sometimes. It can also be terribly exciting. Mostly, it's somewhere in between.

Treatment can be boring, too. But then again, it's not there for entertainment, is it? If that's what you want, try television.

Treatment is supposed to save your life. As long as that happens, what difference does it make if it sometimes lacks dramatic impact?

You think cancer patients don't get bored in chemotherapy? Diabetics don't get tired of giving themselves insulin?

"I'll never be able to get over that." How do you know? In one sense, you have already gotten over it. It's gone, and you're still here. All that's left are memories.

It's ironic: alcoholics and drug addicts, who are famous for forgetting the present (blackouts and short-term memory loss), are also known for dwelling on the past. Maybe that's because time doesn't really pass in an alcoholic haze. It's easy to relive an event that happened five years ago as though it were yesterday.

But no matter how many times you relive it, the pain never seems to go away. It's as though it becomes fixed in the fabric of your toxic brain.

For now, stay with the present. There'll be plenty of opportunities to explore the nooks and crannies of your past, once your nervous system has a chance to recuperate a bit. But if you keep relapsing, you'll probably never get to that point.

"You people have to make some changes too." This sounds as though you're making your recovery conditional on the behavior of others, doesn't it? And that's bad, because they may not meet your expectations.

Look at it this way: What's been your experience up to this point? When you've set standards for people, have they usually measured up? Or have you found yourself frustrated and disappointed at their apparent reluctance to live the way you think they should?

Could there have been anything wrong with your expectations?

Slip the shoe on the other foot: how have you measured up to their expectations?

The best approach to the initial months of recovery is twofold. It involves

1. *strict adherence* to a program for recovery, and
2. a *flexible attitude* in your dealings with other people.

In other words, while you set boundaries on your own activities, you set as few as possible on other people. Let them be themselves. Give them room to make errors, be imperfect, have flaws.

That way, they're more likely to accord you the same privileges. Tolerance works both ways.

How Do I Know When This Task Is Complete?

1. You've anticipated your own weaknesses and begun the process of dealing with each.
2. You've reviewed your approach with your counselor, sponsor, group, or any combination of the above.
3. You've read Chapter 8 on *relapse* and studied the factors most likely to apply to your situation. You've developed a plan to avoid being blinded by your own *defense mechanisms* around the issue of impending relapse.

Task Ten

Put this plan into action.

There's a big difference between planning and action. Lots of things look great on the drawing board. But how do they hold up in the arena of everyday life?

It's the same with recovery. The only way to evaluate your strategy is to try it out.

Of course, you'll encounter problems you didn't anticipate. That's been true for most of your life, and it hasn't changed.

But they'll be fewer in number and probably less severe than before. The biggest change is in your ability to solve problems.

Now that your brain is no longer actively under the influence of a toxin, you'll be able to:

1. *Seek out* good advice
2. *Remember* the advice that's given you

3. *Plan* effective action
4. *Carry out* your plan
5. *Modify* it further if necessary.
Of course, you aren't required to exercise good judgment. If you like, you can mess things up. But at least you now have a choice in the matter.

If you want to succeed, you can. In the past, it was pretty much up to the disease.

How do you know when you're making progress? Look for "little victories" rather than grand triumphs. It's the small successes—that often go unnoticed—that ultimately save your life.

At first, your primary motivation will be the desire to avoid further crises. After awhile, you'll begin to experience the rewards of recovery. There are a lot of them.

A positive program of "staying well" will gradually replace "doing without" alcohol and drugs. Sobriety becomes less of a struggle. Recovery will seem as natural as drinking and drug use did in the past.

But that's a gradual process. To see what it's like, turn to Chapter 7 on the stages of recovery.

Due to the unpredictability of this period, it's crucial to develop a method for assessing strengths and weaknesses in your own program. This allows you to make positive changes and to avoid obvious pitfalls.

It's also important to remember that your still-active defense mechanisms will prevent you from seeing some of the most apparent weaknesses in your program. That makes it extra important that you develop a relationship with someone who is:
1. Knowledgable about addiction and recovery
2. Whom you will allow to tell you the truth
3. With whom you are in daily contact.
This person helps you monitor your own program. No matter how intelligent or determined you may be, you cannot see through your own defenses. It doesn't work that way.

In AA, this role is taken by the *sponsor*. See Chapters 8 and 9 for more on this important topic.

Whatever the source, you will need ongoing feedback from others to avoid unnecessary problems and reduce your risk of relapse.

How Do I Know When This Task Is Complete?

1. You've developed a plan for monitoring your own recovery through daily contact with a person or persons whom you will permit to point out inconsistencies in your behavior.
2. You've begun talking with them daily, either in person or by telephone.
3. You can demonstrate three changes in your recovery program you have made as a result of suggestions from this person.

Chapter Seven

Life in the Months after Addiction

Like the descent into the addiction itself, recovery occurs in stages. The behavior of the alcoholic or addict—especially in response to stress—depends as much upon his or her current stage of recovery as it does upon more obvious factors, such as personality.

Stage One

High augmentation/intensive change.

As elsewhere in this book, we will once again focus primarily on the initial months of recovery, when change is the most dramatic and the risk of relapse highest.

This first stage, known as the "high augmentation" period, ranges from three months (short) to twelve months (extended) in time. There are three keys to understanding behavior during this stage.

The First Key: Understanding Emotional Augmentation

If you read the Preface at the beginning of this book, you already know that we believe most of the credit for developing the

Chronic Disease Model belongs to the pioneering work of Dr. James Milam. Another of Milam's great contributions to the clinical literature was his explanation of alcoholic behavior in terms of augmented emotions. Augmentation—the intensifying and distorting of everyday emotions—begins early in the alcoholic's drinking career and continues (to one degree or another) well into sobriety.

Emotions, like any other brain function, are profoundly influenced by disruptions in the nervous system itself. That's why emotional responses to stress—such as fear, anger, sadness—can be augmented or in some cases _blunted_ by drugs. When you take a tranquilizer, you suppress anxiety by dulling your brain's responsiveness to stress in general. Conversely, when you take a stimulant, you _heighten_ your sensitivity to the environment—and may actually experience added stress.

In addiction, emotions are distorted not only by the drugs you use but, in their absence, by drug _withdrawal._ So much so that even after you've renounced the drug, you may find your emotions augmented—and you may overrespond to everyday events.

Regrettably, our research on humans in this area is limited to autopsy. We've had therefore to rely on laboratory animal studies, which have been conducted despite our distaste for them.

Consider the following experiment: Researchers have taken a cat and implanted electrodes which stimulate the cat's brain with electricity to the point where he experiences the classic animal "fight/flight" response—the same reaction you see when your pet is cornered and can't escape.

electric charge

How does a cat look when he's ready to fight? His backs arches. The fur stands up on the back of his neck. He hisses threateningly. Claws slip from their sheaths.

Because this response is induced by electricity instead of a recognizable antagonist, the cat's anger won't be focused. He will look about for an enemy—but won't find one.

Aha! the researchers conclude: *Our dose of electricity produces a full-blown "fight" response.* They turn off the current, allowing the cat to calm down.

Now it's time for the second stage of the experiment. From the opposite side of the lab, they bring in a yappy, obnoxious dog. The dog begins to bark. The cat, seeing the dog, immediately responds defensively. Back up, claws out, hissing. There's a difference: this time, his anger is directed at the dog.

Why? Because the cat understands that the dog is his natural adversary.

Aha again, the researchers think: *The natural enemy produces a response identical to that elicited by the current.* They then remove the dog from the lab and once again allow the cat to relax.

Now the researchers are ready for the conclusion of the experiment. They bring the dog back into the lab. The cat sees the dog. Just as he's going into his fight response, they turn on the electricity.

electric charge

And what happens?

The cat's response is dramatically augmented. Translation: he goes berserk.

If we could stop the cat in midpanic and ask him why he was responding so forcefully, could we expect him to say, "Well, I don't like dogs, and I'm also being secondarily agitated by that electrical apparatus over there"?

Of course not. He would attribute his entire response to the identified enemy: the dog.

"That is the worst dog I've ever seen," he'd say. "Much worse than ten minutes ago! You substituted a Godzilla of a dog! That's why I'm so upset!"

Let's carry the analogy over to the typical alcoholic or drug addict, the morning after:

We can replace the electrical apparatus with agitated nerve cells—which is what withdrawal represents—and we can replace the dog with the alcoholic's natural enemies: other people.

Suppose one of those "significant others"—say, a spouse—decides to criticize the addict for something said or done the previous evening. The addict, as always, begins to respond defensively. And as he does, his agitated nervous system augments his response.

In other words, instead of getting irritable, he gets really angry. Or rather than feeling disappointed in himself, he becomes deeply depressed.

Suppose that in response to his exaggerated emotionalism, his wife gets angry and begins yelling. Once again his nervous system further augments his emotions, and their argument escalates. Each time she gets angry, he gets "angrier" still.

Suppose again that we could stop this process in mid-debate. If we asked the alcoholic why he was experiencing so much intense emotion, would he say: "Well, I don't feel she's being fair, and also, my emotions are being secondarily augmented by withdrawal-related agitation?"

Of course not. He doesn't understand this. Like the cat, he would blame his reaction on his identified adversary. "My wife is the worst nag in the world," he'd insist. "Anybody would react this way. She provokes it."

Or: "OK, I told my boss to go to hell, but it was his fault. He's just too critical. Everybody feels that way."

Or: "I shouldn't have hit the kid, I know. But he provokes me deliberately. I watch the other kids, and they don't talk to their parents that way."

Or: "It's my parents' fault. The way they get on my case—anybody would have left home. It isn't just me."

But that's only half the problem. Like the alcoholic or drug addict himself, those around him also misinterpret the causes of his behavior.

"I don't know why your father is so irritable," the wife of a cocaine and alcohol addict explains to her teenage daughter. "I guess he's under a lot of stress. I think we all have to try extra hard to be good and not irritate him."

Or this example, from an office supervisor: "I was really surprised to find out he had a drinking problem. He was short-tempered and hard to get along with on the job, and his memory was shot, and he would make a lot of mistakes. But we never saw him drinking, so we never thought about alcoholism. We just came to the conclusion that he was a jerk."

From a fifteen-year-old girl: "I thought Mom just hated me, because she was actually nicer when she'd had something to drink. She was meanest when she was sober. Or sometimes, she was just so depressed she couldn't get out of bed. So to my way of thinking, alcohol actually helped her. It never occurred to me that it was withdrawal that made her so miserable when she was sober."

The same phenomenon continues into sobriety. We see it in hospitals while the alcoholic is undergoing detoxification. Almost any little problem is enough to provoke panic.

One day, walking down the hallway in the Detox Unit, we heard a bloodcurdling scream come from one of the patients' rooms. We rushed in to discover a fifty-year-old alcoholic executive, admitted the previous day, standing beside a hospital dinner tray.

"This is *unbelievable*!!!" he roared. "I ordered peas, and they

send me green beans!! *I hate green beans*!!! What kind of in-
competents run this place, anyway? I demand to see the person
in charge!!!"

It's a legitimate complaint, but the reaction is grossly inappropriate.

Five days later—when detoxification is farther along—the
same error produces no display of temper. What's changed? The
state of his nervous system.

There's another paradox here: because of augmentation,
legitimate tragedies—the death of a loved one, for example—
often elicit a delayed emotional response.

As a result therapists may wrongly conclude that the alcoholic
is out of touch with his or her feelings. If anything, the newly
sober person is phenomenally hyperemotional. But when the
demands on the individual's emotional resources are too great,
you might see a flattened, apparently emotionless response—
followed (several days, weeks, or even months) later by an outpouring of emotion.

One psychotherapist described this syndrome: "My patient
had been in treatment about three weeks when her mother died.
She was really close to her mother, even to the point of being
overdependent. And the death was totally unexpected. So I
thought I would see a great outpouring of emotion when I told
her, and instead, I got nothing—a few questions, a stated desire
to attend the funeral. But that's it. I remember thinking: this
woman is really out of touch. And I don't think it was just denial.
I've seen plenty of that in my work with families, and this was
different. She really wasn't feeling anything.

"This lasted for about six weeks. She arranged for the funeral,
burial, took care of her mother's affairs. No obvious depression,
none of that manic quality you see in people who have just
received an emotional blow and are repressing it, either. Then
finally it hit. I got a phone call in the middle of the night, and she
was on the other end, weeping and throwing things and just
totally grief-stricken. I talked to her for about an hour, and I got a
friend of hers to go over and stay with her. It lasted for about a
week, and then she was all right again. I was amazed she didn't
drink."

Again, this syndrome is a powerful argument for ongoing
treatment. Had this woman not been involved in counseling
or a self-help group, she might well have resumed drinking or
drug use.

The Second Key: Understanding the Physiology of Early Recovery —and Its Effects on Behavior

Most of us are aware of the psychological changes that must occur during the initial recovery stage. But physiological changes may be equally dramatic.

If you observe some of the symptoms outlined below and your doctor can't find a cause, don't be unduly worried. They may be a result of the profound biochemical adjustment the recovering addict undergoes in the first months of sobriety.

Of course, these changes affect you as well as the addict. They're cause for worry and alarm only if you're not prepared for them—if you haven't accepted that you're dealing with a disease rather than a moral or behavioral problem. Every chronic disease has its own timetable for recovery, and it varies from individual to individual. There's only one rule: given time and sobriety, addicts get better.

Here are some of the occurrences commonly reported by newly recovering alcoholics and drug addicts.

Insomnia. This is probably the most commonly reported occurrence in early recovery. Actually, for many addicts the problem is really one of *fractured sleep:* they drift off, wake up frequently, and have some difficulty falling asleep again.

Theories as to the cause are numerous and inconclusive. Some researchers relate it to deficiencies in *serotonin,* a neurohormone often depleted during years of alcohol or drug use and difficult to replenish through normal diet, even once drinking has stopped. That's why a number of treatment programs make use of serotonin precursors such as *L-tryptophan,* which can be purchased at health food stores and produces good results in some cases. In others, however, it appears to have no effect.

Of course, some addicts bring about their own sleep problems—through excessive consumption of caffeine in the form of coffee, tea, or sodas. The remedy: *stop it.*

The main danger is the temptation (to both patient and doctor) to make use of sleeping pills. There are two problems in this area: first, most of them are likely to reawaken the craving for alcohol or other drugs. Second, they aren't effective in the long run, anyway.

Mood Swing and Depressive Episodes. This is a bit different from simple augmentation. Some recovering persons swing between depression and elation; others skip the periods of unrestrained joy but cycle in and out of depression. It's rare to find a newly recovering person who doesn't experience some mood swing. For most, it's simply a byproduct of years of polluting the brain with toxins and abates with time. But for a percentage, it's the sign of coexisting depressive disorder and should be treated by a psychiatrist (one who's familiar with addictive disease and the dangers of medication).

The symptoms of depression are as follows: crying jags or feelings of hopelessness, apathy toward normally rewarding activities, decreased sex drive, difficulty making decisions, poor concentration, loss of desire to care for oneself, persistent sleep disruption, recurrent episodes of anxiety.

These are broad enough that almost everyone will experience several of them. It's when a number are found together at the same time that a coexisting psychiatric problem is most likely.

Fortunately, depressive disorder is treatable. See a physician familiar with both addiction and depression, and follow his or her directions.

Residual Tremors. The recovering person goes to write a check and discovers his hand is shaking. "My God," he thinks. "I haven't had a drink in three months! What's wrong with me?"

Usually, nothing. It's just his nervous system missing its drug of choice. Sometimes, however, it's a sign of poor diet, excessive caffeine consumption or, perhaps, an underlying blood sugar problem.

If the affected person is willing to put up with a somewhat irritating procedure, he can have his blood sugar tested with a *glucose tolerance test,* to see if it falls into either the hyperglycemic or hypoglycemic ranges. See your internist for further information.

Anxiety. Anxiety is a feeling of *dread,* as though something awful were about to happen. The anxious person might experience "butterflies" in her stomach, a rapid pulse, a feeling of lightheadedness bordering on fainting. When this occurs with no obvious precipitating factor, we call it *free-floating* anxiety.

In most cases, episodes of anxiety are relatively short-lived (a matter of minutes) and pass without intervention. Over time, they decrease in severity, frequency, and duration. They constitute one of the most common occurrences in recovery and are one of the best reasons for involvement in the supportive, reassuring fellowship of the self-help group.

If such episodes increase in intensity or become more frequent over the first months, however, it's best to have them evaluated by that same psychiatrist—the one who's familiar with addictive disease. Many of the medications used by clinicians to treat anxiety are strongly *cross-addictive* with alcohol and can promote relapse. There are others available, however, which can be used safely under medical supervision.

Food Cravings. Newly sober people have all sorts of weird food cravings. As one related: "I was just getting off drugs, and my wife was pregnant. It worked out real well: we'd both wake up in the middle of the night with a craving for pistachio ice cream."

The craving that gets the most attention is the one for *sugar*. Many people report their sugar consumption doubles or triples once off drugs. "I never ate sugar when I was drinking," one claimed. "All I wanted was salty foods: potato chips, nuts, stuff like that. But all that changed. I would eat five or six candy bars a day. And dessert at lunch and dinner. I was a thirty-six-year-old man with the sweet tooth of an eight-year-old."

In fact, a sugar-heavy diet is one of the common causes of nervous discomfort in the newly sober. Consider Jack, just out of a treatment program, who's gained ten pounds. Disgusted, he adopts what we have come to call the "Just-Out-of-Detox Quick Weight Loss Plan." He eliminates breakfast, substituting coffee and cigarettes. Then he eliminates lunch, substituting a candy bar, two extra sodas, and still more cigarettes. Then about 7 P.M. that evening, overcome with hunger, he breaks down and goes to a fast-food place. There, over a fifteen-minute period, he consumes a hamburger, fries, apple pie, and a chocolate shake.

Sugar content: about like mainlining a box of Oreos.

Thirty minutes later he's sitting at an AA meeting, downing his third cup of battery-acid coffee, and shaking like a leaf.

"Jeez," he tells his sponsor. "I'm really having a rough time. I think it's all the stress at work."

This is relatively easy to correct. The recovering addict should follow these simple steps:
1. Knock off the megadoses of caffeine.
2. Change his or her diet.

3. Add regular exercise (doesn't have to be vigorous).
4. Take vitamin supplements.

Flashback Experiences. Sometimes, symptoms of drug toxicity—particularly those involving *perceptual distortion*—recur after an extended period of abstinence. For example, a number of young drug users have reported distortions of images on a TV screen, or recurrence of the "trailing" phenomenon, whereby moving objects seem to leave trails of light behind them. Sometimes the flashback experience includes the sensation that someone is calling your name or that moving objects (difficult to identify) flit around the periphery of your vision.

Flashbacks themselves are quite harmless. They provoke anxiety, nonetheless, because the addict can't attribute them to a specific cause and may assume they are an indication of a nervous breakdown of sorts. In most cases they pass quickly and require no medical intervention. If they persist, or prove a source of worry, see a physician familiar with addiction.

Sexual Dysfunction. Most forms of addictive disease are accompanied by some degree of sexual dysfunction. For example, male alcoholics may experience episodic impotence, and females may have difficulty attaining orgasm. Several studies of narcotics addicts have reported dramatically diminished sexual desire in men and severely interrupted menstrual cycles in women.

And of course, the effect of chronic cocaine use on sexual performance is the stuff of legend. Perhaps this is because cocaine makes use of some of the same neurohormones that make sex pleasurable—and when those are depleted, sexual reward is also reduced.

When we think of dysfunction, we normally think of impotence. But newly recovering persons may experience a wide range of problems, such as:
1. Decreased (or in some cases, increased) sex drive.
2. Unpredictable *fluctuations* in desire, from intense to absent.
3. Difficulty reaching orgasm.
4. Exaggerated sensitivity (or lack of it) in erogenous areas.
Along with episodic impotence, as well.

Sex is such a complex behavior that it's impossible in many instances to trace problems to a single cause. Because this is an anxiety-laden subject, there's a tendency to rush off to the sex therapist at the first sign of trouble. But clinical experience tells us that many of these problems resolve over the initial months of sobriety without intervention. And it's important not to let this (or any other) problem distract the newly sober person from the all-important task of avoiding relapse.

Our advice to both the newly recovering person *and* worried partner: be patient. If things don't improve you can always seek professional help. Just remember: this is not worth getting drunk over. If that happens, you'll still have a sexual problem, but you'll be miserable on top of it—as well as back on the road to disaster.

We don't call that progress.

Headaches. The incidence of this symptom varies widely. For some, this is the major difficulty of early recovery. Others have few or no problems. It's often associated with menstrual periods in women. And it's especially common among those whose primary drugs were from the narcotic family.

The principal danger is through the use of cross-addictive medication to treat headache. Again, that's why it's important that the recovering person see a physician who is familiar with the peculiarities of treating patients with a history of addiction. Otherwise, the medications they prescribe may precipitate a relapse.

There really are no universally effective remedies for headache. Aspirin is probably the closest. Other remedies might be a brief period of relaxation and perhaps a self-hypnosis exercise. For the newly sober, the important thing to remember is that their headaches may not persist forever but may be tied to the first months of recovery. So it's important not to overreact: in the absence of convincing evidence, headaches during this period are not the result of an undiscovered brain disease (a common assumption among the emotionally augmented).

Weight Gain and Loss. This is partly due to obvious changes in eating habits. If someone's a cocaine addict who's been getting most of her nourishment through a straw or pipe, she may experience some fairly dramatic changes in weight once she's back on natural stuff. If an alcoholic has spent the past few months picking at food between drinks, he too will probably see his weight change.

Weight variation is also due to changes in the way the body processes food. People who quit smoking, for example, experience weight gain partly as a result of the absence of stimulants that suppress appetite and partly due to a slowed metabolism.

But the biggest culprit in weight gain is probably bad diet. If the recovering addict is worried about getting fat—some people could care less—he should remember to avoid crash diets. They not only don't work, they're liable to drive the dieter a little crazy as well.

Aches, Pains, and Cramping. This is especially likely to occur to the newly sober person who has an old injury that hasn't bothered him in years. That newly awakened nervous system of his may rediscover it.

Fortunately, the discipline of physical medicine has developed all sorts of techniques to alleviate discomfort from aching, cramped, or overtense muscles. There are exercises similar to those given to orthopedic patients; they can be obtained from a doctor or the physical therapy department at a local hospital. There are electrical stimulation units that some people find indispensable. There are relaxing baths and massage. There are self-hypnosis techniques that seem particularly effective in some types of chronic discomfort.

And also once again: there are a number of medications to avoid. A doctor with a background in addictions can help select something safe, if medications are necessary.

Forgetfulness. This may be related to longstanding deficiencies in thiamine and other essential vitamins. Even with supplements, memory deficits can persist far into sobriety.

The most common type of deficit is in the area of *short-term memory.* For purposes of illustration, first, there's *immediate retention:* the ability to recall something that's just been presented to you. Then there's a second level: *short-term postdistractional memory.* That's your ability to recall something after an intervening period of distraction.

This second process is the one most often deficient in recovery. It means that newly recovering people can comprehend and repeat back information but have difficulty recalling it several hours later.

If the recovering addict's job is repetitive—say, pumping gas—this may go unnoticed. If, on the other hand, she's in school, or has to learn new skills at work, it could be a major block to success.

How have people in early recovery dealt with short-term memory deficits? They take notes, for one thing. They write down anything they think may have to be remembered. Especially things like appointments, key dates, schedules. They don't rely on memory.

Allergies, Colds, and Infections. Another commonly reported occurrence is a seemingly increased vulnerability to colds and respiratory infections. Additionally, many addicts report a sudden resurgence of allergies—some virtually inactive since childhood.

"I drank for twenty-five years and never missed a day of work," one man reported. "In the first year I was sober, I used up all my sick leave—and I had three weeks accumulated. I caught every cold, every bug that went around, and it seemed like they all lasted forever. Then, after that first year, it just sort of stopped, and I've been healthy ever since."

"I broke out in pimples," complained a woman. "Thirty years old, and I look like a teenager. Then about four months later, it just disappeared. It was very weird."

There are even more unusual phenomena on record.

"My hair was salt-and-pepper—more salt, actually—and in the year after I quit drinking, it changed color. Grew in dark. I felt like a kid."

"It took me a year before I had a menstrual period," reported a thirty-three-year-old narcotics addict. "And I was pregnant a month after they started up again."

The Third Key: Understanding and Dealing with Craving

Craving is a nonspecific term for any kind of spontaneous desire to use a drug. It's most likely the result of a classic combination of physiology and learning. As a person's body undergoes a transformation from a drug-based to a nondrug "fuel economy," it calls out for its favorite toxins. And of course, there's no more firmly "conditioned" behavior in addiction than drug use itself—think of the overwhelming number of sips, gulps, puffs, or hits that occur during the course of an addict's career.

As a result, newly recovering people find themselves experiencing three types of craving for drugs:

1. *Free-floating craving,* seemingly unrelated to the environment and probably the result of activity on a biological substrate;
2. *Craving due to emotional excitement,* related to allowing the pendulum of one's augmented emotions to swing too far in either direction (elation or depression); and
3. *Conditioned craving,* set off by some environmental cue—anything from seeing old drug-using friends or drinking buddies, to watching a commercial for booze or a documentary on drugs on television.

Cravings vary greatly in form and intensity. One of the more important things people do in recovery is to learn how to recognize and deal with them.

Here are some examples:

Euphoric Memories. Addicts find themselves remembering how wonderful they once felt when they were under the influence of drugs. They forget the bad things that happened later. "I never forgot that first experience," many alcoholics say. "I spent the rest of my life looking for it—unsuccessfully."

Intense Dreams. Sometimes, the dream is so real that people wake up wondering if they've managed to use the drug while they were asleep.

Bothersome Thoughts. The recovering person is doing something unrelated, and thoughts of alcohol or drugs will pop into his mind—and then refuse to leave.

Planning Relapse. "She's leaving town over the weekend," the alcoholic says to himself. "If she goes on Friday, and I get something that same night, I could have myself a little party, and still have all day Saturday to recuperate. When she returns on Sunday, how will she know what happened?"

Acute Drug Hunger. An actual, withdrawal-like craving for the drug. The person can't seem to get comfortable, to rest, to sleep, to concentrate on anything else. By this point, relapse is virtually inevitable.

Some addicts tell themselves that if craving ever gets really severe, then they'll do something about it. Of course, by that time, it's too late.

When craving reaches a certain intensity, *defense mechanisms* reappear, and the ability to perceive one's own problems is greatly diminished. This makes it difficult to take steps necessary to avoid relapse. *After all*, the addict reflects, *why bother? I was never that bad in the first place . . .*

We can't count the number of alcoholics and drug addicts we've met who get prescriptions for Antabuse (disulfiram) or naltrexone and then keep it in the medicine cabinet instead of taking it. "If I ever want a drink," they tell themselves, "I'll take the Antabuse." But by the time they think of the medication, they've already had a drink. And of course, that precludes use of Antabuse.

The best way to deal with craving? We like the *Three "R"* method:

Recognize. Identify a craving as a craving, instead of whatever else it may seem to be. Many therapists indirectly contribute to the problem by helping the addict externalize his craving. Example:

ADDICT: I had a dream last night . . . it was so incredibly real . . . I felt like I must have used cocaine. I could feel the smoke burning my throat, and then that rush coming on . . . Then several times the next day, I would find myself thinking about drugs. What does it mean? Am I going to use again?

THERAPIST: Well, is there anything going on in your life that would cause you to start wanting to do drugs?

ADDICT: Not really . . . well, now that you ask, I've been arguing with my wife lately . . . and I'm still not really happy at work . . . I don't feel my talents are really being used the way they should . . . and I need a raise . . . so I guess I'm pretty frustrated.

Here, the therapist actually contributed to the problem, by linking the craving to a whole array of outside circumstances the addict is not prepared to change. It sets up a false equation: "craving equals problems in relationships and lifestyle." To see the flaw in this reasoning, ask yourself the following question: "This person was on drugs for an extended period. He has been off drugs for a very brief period. If his life were perfect, would he still experience cravings for drugs?"

The answer is yes.

In reality, craving is a natural outcome of addiction. And it would be unrealistic to expect the brain to abruptly stop calling for alcohol and drugs simply because we decide it should. *If we don't satisfy that craving with more drugs, it will diminish and gradually disappear*. If, however, we give in to it—it will grow ever stronger. That's the nature of addictive disease.

So recognize a craving for what it is: a temporary residual complication of addictive disease—and not a sign that the life of the recovering person requires total reorganization.

Reduce. There are dozens of ways to reduce a craving. Here's a partial list:
1. Vigorous aerobic exercise
2. Eat something (preferably not refined sugar)
3. Talk to someone about the craving
4. Distract yourself with some pleasurable activity
5. Use a self-hypnosis/relaxation technique
6. If it's a "cued" craving—leave the situation that is triggering the craving and go to an environment that reduces it.

Different tactics work best for different people. The key is to interrupt the craving as early as possible—in other words, at the level of the intense dream, bothersome thought, or euphoric memory.

Cravings vary tremendously in length. Most that we've seen are relatively short in duration. They "come and go" rather than stay for extended periods.

Refocus. Once the craving is gone, the addict needs to go back to whatever he or she was doing. There's no point in sitting around wondering whether a craving means, as one addict put it, "that I'm hopelessly addicted, and I'll probably always use drugs."

It doesn't. It means the person is recovering. And if he or she maintains abstinence, the experience of cravings will dwindle as the months pass.

Stage Two

Moderate augmentation/involvement.

This stage of recovery is marked by noticeable improvement in most areas of life. Again, there seem to be several "keys" to understanding the behavior seen during it. Since, however, this phase tends to drift beyond the boundaries of our main concern—the early months we call the initial recovery stage—we'll only briefly summarize its highlights.

Key One: A Change in the Nature of Augmentation, from Generalized to Specific Situations

In the high augmentation stage, we noted a pronounced tendency to overreact to most forms of stress. That gradually disappears, and many of the same problems that would once have precipitated relapse are easily handled.

Now, the tendency to augment seems confined to emotionally charged situations—usually involving a specific set of stressful circumstances, or the assumption of new, anxiety-provoking responsibilities.

Key Two: "Waxing and Waning" of Physical Symptoms

Most people continue to have some physiological symptoms for several years. But where they once persisted through days, weeks, or months, they now wax and wane. There may be extended periods during which they are quiescent, followed by episodes of recurrence.

This may also be at the root of the legendary *dry drunk* or *sober hangover syndrome,* the subject of so much discussion in organizations like Alcoholics Anonymous.

The Dry Drunk features the return of symptoms characteristic of active addiction. For no obvious reason, the addict may find himself in the grip of intense craving, or even experiencing what appears to be *acute withdrawal.*

Key Three: Residual Memories of Events from Active Addiction

It has become apparent to us over the years that memory improves during recovery. For some people, this is true not only for *short-term events*, but also for memory of events that occurred long ago.

Listen to the stories of addiction told by recovering addicts as they progress through the stages of recovery. The stories change substantially. Part of this, of course, is because of their improved perspective. Part of it, we believe, is because they are able to remember things they previously had "forgotten."

And occasionally, this may be accompanied by powerful feelings of remorse.

"It was awful," one woman reported. "At about nine months, these memories started coming out of nowhere. I remembered things I'd said and done when I was drinking, that I thought were gone forever. I would have vivid pictures of incidents, and I knew as soon as I had them that they had really happened. I got really depressed, and if it wasn't for my AA sponsor, I probably would have gotten drunk. But she told me to sit down and do a Fourth and Fifth Step all over again. I made an inventory of the things I felt guilty about, and shared it with her, and I started to feel better almost immediately. It's funny—I thought I had already done those Steps. But I hadn't."

Key Four: A Desire for Change

As sobriety becomes stable—thereby requiring less attention—the recovering person usually looks around for something else to become involved with. It may come in the form of a career change, an increased focus on family, or—if single—a desire for an ongoing relationship.

Focus on Family. Where the early stages of recovery may have been marked by absorption in individual goals—with addict and family members moving separately but in the same direction—this stage may feature a reorientation toward the family and relationships in general.

The problems that are encountered—barriers to communication, misunderstanding of each other's intentions, resentments over past events—are the same ones that have been there all along. But in this stage, the addict and family are much better equipped to deal with them.

That is, provided the family hasn't made the crucial mistake of assuming that recovery is entirely the alcoholic's problem and has simply been waiting—resentments and demands at the ready—for him or her to show some interest in renewing the relationship.

In that case, the "family" as such may not survive this period. If they insist on holding the alcoholic accountable for everything he said or did while in the grip of the disease, the family unit may break apart. Families are not meant to take that kind of strain.

Sure, alcoholism is not a defense in the eyes of the law—*but we're not in court, remember?*

Stage Three

Low augmentation/maintenance.

By this point, it would be difficult to separate alcoholics from nonalcoholics on most psychological scales. Pronounced craving is a thing of the past. Most of the recovery symptoms have abated. It is increasingly easy for the addict to accept himself as a recovering person. Mood swings are diminished.

The recovery program has become one of maintenance. Like the stable diabetic or heart patient, the real key is to provide continuing motivation for adhering to the recovery program.

There's still a danger of relapse, though it's greatly reduced. It comes largely through two factors we discussed previously: *overconfidence* and *overinvolvement in other activities*.

It's hard for people to understand how someone who's doing well might choose to start using alcohol or drugs again. But that's precisely the reason they do: *because* they are doing well. Such false confidence can lull them into taking that "one drink" which turns into a major relapse.

That's one of the principal reasons why alcoholics remind themselves they are "just one drink away from a drunk."

Sometimes, the recovering person's desire for further involvement in life represents another risk, since it's really an effort to "make up for time lost" through years of drinking or drug use.

That too can be dangerous. What's gone is gone, and no amount of frenzied activity can make up for it. It can provoke relapse, however, if unchecked, simply by providing enough distraction to make it impossible to concentrate on the tasks of recovery.

The Common Questions Asked by Family, Friends, and Associates during Early Recovery

1. Should we remove all alcoholic beverages from our home? What about restricting money?

With most adults, it's a waste of time and energy. Once an alcoholic decides to drink, that person won't be stopped by a little obstacle like having none in the house. Our cities are absolutely jam-packed with places to buy liquor. If you're *really* lazy, you can get it delivered.

The same is true for other drugs. Even being flat broke isn't a deterrent. Most coke users can find somebody to "front" them cocaine. Most narcotics addicts can find someone who'll trade heroin for some type of service.

There is an exception. In cases where drinking or drug use is typically an act of unbridled impulse—without much premeditation or effort to control—then simply limiting the availability of the drug may inhibit relapse. One example would be where the alcoholism is *severely late-stage*—and the alcoholic is an older person suffering from some organic brain impairment, with limited access to funds or transportation. Another would be that of an *adolescent* who lacks significant impulse control and drinks or takes drugs on the spur of the moment.

Just remember: without the addict's cooperation, relapse will inevitably occur, no matter what precautions are taken by those around him. The key to recovery is the *alcoholic's* attitude.

2. Then is it all right to drink in front of an alcoholic?

Some recovering alcoholics feel very strongly that they do not want their disease to interfere with the pleasure of other people.

They will insist that others go ahead and drink as they normally would.

Others find it very uncomfortable to be around people who are drinking. Not so much because they're jealous, but because most nonalcoholics act a little funny when they drink. If you don't believe us, try staying sober at a party where everyone else is drinking. See if it doesn't seem a bit *stupid* to you.

The only way to figure out how your alcoholic feels about this issue is to ask.

3. Is it okay for a recovering cocaine addict to be around his old drug friends?

This doesn't seem to work, especially where the addict's primary drug is one noted for its ability to produce a strong craving—cocaine or a narcotic, to name two. Being around others who are using these drugs is an almost inevitable prelude to relapse (if not at that moment, then shortly afterward).

4. Does he really have to go out to meetings all the time?

In this stage, it's a good idea. The needs of the newly recovering aren't easy to meet through the "normal channels" of family, friends, and work. He needs advice and guidance that a counselor or a group provides. Don't let yourself get jealous—they don't want to take him away from you.

5. Why do I have to go to meetings?

If you're still asking this question, you haven't read Chapter 5 on the ten tasks of recovery for the family. Turn there now and read it. Our position in brief: you have to change, too. The nature of addictive disease is to make you either part of the solution or part of the problem. It won't let you be neutral.

6. What can he or she handle in the way of responsibilities at work, and so on?

Being an adult means assuming responsibility for your life. Every human being has responsibilities to family, work, friends, the law, government, and so forth. If we don't meet them, we get in trouble.

Being an alcoholic or addict means having a disease that *interferes,* to a greater or lesser degree, with one's ability to meet these responsibilities. It doesn't much matter how strong willed or determined or principled a person might otherwise be—addiction will turn these strengths to its own ends.

When someone first gets sober, it's tempting to try to assume a number of new responsibilities in an effort to make up for the follies of the past. This won't work, of course. Quitting drugs or alcohol doesn't turn anyone into Superman. It turns that person into a recovering alcoholic or drug addict. That's good—especially compared to the state he or she was in before making that choice—but there's a long way to go.

As a matter of fact, family members and even employers can be tempted by the same false promise. "Now that he's drug free," they tell themselves, "he can do this job, and he can handle this, as well, and he can take over this, too . . . " There may even be a hint of revenge: "Besides, I need a rest, and he should have been doing it all along . . . "

The reality: neither the alcoholic nor those around him know for sure what he is capable of handling. The only way to find out is through trial and error.

If you were running a business and were planning a new project that you weren't certain was going to work, wouldn't you start *small* and see how things went? Recovery is like that.

There's a paradox here. Some people have expressed fear that the disease model removes responsibility from the addict. In reality, it places a host of new tasks and duties squarely on the addict's shoulders. He or she is totally accountable for them.

Recovery itself is the assumption of responsibility: for abstinence, for sticking with treatment, for changing lifestyle, for avoiding relapse. As long as those responsibilities are met, others will fall into place as time passes.

If, on the other hand, those primary responsibilities aren't met—few others will be, either.

7. *He's still irritable. Will that change?*

Yes. Irritability is characteristic of most addicts during the initial months of recovery. It doesn't much matter whether they've given up alcohol or cocaine or cigarettes. Of course, some are a little better at adjusting to it than others.

One thing to remember: newly recovering people tend to have more trouble with minor inconsistencies than with major problems. Many come through actual crises with flying colors but fly off the handle at some small irregularity in daily routine, or at being assigned some new task they didn't anticipate. They're not likely to be *patient* when confronted with delays, and they can be awful *perfectionists* regarding both their own actions and those of other people. That's one reason for the popularity of the slogan, "Live and Let Live," within self-help groups.

It's generally not a good idea to go out of one's way in an attempt to *please* a family member who is experiencing this degree of irritability. There are two reasons. First, it won't prevent future displays of the same behavior (in fact, it may encourage them). Second, it creates an unequal relationship, wherein one person is constantly (and unsuccessfully) trying to meet the demands of another. That's a good breeding ground for resentment.

Strive to be *reasonable*. If you don't know what to do in a particular situation, ask for advice from a counselor or sponsor in a self-help group.

8. *She seems so moody. Is this normal?*

It's normal for newly recovering people to experience a certain degree of fluctuation in mood. They're known for it. It's sometimes hard to distinguish these swings from those characteristic of more serious conditions, such as depressive or bipolar disorder. That's why so many have been misdiagnosed as suffering from these conditions.

That's another advantage of a strong aftercare program. A counselor or physician can be enlisted to evaluate the alcoholic in this respect, so that if treatment is necessary, it can be initiated.

9. *What can we do if we suspect he or she is drinking again?*

Once again, see Chapter 5 on the tasks for the family. In brief, if the addict relapses it will soon enough become obvious. If he or she is involved in an aftercare program, work with the counselor to intervene and to restore his or her involvement in treatment. If the addict's not in an aftercare program, contact a counselor for training in intervention.

If it's a family member, avoid the role of "detective." You'll probably just drive the drinking or drug use further under cover. Contact the professionals for advice.

> *10. Sometimes I see him doing some of the things he did before he stopped drinking—like working long hours and missing AA meetings and getting defensive whenever somebody criticizes him. What should I do?*

In brief: yes, these *can* be signs that an alcoholic is building toward a relapse. And it's true that some form of intervention is required.

But in most cases, the family by itself is not the best intervention tool. When a wife, husband, or child attempts to control or change the alcoholic or addict's behavior—to manipulate him or her into attending more meetings, or working fewer hours, or being less defensive—old patterns of enabling and provoking may emerge. This creates an atmosphere of conflict that can actually feed *into* the relapse dynamic.

So the best approach is to discuss the situation with an aftercare counselor or with others at a self-help group. Wherever possible, let the professionals take the lead in planning intervention.

Quitting Smoking

"I spent ten years telling people how great it felt to be drug free before I realized that I couldn't last twelve hours without a cigarette."

—a former smoker in AA

It's both tragic and ironic that so many people recover from alcoholism and drug dependence only to die eventually because of yet another addictive disorder: smoking. The scope of the problem is staggering: Cocaine may kill six thousand Americans a year, but tobacco-related illnesses kill more than that every *week*. And it's of special interest to the recovering community: 80 percent of our former patients continue to smoke well into sobriety. Although quitting smoking isn't a requirement for sobriety (if it was, there would be far fewer people in Twelve Step programs), we think it makes a terrific project—both rewarding and possibly life-saving—for your second or third year of sobriety.

If you or someone you love still smokes, here's a seven-step plan for quitting.

Step One

Learn About Nicotine Addiction.

Most of us regard alcoholism as a disease and smoking as a bad habit. But if anything, nicotine is even more addictive than heroin or alcohol. It's a stimulant, like cocaine or amphetamines, and a cigarette is to the nicotine addict what the pipe is to the crackhead—a cheap, effective way to get the drug to a hungry brain.

But does nicotine addiction qualify as an addictive disease, to be classified alongside alcoholism and drug dependence? Let's see if it meets the usual criteria.

1. *It's chronic and progressive.* Most smokers begin in their late teens and continue to smoke for at least ten years before they quit. The negative aspects of smoking (shortness of breath, irritability) become more apparent as they age.

2. *It's potentially fatal.* As noted above, smoking was tied to more than four hundred thousand deaths in 1990.

3. *Addicts experience tolerance and withdrawal.* Most smokers start with an occasional cigarette and gradually increase consumption until they approach a pack every day. A minority may consume as many as two, three, or even four packs in a twenty-four hour period. When they attempt to stop or cut down, they experience irritability, craving, and restlessness associated with decreasing levels of nicotine in their bloodstream. The symptoms are never as intense as heroin withdrawal, but persist for weeks and may be equally likely to produce relapse.

Progression of Nicotine Addiction

EXPERIMENTATION STAGE

Recreational smoking, usually with others

Smokes regularly at social occasions

Begins to crave cigarettes in certain settings

Starts buying cigarettes

Amount and frequency increases

Becomes more tolerant to nicotine (less effect per cigarette)

Regularly experiences craving for tobacco

DEPENDENT STAGE

Experiences mild irritability when unable to smoke

Makes sure tobacco is always available or close at hand

Develops "maintenance pattern"

Withdrawal worsens, becomes actual physical discomfort

Avoids situations where smoking is prohibited

Defensive about criticism of smoking

Avoids discussing health consequences of smoking

Experiences shortness of breath, rapid heartbeat due to smoking

Guilt feelings about "smoking too much," "should cut back"

DETERIORATIVE STAGE

Cuts down on consumption to reduce risk to health

Soon resumes consumption at higher levels

Switches to low-tar brand

Increases consumption further

Makes attempt to quit

Returns to smoking

Health problems increase

Chronic remorse about smoking

Failure of repeated attempts to quit without assistance

REHABILITATIVE STAGE

Seeks help for smoking cessation

Abstinence

4. *It's compulsive*. Smokers who've made an attempt to quit and have relapsed may experience this compulsion in a very powerful way—they find themselves consuming many more cigarettes than formerly. One psychiatrist we know smoked a pack of cigarettes in *two hours* following six weeks of abstinence.

5. *Addicts continue to smoke despite adverse consequences.* There are thousands of documented cases of smokers who persist in the face of severe, even life-threatening medical conditions. Do you know someone ordered to stop because of lung or heart disease who still smokes? Someone who stands outside his smoke-free workplace in the dead of winter, puffing on a cigarette? Someone who grouses about every price increase yet still forks over thirty to sixty dollars a month for tobacco?

Clearly, nicotine dependence is related to the addictions we describe in this book. Therefore, you'll need to *self-diagnose* as part of recovery. To assist you, turn to the Progression Chart and make a list of the symptoms you have experienced.

Step Two

Investigate Smoking Cessation Programs in Your Area.

You've probably heard or read that all smoking cessation programs are equally ineffective—one year after completion, only 30 percent of graduates remain smoke free. This can be misleading. Studies often fail to take into account the number of people who have one or more relapses before subsequently establishing stable abstinence from nicotine—a population your own experience should tell you is quite large.

A smoking cessation program can do several things that you can't do by yourself. First, it's a quick and convenient source of information about the detoxification process. Second, it provides group support. Third, it helps structure the behavior change which accompanies abstinence.

Most outpatient programs are inexpensive, convenient, and can be found by calling the local hospital or heart, lung, or cancer information center.

Step Three

Stop Smoking.

If you were to stop abruptly, you'd probably experience something like the following withdrawal syndrome:

Stage One: Agitation

Begins three to four hours after the last dose. Features anxiety, muscular tension, irritability, difficulty sleeping, high craving.

Stage Two: Reactive Depression

Begins about twenty-four hours after last dose. Symptoms are nervousness, difficulty concentrating, forgetfulness, short temper, mild periodic anxiety, mild craving, emotional volatility, fatigue, insomnia.

Stage Three: Honeymoon

Begins approximately three to ten days after last dose. Improved mood, energy level, sleep pattern; craving present but manageable.

Stage Four: Post Acute Withdrawal Phase

Begins two to four weeks after last dose. Craving relatively mild but many symptoms of rebalancing physiology: periodic nervousness, irritability, sleep disruption, cold symptoms, fluctuations in energy.

Stage Five: Second Honeymoon

Begins four to six weeks after last dose. Improvement in above symptoms leads to conclusion that danger of relapse has passed and withdrawal is over.

Stage Six: Relapse Phase

Begins approximately six to ten weeks after last dose. Return of craving, emotional lability. Very high risk of relapse. Much "covert" craving: That is, the former smoker doesn't realize he is setting up a relapse and unconsciously exposes himself to risky situations.

Stage Seven: Stabilization

Begins ten to fifteen weeks after last dose. Craving is largely the result of conditioned responses to certain situations or environments, and these can be avoided. Abstinence is fairly comfortable with a few exceptions: periods of unusual stress, periodic (often every few months) episodes of recurrent craving, occasional strong memories of pleasures associated with smoking.

Some of this is unavoidable: the price you pay for months or years of addiction. But to ease the discomfort of detox, try decreasing consumption *gradually,* in much the same way a physician might advise. A simple method: For two weeks, carry a piece of paper with your cigarettes, folded in the cellophane around the pack. Smoke as usual. Every time you light up—no matter where or when—write down your location, the time of day, what you are doing, and the intensity of your desire, on a scale from one to four, as below.

1. You really didn't want the cigarette but lit up mostly out of habit.
2. You felt like having a cigarette but could just as easily have done without it.
3. You wanted a cigarette and would have felt deprived if you hadn't been able to have one.
4. You really needed a cigarette or you would have felt physically uncomfortable.

After two weeks of this, you should have learned something about your own pattern of addiction. How many do you rate in each category? In week three, eliminate all the ones and twos, so that you're only smoking cigarettes you need in order to feel comfortable. The following week, cut out the threes. Hold yourself to fours for a week, then quit entirely.

There are also medications and behavioral techniques that can reduce the discomfort of withdrawal. *Clonidine* is a heart medication often used to reduce withdrawal symptoms; it can be prescribed orally or in the form of a time-release skin patch. Nicotine gum is also useful for some. Your doctor can provide more information. Hypnosis is effective for some smokers to aid in the initial stage of abstinence. Normally, hypnosis requires one to four visits to a certified hypnotherapist for full effectiveness. Contact your local lung association or medical society to see if they have a list of approved practitioners.

Step Four

Get a Buddy in a Twelve Step Group.

Find someone else in AA or NA to act as your "temporary sponsor" in quitting smoking—an individual with experience in successful recovery from alcohol and drugs as well as from tobacco. A hint: You're more likely to find such a person at a nonsmoking meeting. Discuss your plans and ask for his experience, strength, and hope in terms of nicotine addiction. Arrange to meet regularly at meetings or talk on the phone. Use this person as a role model—someone who succeeded in doing what you would like to do while coming from a similar background to your own.

Step Five

Change Your Environment to Support Abstinence.

In other words, make things easy on yourself by altering behavior patterns which are strongly associated with smoking. If coffee and cigarettes are synonymous in your mind, do something to break that pattern: switch to tea, or walk around rather than sit at the table while drinking it. After meals, get up and brush your teeth, then do something distracting: exercise or get out of the house for a while.

Remember: Smoking a pack a day means taking as many as 75,000 puffs a year, each bringing immediate relief from withdrawal. It's hard to imagine a more strongly conditioned behavior. It will take awhile for your brain to accept the fact that you're no longer feeding it doses of nicotine.

Step Six

Study the Causes of Relapse.

Relapse is not at all mysterious. It happens because nicotine addiction is very persistent and because smokers are human beings, with all the attendant weaknesses. When relapse occurs, it is almost always surrounded by defense mechanisms: the same denial, rationalization, externalization, and minimizing which surround drinking and using drugs. That's the best reason to seek outside help—none of us is so insightful that we can penetrate our own rationalizations without feedback from others.

Here are a few scenarios in which relapse occurs.

No self-diagnosis: Many people quit smoking for the "wrong" reasons—for example, to get someone else off their backs. That's fine as long as they eventually come to understand the need to *remain* abstinent after the nagging stops. Without this realization, relapse will follow. Here's an example.

Darla's husband and children nagged her for several years about her smoking. Finally, she gave in. "I'm going to quit just to shut them up," she told herself.

Needless to say, her family was overjoyed. They all praised and rewarded Darla for exhibiting the willpower to stop cold turkey. Darla enjoyed this but knew in her heart that if it hadn't been for their nagging, she never would have found the motivation to remain smoke free. Darla had never seen much of a downside to smoking: She couldn't understand smokers who complained about coughing, or the cost of a pack of cigarettes. To her, they were small sacrifices for the pleasure of tobacco and the relaxation it brought.

After Darla had gone a year without smoking, her eldest son (a leader of the get-Mom-off-cigarettes campaign) went off to college, her two daughters became involved in more school activities, and her husband's job required more travel. This meant Darla spent a great deal of time alone. She didn't mind—after years of taking care of others, it seemed like a vacation—but she did find herself thinking about smoking more than she had in months.

One evening Darla watched a friend light a cigarette after

dinner. It happened to have been Darla's favorite brand, and as soon as she saw the pattern on the filter, she found herself unable to recall why she had denied herself the pleasure of tobacco. What the heck, she decided. Just this once. Who's it going to hurt? They're all at school or on the road, anyway.

That cigarette came and went, but others followed. To her astonishment, Darla discovered that her craving for nicotine was far greater than it had ever been. She kept telling herself that if she quit once on her own, she could of course do it again. That was only common sense. But each time she tried, she found herself thinking up reasons to have just one more. . . . Until, one month later, she simply gave up and resumed smoking in front of other people again. Her family was deeply disappointed, and the complaints about the noxious smoke were worse than ever. But Darla knew that quitting was not something she felt strong enough to do at that particular point. And all she could think to do was wait and hope and pray that another opportunity would come, and that she would have sense enough, if she got off tobacco a second time, not to go back.

Slippery people and places: Sometimes relapse occurs because smokers insist on hanging around other smokers. Betsy and Ben, both heavy smokers, had been married for twenty years. Betsy had been advised by her doctor to quit, since she had signs of emphysema. Ben, on the other hand, felt quitting wasn't possible at that point. Betsy felt that she had no right to ask him to quit for her sake—"I don't think I could have done it for Ben's sake if it was me," she said—so she repeatedly made attempts to quit without influencing his use of tobacco. Inevitably, she relapsed. The situation was always the same: She and Ben would go out to dinner with friends who also smoked. Betsy would begin experiencing her craving during the meal, anticipating that everyone else would smoke as soon as they were done. By the time they lit up, she was "dying" for a cigarette. Within three days, she would smoke again.

Forgetting the addiction: Sometimes smokers relapse out of simple, destructive curiosity—the kind that killed the cat. Lee quit smoking on a dare, because her son bet her she couldn't. The withdrawal she feared proved to be largely imaginary.

After about four months, she began to wonder whether or

not her reaction to nicotine might have changed. After all, she was no longer addicted. What would happen if she tried to smoke? One day she was sitting around the kitchen table with a couple of her friends and took a drag from one of their cigarettes. It nauseated her. *Isn't that interesting?* she thought to herself. *I've really changed. My body rejects tobacco.*

A couple weeks later, she was sitting around the same table with her girlfriend Lucy, who was smoking one of the new long cigarettes Lee had heard about. Once again she took a puff, and once again felt sick. This experience was a revelation. *You know,* she decided, *if I get sick from smoking, then it must be okay for me to have an occasional cigarette. If I don't even enjoy it, how can I possibly get addicted?*

So she began smoking again because she didn't want a cigarette. This meant in her mind that it was safe to have one.

Within three weeks she was smoking at least one cigarette every day, and craving more. She tried to quit and somehow couldn't. Before she knew what she was doing, she found herself lighting another one. Finally she gave up and went back to smoking full time—at a level twice what she had consumed before her initial attempt to quit.

Distracting medical difficulties: Smokers often suffer from other medical problems, and sometimes these problems motivate relapse. Vern quit smoking for a year. He experienced little difficulty and enthusiastically praised the benefits of not smoking to his friends. After a while, however, he began to experience some difficulty with his lung capacity, reminiscent of what he suffered while he was still smoking. He visited the pulmonary specialist and was told he suffered from emphysema—that quitting smoking was not going to be enough to stem the advance of this disease, and that he would probably experience more problems in the future.

That night Vern was sitting alone in his living room, pretending to watch TV, thinking about the rest of his life. *If I'm going to die anyway,* he reasoned, *why not smoke?* He bought a pack of cigarettes and smoked half of one. He immediately regretted it, threw the pack away, and swore that he would never touch another. But the hunger had been reawakened, and Vern found himself unable to stop this time; he died of emphysema two years later.

Step Seven

Share Your Recovery with Others.

Rather than sit around hoping you can stay away from cigarettes, become proactive. A suggestion from AA: After you've been smoke free for six months, help somebody else. Perhaps you might volunteer at the local cancer society. Train to become a smoking cessation instructor. Start a smoking cessation group in your workplace, for which you serve as a resource person. Offer to help someone else in your home group who wants to try to quit. By aiding a fellow sufferer, you directly increase the chances of your own success. Remember the slogan—*the best way to keep it is to give it away.*

Chapter Eight

Coping with Relapse

What you get when an addict relapses isn't much different from what you saw before initial treatment. *It's just worse.* In fact, each relapse will be a little more damaging than the last.

There'll be increases in drinking and drug use, of course. Accompanied by loss of control and probably blackouts. If anything, the alcoholic will seem even more defensive than before. The problems that result—medical, legal, financial, work-related, marital, what-have-you—usually hit new highs.

It's a lousy way to live, of course. But it's nothing very new.

In some ways the worst thing about relapse is the *sense of failure* everyone feels—particularly the family. "Treatment didn't work," they decide. "The whole thing was useless. There's no point in even trying. There's nothing we can do anyway."

And in many instances that's exactly what the family does: *nothing.* Meanwhile the addict plunges deeper and deeper into the addiction, spiraling downward at a faster rate than ever before.

Here's our point: because relapse is little more than a return to drinking and drug use—no matter how severe that may be—the principles of intervention are still valid. They work about as well for the relapser as they do for the person who's never been treated.

If you read Chapter 3 on intervention and getting an alcoholic into treatment, you may recall the three common mistakes families make in dealing with resistant addicts. Those were:

1. *Not being clear,* either in describing the problem or in setting forth the solution.
2. *Dealing with the addict as individuals* instead of as a united front.
3. *Giving up too easily* in the face of resistance.

Not surprisingly, many families make exactly the same mistakes in their response to relapse.

Likewise, those around the relapser have the same advantages to help them overcome the addict's defenses:

1. They are not actively under the influence of toxic chemicals—so their thinking should be clearer than the addict's.
2. The relapser's behavior is unusually predictable—which means the family can anticipate and overcome defenses.
3. They should be able to identify and make use of leverage and influence to get the addict back into treatment.

The key to intervention is cooperation, and the single most pronounced obstacle to its success is the belief on the part of family members that relapse is a final, unequivocal sign that treatment has failed.

Which, of course, it isn't.

It does mean that treatment hasn't succeeded, this time. But it doesn't imply that the relapser can't or won't once again get sober.

Most of the first members of AA were alcoholics with innumerable relapses. Many of the counselors working in the nation's treatment programs have had one or more relapses; yet they now enjoy stable sobriety.

The first step in terminating a relapse usually involves overcoming the family's resistance to further intervention.

Here's an example. A counselor received a call from a woman whose husband had been discharged from an outpatient treatment program approximately three months before. We'll pick up the conversation after the woman has described the antecedents of the relapse—which has been in progress for about a month.

WIFE: So that's the story, I guess. I had such high hopes he was going to make it.

COUNSELOR: I think there's a good chance you could get him back into treatment.

WIFE:	What? I don't see how. He won't go. He doesn't even come home half the time. The minute I brought up treatment, he'd explode. Or just leave and go to a motel.
COUNSELOR:	It took an intervention to get him into treatment in the first place. I think we could do a second intervention to stop this relapse.
WIFE:	There's absolutely no chance. I wouldn't even dare bring it up to the kids. Do you know my son flew in from Phoenix for the intervention? I couldn't ask him to do that again.
COUNSELOR:	Maybe you wouldn't have to. Aren't there several of your children here in the area?
WIFE:	Hah. My oldest daughter is so mad at him she won't even let him see the grandkids. She's washed her hands of his problem. The others don't want anything to do with him, either.
COUNSELOR:	I can understand that. But that pretty much leaves you stuck, doesn't it? I'd be glad to sit down with all of you and see if I can't provide a solution.
WIFE:	(angry) Doesn't this ever end? Why do I always have to be the one to take care of everything? I have needs of my own, you know. I'm sick and tired of having to run things.
COUNSELOR:	I can understand that, too. All I'm saying is there may be a way to get him back into treatment, and then you wouldn't have to worry.
WIFE:	That's what we thought would happen the first time. And it didn't last. Why don't you just admit it? The program didn't work. As far as I'm concerned, nothing ever will. At least until he reaches the point where he's so miserable even he doesn't want to drink anymore. And I can't imagine that happening until he's on his deathbed.
COUNSELOR:	So what are you going to do?
WIFE:	Do? There's nothing I can do.

COUNSELOR: With all due respect, I think there is.

WIFE: Well, that's your opinion. You're not the one who has to live with him.

As understandable as this woman's feelings may be, the practical result of her attitude will be an extended relapse. And who'll bear the brunt of the consequences?

She will, of course.

The alternative? Here's an example where intervention successfully terminated a painful relapse.

Jared is a twenty-six-year-old electrician who relapsed two months after discharge from a treatment program. Since that initial relapse—about three months ago—he's used cocaine half a dozen times, usually in the form of weekend binges that he funds with the family's savings or through selling family possessions such as the television or stereo. He has no children. His wife is a secretary with a good job, and his mother runs her own day-care business. They are the ones most directly affected by his relapses, and it is they who contact the counselor for help.

COUNSELOR: Well, I think I'm pretty clear on what caused Jared's relapse. He wanted to make a lot of money quickly, so he volunteered to work overtime every night and stopped going to meetings. Then he started having a beer when he got off work because he was so exhausted, and one night he got a little drunk and decided to buy some coke. Since then, he's been going on a binge every couple of weeks. He empties out the bank account, or steals something from the family—he doesn't own anything himself— and sells or trades it for crack. Then he disappears for the weekend—nobody knows where. And staggers back to the house, where he crashes for most of a day. He refuses to discuss the problem with you, and if you bring it up, he loses his temper and stalks out of the house. He's getting paranoid again and thinks everyone is plotting against him.

WIFE: One other thing: he got fired from his job a month ago.

COUNSELOR: Had he been there long?

WIFE: About eight months. He's had three jobs in two years. I think he's actually spent more time out of a job than he's had one. That's the cocaine. He gets into arguments with his boss, or he just stops showing up, and they fire him.

MOTHER: That's why they moved in with me. She couldn't pay all the bills. So she pays me rent. He's supposed to, but he hasn't made a payment in months. And he's always borrowing money but he never pays it back. He won't even have enough money to take the bus to work, sometimes. As soon as he gets paid, he takes the check to a bar and gets it cashed so he can buy cocaine. So we never see any of that money.

COUNSELOR: What would you all like him to do?

WIFE: We want him to stop using drugs, forever.

MOTHER: And learn to communicate with us. He never talks at all.

WIFE: That's true . . . he doesn't let me know how he's feeling.

MOTHER: And we want him to take some responsibility for himself. We want him to pay some of the bills and take care of himself more in general.

WIFE: And I wish he would be *happier*. He's always complaining. But he doesn't do anything for himself—he's like a big baby.

MOTHER: He's been that way since he was a child, girl . . . he needs to grow up. He's a case of arrested development.

COUNSELOR: Is this what you tell him you want?

WIFE: Yes. But he just ignores us.

No wonder. They're violating the first law of successful intervention: *have a reasonable goal.*

Instead, they've fallen into the trap of trying to change the alcoholic's entire personality. Even if Jared weren't a drug addict, he couldn't possibly meet all these demands.

COUNSELOR: I think you're asking too much of Jared. You can't expect him to transform himself into a completely different human being. People simply can't do that.

WIFE: I guess you're right. But what is fair, then?

COUNSELOR: Well, what would make your lives better almost immediately?

WIFE: That's easy. If he stopped using cocaine.

COUNSELOR: Can he do that on demand?

WIFE: I don't know. I guess not. He needs some kind of help. Now that I think about it, I *know* he can't do it by himself.

MOTHER: No, he needs help, all right.

COUNSELOR: So why don't we see if we can't get him back into a treatment program?

MOTHER: That sounds good to me.

COUNSELOR: Okay, then, that's our goal. To get him back into treatment. In order to do that, we're going to have to forget about the other goals for awhile.

WIFE: That's okay. If he quits the cocaine, I could deal with the rest of the stuff.

The counselor has crystallized the family into the beginnings of an *intervention team:* the group, as we learned from Chapter 3, organized specifically to get the resistant addict into treatment.

As the session continues the counselor relates all of Jared's current troubles to his relapse. The counselor asks how Jared manages to survive these crises and stay out of trouble with no resources of his own. This leads Jared's wife and mother to recognize it's they who are propping him up. Their fear that he'll end up in the streets—or dead—pressures them into giving him money and shelter. The counselor has pinpointed their strongest leverage over Jared.

COUNSELOR: What if you confronted Jared with the possibility that you were going to withdraw your support? Gave him the choice between going back in treatment or supporting his drug use by himself?

WIFE: We've done that. I mean, I've told him that if he doesn't stop drugs, our marriage won't last. I've said that a thousand times.

MOTHER: I have told my son that I cannot continue on an indefinite basis to support him and let him live in my house and keep using my money for drugs.

COUNSELOR: And how did he react?

WIFE: He ignored us. Or he yelled at me and called me a bitch.

COUNSELOR: Let me ask two questions. First, when did you discuss this with Jared? Was it by any chance when he was loaded?

WIFE: Most of the time, yes. He'd come home all liquored up and I'd get furious with him. And it didn't do any good.

MOTHER: Well, I only talked to him once. It was after he stole my good jewelry and sold it for drugs. I really let him have it. He just paid me no mind.

COUNSELOR: Did you ever think of talking to him when he's sober?

WIFE: No, he's too irritable. You can't talk to him then.

Here's the second mistake. They're attempting intervention on someone who's under the influence. There's no way they can know for certain if Jared even *recalls* their conversation the following day.

COUNSELOR: Now for the second question: did you ever talk with him together?

MOTHER: No, we never have.

COUNSELOR: And lastly, have you ever followed through on any of those threats? I mean, you said he had to move, or you told him you'd withhold the money, or you said you'd file for divorce—did you ever actually do any of those things?

WIFE: I never did.

MOTHER: I haven't yet.

COUNSELOR: That's your problem, then. First, after he got out of treatment, you went back to being _enablers_. And because you approach him separately rather than together, you don't have any impact. And lastly, you've taught him not to listen to you, by making threats and then not following through on them. He doesn't listen to you because he doesn't believe you'll actually do what you say you will. _You've taught him that you won't._

WIFE: So what do we do?

COUNSELOR: Well, first we identify all the enabling behaviors you've fallen back into. Then we change those, so that when the disease creates problems, it's Jared who suffers, not you. That should increase his motivation and put a dent in his denial.

Then we see who we can get to participate in an intervention. We plan and orchestrate the whole thing so that whatever Jared says, we're ready for it.

Before we spring it on him, we have it arranged so he goes directly into treatment, without a lot of time to think of excuses to stay out and use more drugs.

WIFE: Do you really think it would work?

COUNSELOR: Can you think of an alternative?

WIFE: I suppose not. Even if it doesn't work, I'm no worse off than I am now. And at least I'll know that I've tried everything. That will make it easier to leave, if I have to.

It did work. A team of four persons designed, trained, rehearsed, and completed a successful intervention that got Jared back into treatment despite his lack of motivation.

But the process didn't end there. When you know someone is a candidate for failure—and there's no better indicator than a history of relapse—it's best to include a "contingency plan" to offset the damage to others in case the addict returns to drugs.

Thus, when it was time for Jared to be discharged, the family and the counselor held a second meeting.

WIFE: Well, he sounds terrific. But he sounded great the first time he left the program, too.

COUNSELOR: That's true. Jared's problem isn't his attitude while he's in treatment. It's what happens to that attitude after he leaves. So to make it less likely he'll go through the same thing again, I think you ought to set some clear boundaries right off the bat.

MOTHER: What do you mean?

COUNSELOR: Well, your big complaint is that Jared is too dependent on the two of you. You want him to take more responsibility for himself.

WIFE: You can say that again.

COUNSELOR: And you remember that Jared's big complaint about you two is that you nag him all the time and you're always watching him to make sure he goes to meetings. He says you're more like police than family.

MOTHER: Well, we wouldn't do that if he took some responsibility for himself.

COUNSELOR: That's not the point. You say you don't want to be responsible for Jared. But the only way to accomplish that is to give the responsibility back to him. Otherwise, he'll *always* be depending on you. If *you* change, he'll have to come up with other solutions to problems, instead of running to you.

MOTHER: I see what you mean. But does it have to be all at once? What if he fails?

COUNSELOR: Then it's *his* failure. He can't blame you for it. See, one of your illusions is that you can keep Jared off drugs. You can't. He's the only one who can do it.

WIFE: I know that. But if he uses cocaine again, he'll be taking money from me, and doing all sorts of bad things. So I feel like I have to know if he's starting to backslide.

COUNSELOR: What would it take to satisfy you he was clean?

MOTHER: Well, suppose we kept all the money away from him? That way, it would be hard for him to buy drugs.

WIFE: Oh, Mama, that doesn't work. He's got friends. He'd do somebody a favor so they'd give him some.

COUNSELOR: Besides, you're his family. If you keep putting yourself in the position of parole officer, he's going to resent you terribly.

WIFE: What can we do?

COUNSELOR: Suppose Jared signs an agreement—which he volunteered to do, by the way—that you will be notified if he drops out of treatment?

WIFE: He'd do that?

COUNSELOR: It was his idea. But he wants something from you, as well.

MOTHER: Here it comes. What does he want? Money?

COUNSELOR: He wants you to agree to go to family sessions. He wants you to stop nagging him so much. And he wants you to leave his recovery entirely up to him.

WIFE: What does that mean?

COUNSELOR: It means you wouldn't monitor him, outside of knowing whether or not he was in treatment.

MOTHER: But if he dropped out, we would know?

COUNSELOR: Immediately.

MOTHER: And suppose he did drop out? What then?

COUNSELOR: It's up to you. What will the two of you do if he relapses again?

MOTHER: I would say he has to agree to move out of my house immediately. His wife can stay, but he has to leave.

WIFE: I thought about this. I talked to a lawyer, and I've decided that if he goes back to drugs, I'm getting a legal separation as soon as I can. And then I'll file for divorce.

COUNSELOR: That's your final decision?

MOTHER: Yes. It's up to him. If he wants to use drugs, I've come to realize we can't stop him. But we aren't going to leave ourselves wide open for trouble, either.

COUNSELOR: And you'll agree to Jared's requests?

WIFE: Of course. If I felt there was some way I would know if he relapsed—instead of relying on his word—I would be willing to stop nagging him.

MOTHER: I suppose we could go to those meetings, as well. Though it's hard to find the time.

COUNSELOR: I think you should remember one thing: if you don't keep to your side of the bargain, neither will he.

WIFE: You mean if we don't go to the meetings, he won't either?

COUNSELOR: I'd say that could happen.

WIFE: I guess that's fair. We'll stick to our side. But if he doesn't keep up his end, we're taking action.

COUNSELOR: Good. You should. Why don't we get Jared and draw up a contract?

This time Jared made it.

Of course, the best defense against relapse is the sober alcoholic or addict who remains on his program from the start and stays vigilant for the presence of "slippery" situations that may invite disaster. Yet because people like Jared relapse so frequently, it's tempting to conclude they never had any intention of remaining sober in the first place. This attitude minimizes the degree to which it is difficult for anyone to consciously police themselves *all the time* in *all situations*.

Is there a solution to this dilemma?

The Key to Avoiding Relapse: Developing a Personal Feedback System

When alcoholics begin to appreciate the extent to which their thinking has been dominated by defense mechanisms, their first response is to look for a way to avoid them in the future. "I want to learn how to see through my own denial," they insist. "How do I recognize when I'm rationalizing or externalizing?"

But of course, this won't work. It's virtually impossible for anybody to recognize their own rationalizations, except after the fact. Or to put it simply: you can't see you're in denial because you're in denial.

Example: a smoker is desperately trying to quit. It's been five days since his last cigarette. He's sitting at his desk counting the hours before the workday ends.

Just then, his boss walks in the office. "Jeff," the boss says, "I'm afraid you're going to have to help me out. The Vice-President is coming down for a review on the Centex project, and you're the only one who can brief him. Be ready in fifteen minutes."

Jeff panics. *Oh my God, I can't let them see me like this. I'll be a nervous wreck.*

I need a cigarette. But I quit, damn it . . . what am I gonna do? Wait a minute—suppose I bum one from Gary? And smoke just a few puffs, and throw it away? That's only half a cigarette, after all . . . it's not like I bought a pack or anything. I can quit right after the presentation. It's not even like I started again, because it's just for this one problem I have to take care of . . . I won't have any trouble stopping, once the pressure is off. I can go home and relax, have dinner. I probably won't even think about a cigarette . . .

Three hours later he's sitting in his apartment in the grip of an overwhelming craving for nicotine. Now he thinks: *God, I forgot what this was like. I can't seem to relax. If I don't think of something to do, I'm going to have to have another cigarette, or I won't sleep tonight . . . I can't believe I smoked this afternoon. I was doing so well . . . now I feel like it's the first day of withdrawal again. . . . What in the world was I thinking when I had that cigarette?*

The only practical solution is to develop a sort of "feedback system"—which allows people in this situation to test their thinking before they act on it.

Put yourself in the place of a newly sober alcoholic or addict. This is what we would instruct you to do: create a system with the following components:

1. A willingness on your part to ask others for advice before you proceed.
2. A network of persons
   a. whose judgment you trust,
   b. who are generally available to you,
   c. who are familiar with addictive disease and addictive defenses,
   d. with whom you will be honest, and
   e. who are willing to tell you the truth, whether or not you react favorably to it.
3. A commitment on your part to follow their advice, especially in situations where your sobriety may be at risk.

Components 1 and 3 must come from the alcoholic. If he wants advice, he has to learn to ask for it. Otherwise, people may withhold it for fear of butting in where they aren't wanted.

And of course, if a person isn't willing to *follow* good advice, what was the point of asking for it in the first place?

It's the second component which takes a bit more planning.

Look at each qualification:

Someone whose judgment you (the addict) trust.

Notice we didn't say "people you like." There's a difference between feeling affection for someone and trusting their judgment. People with good judgment are usually pretty easy to pick out of the crowd because their lives work a little better than the average. They experience fewer crises and seem less anguished when problems do occur.

Good judgment, however, has very little to do with material

success. There are a lot of very wealthy people whose personal lives are in utter disarray. There are an equal number of blue-collar workers who possess exceptional understanding of human nature.

Someone who is generally available to you.

What good is a friend with the wisdom of Solomon if you can't ever reach him by phone to find out what he thinks?

Someone who is familiar with addictive disease and addictive defenses.

Now we're searching for people with good judgment who also have a knowledge of addiction. That narrows the field considerably.

There are two places to find folks who know a lot about alcoholism and drug dependency. One is from among the ranks of professionals: counselors, therapists, social workers, physicians. The second is among nonprofessionals who have some experience of addiction: recovering addicts and their loved ones.

Of course, addiction treatment is a specialty. You can't assume that all health professionals are familiar with treatment, any more than you can presume all doctors perform plastic surgery. It simply isn't true. The addict will have to search out those with expertise in addictions.

Obviously, some professionals and some persons with personal experience also possess the kind of good judgment that's needed in the early months of recovery.

Someone with whom you will be honest.

We can't withhold large chunks of information from people and then ask them for their opinion on a course of action. We haven't given them enough data for an informed response. Thus a lack of openness on our part detracts from the quality of the feedback we receive.

Yet it's difficult to be honest. There's always the risk of alienating the listener. Thus we're most *likely* to be open with someone who:

1. maintains a certain degree of emotional uninvolvement with our situation,

2. isn't looking for us to meet emotional (or material) needs of his or her own, and
3. we don't expect any financial or material gain from.

We specify these conditions because they are the things which usually interfere with honest communication in the first place.

If we think somebody will be deeply affected on an emotional level by something we say, we'll be much more hesitant about saying it. If we believe they look to us for emotional support or gratification, we'll tend to think about *their* needs instead of our own. If we're looking for money, promotion, or other material gain—well, are most people terribly honest with the company president or a rich uncle?

Someone who is willing to tell you the truth, even if you don't react favorably.

This of course is the most difficult of all. Nobody likes to be the "bad guy." There are lots of folks out there who possess good judgment, know something about addiction, and will allow us to communicate honestly. However, quite a few can't bring themselves to tell us when we're full of it.

But that's exactly what someone coming out of alcoholism or drug abuse needs, isn't it? Alcoholic defenses distort reality. When we aren't thinking clearly, we need to know somebody is there to tell us how things really stand.

When the alcoholic is setting himself up for a relapse, he doesn't need someone to provide him with emotional support. He needs someone who'll say, "I think you're setting yourself up for a relapse."

When we've fallen back into rationalizing and somebody points that out, we'll probably get mad. There's no need to feel bad about it. Everybody does.

Just recognize that when that moment comes, we all need the feedback of a person who isn't afraid of our reaction. We must make sure we include people like this in our feedback system.

Whether it's a counselor, a physician, a friend, somebody in a self-help group, or a combination of all four—these are the most important people in recovery.

This feedback system becomes the sounding board for the initial months of recovery. Whenever an addict doubts his or her own judgment—which should be frequently—this model provides ready access to clearer thinking.

Caution: one group who probably can't serve in this capacity is the alcoholic's immediate family. It's virtually impossible for you to meet the requirements of an effective feedback system.

For one thing, you care *too* much. Whether you want to or not, you tend to react emotionally, and to look to the recovering spouse for your own emotional needs. Second, your relationship may be inextricably tied to financial and material security.

Lastly, it's a rare family that isn't struggling with its own problems and needs during the early months. You need to pay attention to yourself. The worst thing you can do is attempt to be everything to everybody else.

Therefore, the best way to look at the family is as fellow-sufferers rather than a therapeutic tool.

A Note to You

It may have occurred to you that a feedback system would be as useful to you as a family member as it is for the recovering addict. That happens to be true. We suggest you develop such a system, following the same guidelines. You won't regret it.

PART IV

A PROGRAM FOR THE REST OF YOUR LIFE

Chapter Nine

The Twelve Step Programs

If there's one big advantage that the newly recovering addicted person and family have over the diabetic or the heart patient, it's the availability of Twelve Step fellowships.

It would be impossible to overstate their importance to the lives of their members. In fact, the proliferation of Twelve Step groups is, along with the disease model itself, probably the twentieth century's major contribution to addictions treatment. Without them, it would be much more difficult to recover from alcoholism or drug addiction in America today.

But to the outsider—and unfortunately, to many newly sober addicts and their families—the Twelve Step fellowship can seem mysterious and even intimidating. Contrary to popular belief, it isn't enough to simply attend meetings of Alcoholics or Narcotics Anonymous and hope for a sort of spiritual osmosis. Making use of a Twelve Step fellowship requires a certain degree of motivation, as well as some understanding of how the program works— its language, structure, philosophy, and intent.

The more we learn, the more benefits we experience. And the less likely it is that the recovering addict will drop out.

Of course, if you're actively involved in a Step program such as Alanon, it will be a lot easier to understand. But we also encourage you to familiarize yourself with the addict's program of recovery, as well—perhaps by attending some open meetings, or meetings that *combine* AA or NA with Alanon or Naranon.

Let's take a brief tour of the Twelve Step movement as it exists today, concentrating on those groups that are most closely connected to the treatment of alcoholism and drug dependency. We'll look at some of the questions newcomers have about these programs, and then at the meat of the program itself—the Twelve Steps.

Why Is It So Important that the Newly Sober Attend Twelve Step Programs?

Put *yourself* in the place of somebody just getting off alcohol or drugs: over the years the disease has probably heavily influenced your selection of associates. If you've been using street drugs, this will be obvious: there's an entire subculture built around illicit drug use, with its own rules, economic strategies, language, values, and dress code. If you're an alcoholic, that subculture is less apparent but still very real.

One important criteria for membership in your social circle will be a willingness on the part of newcomers to drink as you do, or to keep quiet about your drinking. You'll avoid (wherever possible, unless you're a masochist) people who are critical of your behavior.

That's why many alcoholics can honestly state that they "don't drink that much more than [their] friends do." It may be true, but more as a reflection of their choice of friends than on the presence or absence of alcoholism.

To continue: assume that despite this congenial environment, your disease progresses to the point that you're experiencing frequent episodes of loss of control. This results in the usual array of legal, social, family, and medical problems. You find to your horror that you're bottoming out—reaching the conclusion that you must abstain totally from alcohol and drugs.

This decision will save your life, but it does create a dilemma of sorts: you no longer belong to your own peer group. Yours is a circle of people brought together in part by a mutual fondness for drugs and alcohol. You may still have the fondness—but you've renounced the active ingredient, in favor of survival.

So where do you belong? With the nondrinking elements of society? It's a sizable contingent—in fact, about 30 percent of the adults in America are virtual nondrinkers—but how well do you really fit in? How do you explain a drinking (or cocaine) binge to someone who never even wants a second glass of beer? How do you make someone understand the idea that "having just one" is as easy for you as flying to the moon on a broomstick?

This is where the Twelve Step programs come in. At the most basic level, they provide companionship, acceptance, and fellowship from people whose experience is very much like that of other alcoholics or drug addicts trying to break from their past.

People who not only abstain from alcohol and drugs, but *do so for the same reasons the newcomer does.*

The addicted person in your life will find the same safe haven and mutual understanding in the Twelve Step group. Later on, perhaps, when the addict's sobriety is more stable, he or she will find the experience of addiction isn't much of a barrier to close relationships with nonalcoholics. But for a newcomer, the Twelve Step group serves as an all-important alternative to the society of active addiction.

How Did Twelve Step Programs Originate?

Self-help groups for addictions actually got their start from the Christian self-help movements of the late nineteenth and early twentieth century. The one that played the most significant role was the so-called Oxford Movement, which encouraged the formation of small discussion groups in England and America that met to practice a simple program of spiritual self-improvement. The Oxford Groups attracted a number of alcoholics, one of whom was a fellow named Bill Wilson, who found the program helped him establish—for the first time in his life—something resembling comfortable sobriety. He in turn carried the message to an alcoholic surgeon named Bob Smith and, over the next few years, the two of them helped give birth to the organization known as *Alcoholics Anonymous*. The Oxford Movement died, but its spinoff became one of the great social and health movements of the era.

Many of the original members of AA were Roman Catholics, but most of the early meetings were held in Protestant churches.

Despite the close ties between AA and organized religion, it remains profoundly nondenominational and nonsectarian—a "spiritual" rather than a "religious" program.

The organization itself is "protected" by the Twelve Traditions, which grew from the early experience of the fellowship and which set guidelines for AA groups and for individual members in their contacts with the larger society. One tradition, for example, involves the refusal to accept outside contributions beyond what can be collected by "passing the hat" at meetings. Another is designed to preserve the anonymity of members at the level of press, radio, and other media—that tradition, as you may have noticed, is sometimes violated by celebrity alcoholics. The Traditions help AA to maintain the integrity of its primary purpose—which is to carry the message of hope and recovery to the alcoholic who still suffers.

Narcotics Anonymous is in turn a spinoff from AA. The program of NA is virtually identical to that of AA. Why the need for a separate organization? Because the experience of being an alcoholic in America is substantially different from that of someone who is addicted to an illegal narcotic, such as heroin. Though the disease process itself is the same, recovering addicts found that they could better attract the suffering addict by concentrating on this experience.

Cocaine Anonymous is the product of the cocaine epidemic of the 1970s and 1980s. Once again, the program is the same. It's only the experiences that differ.

Alanon was founded by Bill Wilson's wife and is geared toward those who love an alcoholic. Their Twelve Step program centers around giving up futile attempts to control the alcoholic's behavior—and the development of a degree of "detachment" that allows the Alanon member to maintain some degree of sanity in the face of unpredictable addiction.

Does Alanon Have Its Own Twelve Steps?

The Alanon, Naranon, Cocanon, and Alateen programs use a Twelve Step format adapted from AA. That's a good illustration of the flexibility of the Steps themselves—they're designed to improve the quality of life, and alcoholism is only *one* of many applications.

The key to the program is in the first three Steps. They're incredibly simple and remarkably effective. Let's review them as they apply to the family member of a recovering alcoholic—bearing in mind that they apply exactly the same way to a recovering drug addict.

> **Step One:** *We admitted we were powerless over alcohol—that our lives had become unmanageable.*

When the alcoholic takes this Step, he means that he's lost the ability to control his drinking. Step One to an Alanon member is an admission of powerlessness over *the alcoholic's* drinking.

Remember that family members go through a stage (sometimes lasting years or even decades) where they try to limit the alcoholic's consumption or minimize the damage drinking brings about. They nag, plead, beg, criticize, police, threaten, and sometimes even assault the alcoholic in an effort to get him or her to change. This doesn't work for several reasons.

First: it's impossible to watch somebody all the time. Anybody who sincerely wants to drink or use drugs can get around anybody who tries to stop them.

Second: because alcoholics can't understand what you're so upset about—their defenses make it impossible for them to appreciate what you're going through—your message doesn't get through clearly enough to have an impact.

Third: it creates a "war zone" within the family which usually alternates between "firefights" (skirmishes that provide the alcoholic with endless excuses for drinking) and periods of "truce" (superficial cooperation with hostility just below the surface).

The outcome is generally twofold: an alcoholic who feels totally misunderstood, resentful, angry, and hurt, along with a family dogged by futility and a sense of hopelessness.

Thus the first step in recovery, for the family as well as the alcoholic, is to *quit fighting*.

That's right: the best way to win this battle is to surrender.

Again, think of this as a disease. Suppose your loved one suffered from uncontrolled, undiagnosed diabetes? You'd see the signs: confusion, extreme fluctuation of moods, physical and psychological complaints, and often, *denial* of such symptoms. What would happen if you undertook to control these occurrences through nagging, criticizing, arguing, or threatening divorce?

Wouldn't you simply make things worse? Wouldn't you damage your relationship, and probably drive yourself crazy in the process?

By admitting your own powerlessness, you open up a door to help—which comes in the second Step.

Step Two: *Came to believe that a Power greater than ourselves could restore us to sanity.*

It's pretty hard, if not impossible, to live with addictive disease and not get a little crazy yourself. After all, you're trying to manage a life that is becoming increasingly unmanageable. Just about everything you try fails. You live with the knowledge that the next crisis could be even worse than the last.

And worst of all, you find yourself running out of energy. Your will to fight is sapped by repeated defeat. Just under the surface is a profound feeling of hopelessness—and it gets harder and harder to keep it at bay.

What you need is a Higher Power. Something to rely on other than your own dwindling resources.

This doesn't have to be God. There are no entrance requirements for being a Higher Power, except these:
1. it has to be something you can put your faith in, and
2. it can't be you.

Most people have a picture of a Higher Power somewhere in their conscious or unconscious thoughts. It's pretty hard to get through childhood without one. You may have forgotten what it looks like. Think about it. What gave you strength when you were *really* afraid?

Or if you prefer: use the Alanon group itself as your Higher Power. Not individual members—but its larger principles and purpose.

Got it? Now, tell yourself every day that there is a way out of your dilemma, and your Higher Power will show you, if you so allow.

> **Step Three:** *Made a decision to turn our will and our lives over to the care of God, as we understood Him.*

Okay, now begin living differently.

You know all those decisions you find yourself having to make? The ones you agonize over for weeks or months, trying to figure out how to avoid making things worse? Or the other kind: where you just act because you feel you have to do or say *something* or you'll go nuts?

Turn those over to the Higher Power. Discuss your awful dilemmas at Alanon meetings and make a conscious effort *not to dwell on them* during the day (what good is it anyway?). And before you act impulsively, call your sponsor or somebody else in the group. Talk it out with them *first*.

See if this doesn't make life work better. And when you find yourself wondering if things will ever change, or if you're going in the right direction, tell yourself: *Leave it alone. The Higher Power will get me out of this. Just listen.*

What Do People Talk About at Meetings?

Basically, they share the "experience, strength, and hope" of recovery. When members tell their story, they usually follow a simple format. First, they describe the course of their illness, from beginning to end. Then, they relate the events that led them to AA and to sobriety. Lastly, they talk about what's happened since they joined the fellowship.

In discussion or Step meetings, the format varies. The leader for that evening will offer a topic for discussion—one of the Twelve Steps, perhaps, or something else of relevance to the members.

Throughout, the participants' emphasis is on *self-disclosure:* revealing the truth about themselves and their addiction. You'll notice that even when someone disagrees with something that's been said, they'll usually couch it in terms of their own experience rather than criticizing the speaker's.

Why Are There So Many Meetings? And So Many Different Kinds of Meetings?

There are so many meetings because there are so many people with addictive problems, and they need so much in the way of help. Additionally, many members prefer small meetings where there's an opportunity for discussion, and that encourages proliferation of groups. Twelve Step fellowships make it easy to start meetings, and they tend to allow each meeting to govern itself. The Twelve Step movement is a perfect example of the survival capabilities of decentralized, grass-roots organizations that don't rely on policies majestically dispensed from a central headquarters.

There are so many types of meetings because Twelve Step groups operate on a principle of "attraction rather than promotion." The tremendous diversity of persons with addictive disease—who, you'll remember, come from every conceivable background—encourages the formation of subgroups that attract different segments of society. Stag, women's, gay, professional, and foreign language meetings serve as an example. The program itself, however, is essentially unchanged.

What's the Purpose of a Sponsor?

The relationship between a member and his or her sponsor is one of the real strengths of the fellowship. The sponsor helps you to *personalize* your view of the program and to individualize its many lessons in terms of your needs, wants, goals, and aspirations. A sponsor helps you interpret the Steps and guides you through the ups and downs involved in their completion. Lastly, a sponsor reminds you what it's like to have a friend, in the best sense of that term.

Think back to Chapter 8, in which we spoke of the need to find a special "adviser" with very specific characteristics. This person would supply the kind of honest feedback that helps the addict defend against the tendency to relapse, a kind of honesty not easy to find. In a sense, the Twelve Step environment is designed to help the recovering addict—or the significant other in Alanon—find just such a person in the form of a sponsor.

Best of all, you owe the sponsor nothing but your time, your honesty, and your willingness to listen. His or her reward comes from the role of sponsorship itself. As is often said, "We keep our sobriety by giving it away."

The Steps—which AA takes pains to explain are suggestions rather than directions—were adapted from the Oxford Movement. The majority are not specifically geared to recovery from alcoholism—though that has been the area of greatest application. In fact, this is also why Twelve Step programs have proliferated in response to a variety of life problems, from overeating to parenting.

The Steps provide a foundation for a way of living that is, as one AA member described it, "the polar opposite of the way you live when you're drinking."

Another thing to remember: the Steps were written in the mid- to late 1930s, and were adapted from a program rooted in the attitudes of the late nineteenth century. The language of the Steps reflects their origins. It certainly isn't the language of the 1980s or 1990s and therefore requires some translation in order for many newcomers to make use of them. Nevertheless, the principles behind the Steps remain essentially intact.

Here's a list of the Twelve Steps of Alcoholics Anonymous, with brief comments on the role of each in the larger picture of recovery. Before we continue, we ought to warn you that there's no one right way to work the Steps.

In fact, it may be true that no two people ever work the Steps in precisely the same way. And of course, "whatever works" is the only real standard by which to judge anything in recovery.

And remember, these Twelve Steps can be adapted to *any* addictive disease situation.

So these are just a few of our suggestions about the suggestions of AA's founders—as embodied in the Twelve Steps. We'll have to give them short shrift here. For a more complete discussion, see our book *The Twelve Steps Revisited: AA and the Disease of Alcoholism* (Seattle: Madrona Press, 1988). (See Suggested Reading.)

Step One

Powerlessness and unmanageability.

*"We admitted we were powerless over alcohol—
that our lives had become unmanageable."*

All Step programs hinge on the individual's willingness to admit powerlessness and unmanageability. Why? Because it is this self-recognition that provides the motivation for working the remaining Steps.

Look at it this way: recovery from addiction involves a considerable amount of effort, which is supposed to culminate in profound personal change. If you're addicted to a drug, you have to give it up. In order to stay off, you're asked to critically examine the way you live—something most people don't like to do. Thus your recovering addict will probably have to disclose things about himself (or herself) that he would rather keep hidden. He needs to stick with a treatment regimen, even if it's occasionally inconvenient or even dull. Somewhere along the line, he'll be asked to learn to pray (or at least meditate—popular in Eastern cultures, but not exactly the average Westerner's idea of a good time).

Why would anyone go to such lengths unless it was *absolutely necessary?* They wouldn't. That's why addicts and alcoholics do the First Step—to show themselves that change is required *because* they're powerless over a drug, and this is making life unmanageable.

But when addicts try to examine their lives for signs of powerlessness and unmanageability, they run smack into one of the signs of their illness—denial. The nature of addictive disease is to conceal itself from its victims. That's how it kills, remember. Not because it isn't treatable—but because people refuse to treat it.

In fact, a number of the Tasks of Recovery (for both alcoholic and family) have to do with overcoming defense mechanisms such as denial, rationalization, externalization, and minimizing. During this process, you reveal to yourself the extent and severity of your problem. When you complete the traditional First Step, you do in essence the same thing.

And in fact, many alcoholics and addicts relapse because they don't take the time to go through this process of *self-examination* and *self-diagnosis*. They go on the wagon because of some immediate dilemma—the wife is talking divorce, the judge is threatening jail, the finance company is scratching at the door— and discover that when the crisis abates, their motivation for sobriety disappears with it.

Step Two

The Higher Power.

> *"Came to believe that a Power greater than ourselves could restore us to sanity."*

Once we've completed Step One, we're ready for the second issue. Which in a Twelve Step program involves the substitution of a "Power greater than ourselves" for our own will.

Elsewhere in this book we make the point that contrary to popular mythology, alcoholics and drug addicts are not weak willed. The addicted person instead represents a superb example of considerable determination put to the wrong use—the service of an addiction.

During the course of the disease, a conflict develops within the addict. On one hand, he may want sincerely to live a better life. On the other hand, he wants to continue his dependency, no matter what the obstacles. The addict's motivation to keep on using drugs is simple, but it's also incredibly powerful: he doesn't feel good without them.

Once this conflict matures, he has, in essence, *two wills*. The disease makes sure that as long as alcohol or drugs are present, the "sick will" comes out on top. Sure, there are brief periods of respite, when he can again delude himself into thinking he is in charge of the addiction. But ultimately, he is unable to overcome his own desire for the drug.

So why is it that alcohols can't control their drinking through willpower? The disease won't let them. Why can't they simply stop drinking or using drugs through an exercise of that same willpower? They in fact can, but only for short periods. However, there exists another, stronger will that eventually overrides their resolve.

By the time they reach a treatment program many alcoholics and addicts have "quit" a thousand times, only to relapse shortly afterward. There's nothing quite as damaging to one's self-esteem as repeated failure.

So, according to the Steps, what gives the addict the power to succeed where his own will has failed?

A Higher Power.

Early on, people in Alcoholics Anonymous realized that to specify the exact nature of the Higher Power would effectively eliminate a tremendous number of alcoholics—principally, those whose definitions of a Higher Power were different. And since the obvious purpose of the organization was to include rather than exclude suffering alcoholics, the Steps were designed so that they permit the alcoholic to choose a Higher Power for himself.

The desire not to exclude is one of the reasons why members refer to AA as a "spiritual" rather than a "religious" program. It's also the reason why AA so easily absorbs people of many faiths, without interfering with their religious beliefs. You can continue to practice Catholicism, Protestantism, Buddhism, or no-ism-at-all, if you so choose, while remaining an AA member in good standing.

Can an atheist or an agnostic survive in the spiritual atmosphere of AA or NA? Sure. Agnostics already believe in something, though it may not be God. The atheists we've known may renounce the idea of a deity, but they're often unusually moral persons in their approach to life. Many adopt the principles embodied in the Steps—with or without including God—as a sort of Higher Power, and seem to do quite well.

The key point: there has to be something addicts can believe in, other than themselves, to carry them through the rough times on the road to recovery.

Why can't they rely solely on their own judgment, their own determination? Because—as an old AA member once told us—a part of them still belongs to the disease.

Step Three

Turning your will over.

"Made a decision to turn our will and our lives over to the care of God as we understood Him."

This is the big, important Step in which the recovering person turns his or her will over to the care of the Higher Power. Watching someone go through it, we find ourselves wishing that the myth about alcoholics being weak willed were true. It would make this process so much easier.

But of course, they aren't. In fact, by the time they reach the point where they reach out for help, many alcoholics are little short of what AA members call "self-will run riot."

In other words, they have trouble doing anything other than what they want to do, when they want to do it. Have problems seeing things from any perspective other than that of their immediate situation. Have great difficulty acceding to any limits placed on them at work, at home, or in the treatment program.

So even as they reach out, they have considerable difficulty accepting the help that's offered.

You hear it over and over again from newcomers. "I'll do anything to recover," they insist. "Except . . ." followed by a long list of what they *won't* do.

In AA, this willfulness is seen as interfering with the ability to make use of a Higher Power. "I wanted to open up and make room for faith in my life," one alcoholic told us. "But my ego was taking up all the chairs."

"It's hard to describe what happens when you first turn your will over to a Higher Power," a recovering narcotics addict explained. "It's not something you can express in words. I think you just discover that somehow you've slipped out of the driver's seat, and that contrary to expectations, you're not crashing. Something else is driving, and it's doing a better job than you did."

Other addicts find this explanation entirely too spiritual. "There was nothing mystical about it," a woman asserted. "The Third Step is a matter of deciding to follow the directions that people have been giving you all along, but that you were just too stubborn to listen to."

Whatever your interpretation, the message seems clear: it isn't enough to have faith in a Higher Power, if you aren't willing to live by it.

Step Four

The inventory.

> *"Made a searching and fearless moral inventory of ourselves."*

There's no two ways about it. The experience of addictive disease changes people—addicts themselves and, as you are well aware, the people involved with them.

We don't think anyone can be an alcoholic or drug addict without some adverse effect on their mood, judgment, and thinking processes. There's nothing particularly mysterious about this. The addict can't avoid it, any more than a diabetic can avoid being influenced by peaks and valleys in his blood sugar. It just happens.

Surround this with defense mechanisms, and the effect is profound. It becomes hard to differentiate personality from disease.

Families notice it: *It's as though he isn't even the same person,* they'll say. *We don't know how he'll react to things anymore.*

The family, too, undergoes a transformation. *Enabling* and *provoking* behaviors begin to appear, coloring relationships with the alcoholic. Eventually, we see the classic picture of the co-dependent in crisis: anxious, obsessively worried, unable to take action.

The defenses, attitudes, and beliefs born and nurtured in the experience of addiction don't automatically disappear once an alcoholic or addict gets sober. They linger on into recovery—and if not addressed, can sabotage it. As they once protected, justified, and excused drinking and drug use, they can serve the same role in relapse.

These behaviors form the subject of the Fourth Step. Its purpose: to carry the process of self-examination beyond the simple acknowledgment of powerlessness and unmanageability.

In other words: to identify some of the attitudes, beliefs, and feelings that might interfere with recovery.

Or, to borrow a phrase used by one AA member, "the things that block our access to the Higher Power."

Older AA members often interpret this as referring to character defects: negative personality traits such as false pride, resentment, intellectual arrogance, procrastination, and even simple laziness. Accordingly, their Fourth Step inventories range far and wide, and may make little mention of alcoholism or its direct effects.

Some members see this as an opportunity to rid themselves of psychological debris—a sort of "spring cleaning" for the brain that leaves them less burdened with resentment or remorse.

In our view, the proper subject of the inventory is the set of defense mechanisms and irrational beliefs that grow to surround addiction—and which, left unexamined, provide fertile ground for relapse.

Whatever the interpretation, most Twelve Steppers agree that the content of this inventory changes as dramatically as the person does. In other words, a Fourth Step done at six weeks sober bears little resemblance to the same exercise after a year of abstinence.

Step Five

Sharing the inventory.

"Admitted to God, to ourselves, and to another human being the exact nature of our wrongs."

Once you've completed the inventory, Twelve Step programs suggest that you share it with other people—and with your Higher Power, whatever that may be.

There are a variety of reasons for this. First, it does help to put an end to the isolation experienced by most addicts—and by most co-dependents. Second, it can aid in establishing a strong, open relationship with a sponsor—if that's with whom you choose to share it. For many newly recovering people, the Fifth

Step becomes something of a confessional—a place to reveal things they hitherto kept hidden.

The most important single benefit of the Fifth Step is the opportunity it presents to "see" ourselves through the eyes of another. Most people are surprised at how seldom their tales of wrongdoing and self-delusion evoke shock or disgust from their listener.

Step Six

A state of readiness.

"Were entirely ready to have God remove all these defects of character."

To most Americans, change is purely a matter of taking action. They ignore an essential ingredient in determining whether or not that change becomes permanent: the achievement of a state of readiness.

Every New Year, most of us make half a dozen resolutions about personal change. We promise to diet, to organize our schedules, to live within a budget, to make up with friends, to quit smoking. We can say with certainty that achieving any one of these goals would substantially improve our lives. Yet within short order, most of us have abandoned our resolutions in favor of doing the same things we've always done.

We see the same thing with attempts at recovery from various addictions. Think of all the alcoholics who gave up alcohol "forever" at least a hundred times before it finally took. Why so many failures? Their intentions were good, at least some of the time. And what, finally, allowed them to succeed, where previously they had only found failure?

Most will express it as did this fellow: "I guess I just wasn't ready those other times."

To our way of thinking, success comes when the alcoholic, the addict, the overeater, the co-dependent, the gambler stops making change conditional. In other words, when he or she gives up saying, "I'll act differently if . . . " and replaces it with, "I'll act differently, one day at a time, no matter what."

Step Seven

Changing.

> *"Humbly asked Him to remove our short-comings."*

Perhaps no Step is more strongly tied to the philosophy and traditions of the Oxford Movement than this. The original idea was to open one's life to God, who would then enter and rid the sufferer of spiritual failings in much the same way a surgeon removes a diseased organ.

And indeed, there are many people whose conception of God allows them to think in exactly this way. But most modern Americans interpret it differently—that the Higher Power, rather than removing flaws for us, presents us with an opportunity to do a little minor surgery on ourselves.

The recovering addict has the raw material: the First and Fourth Steps provided it. He understands, through the experience of the Fifth Step, that he's not alone—others have seen, done, and survived what he has. He's achieved something resembling a state of readiness for change. Now it's time for him to translate this into action. He can begin to live differently than before.

Of course, the addict is still the same person, and such profound alteration in behavior isn't accomplished overnight. Most Twelve Step programs emphasize *progress over perfection*. The only legitimate comparison is with the way one used to be—and if you're better than you were, you're a success. Greater rewards, you may assume, will come with time.

Step Eight

Willing to make amends.

> *"Made a list of all persons we had harmed, and became willing to make amends to them all."*

Somewhere along the line, it will probably occur to the sober addict that his behavior has brought grief not only to him, but to those around him. That may elicit some feelings of remorse. Thus, this is a Step that relates profoundly to you as the significant other.

Step Eight is designed to help AA members handle that in a systematic fashion. Instead of wallowing in (or going out of their way to avoid) such sentiments, they can strive to resolve unfinished situations through a process of making amends.

In essence, it's a way of confronting the past. Just making a list of the people the alcoholic has harmed is a cathartic experience. The point is to be honest, but it's not necessary to put on a hair-shirt —the fact is, the alcoholic was under the influence of a potentially fatal disease, and if he or she is like most alcoholics, co-dependents, gamblers, overeaters, and so forth, he did as much harm to himself as anybody.

Of course, there are any number of situations where amends might be advisable, as there are an equal number that are probably better off left alone. Step Eight only suggests that the addict become willing to make amends, as he became "ready" to have his defects removed in Step Six. The assumption of this posture of willingness is half the battle. Even if the opportunity for amends doesn't present itself, at least we know we were ready to take that Step.

Step Nine

Making amends.

> *"Made direct amends to such people wherever possible, except when to do so would injure them or others."*

Here, people are given the criteria for making amends. Notice that it has to do with the possible effect of one's actions on other people, rather than on oneself. An interesting contrast to the self-absorption of active drinking or drug use.

How does the sober alcoholic make amends? In some instances, a simple apology will do. In others, he might want to try to do something nice for the person he believes he harmed. In still other instances, he might conclude that no amends are possible, beyond his sincere intention to avoid repeating the experience.

The Ninth Step is a way of putting the past to rest, in favor of living in the present.

Step Ten

Continuing inventory.

> *"Continued to take personal inventory and when we were wrong promptly admitted it."*

Whew! This is too much! Give up drinking, sure—other drugs, too, if you want. Acknowledge our flaws, and even share them with other people. That's tough, but we can do it.

But admit it when we're wrong, on a daily basis? That's going too far. Isn't it?

The truth is, most of us are absolute junkies when it comes to being "right." We get to the point where we want to be right all the time. We want to win all the arguments, make all the correct decisions, always be on the winning side.

Some of us even get to the point of believing we've achieved this lofty goal. Of course, shortly thereafter we're probably committed to a mental hospital.

The nature of events is to prove us wrong on some occasions. Let's be honest—on many occasions. Nevertheless, most of us go out of our way to try and hide how frequently it happens—as if it weren't happening to everyone, every day of our lives.

This is part of the process of "ego deflation" inherent in the Steps. But it isn't our real self-esteem that's diminished. Instead, it's the false, unrealistic arrogance that has to go.

Step Eleven

Looking inward.

> *"Sought through prayer and meditation to improve our conscious contact with God <u>as we understood Him</u>, praying only for knowledge of His will for us and the power to carry that out."*

Externalization is one of the most popular defense mechanisms, not only for alcoholics but for everyone. This Step suggests counteracting the tendency to look outside yourself for answers by turning your focus inward.

A more spiritual interpretation might emphasize prayer and meditation as the only way to maintain strong contact with the Higher Power—which, after all, is what gives people the strength to maintain a program of recovery.

Note that once again the phrase, *as we understood Him*, is underlined. In our view, this is a way of emphasizing that there is no single correct way to understand God, or the Higher Power, or whatever you choose to call it. There are no standards to meet, no dogma to memorize, no commandments to live by. Just a series of suggestions to be interpreted by the individual in any one of a number of ways. In a sense, it's the ultimate in individualizing a program of recovery. Make your recommendations as broad as possible, and let people fit them to their own circumstances, their own needs.

It's so incredibly simple it's hard to understand why highly educated professionals—doctors, psychologists, and others—didn't figure it out for themselves.

Then again, maybe it isn't.

Step Twelve

Carry the message.

> *"Having had a spiritual awakening as the result of these Steps, we tried to carry this message to alcoholics, and to practice these principles in all our affairs."*

It's one of the oldest slogans in education. *The best way to learn is to teach.*

Right from the beginning, the founders of AA recognized the value of turning every recovering alcoholic into a messenger for the principles of AA. It didn't guarantee that the message was heard by the listener. It did make it nearly impossible for the messenger himself to ignore it.

And if nothing else, it might keep him sober.

Actually, most of us probably spend too much time looking for people to help us. We might benefit from devoting more energy to sharing what we know with others who have yet to figure it out.

Think about it: as messed up as we may be, there's probably somebody within a three-block radius who's even more confused. Striving to get through to them is often the best way to understand our own difficulties.

And of course, the most difficult part of the Steps comes in the final passage, which suggests we "practice these principles in all our affairs." It's a tall order; just the part about promptly admitting when we're wrong is enough to send some people scurrying to the showers.

Nevertheless, that's what recovery involves.

Chapter Ten

Intervention in Action

Mary Louise Delaney has just noticed she no longer feels alone. As a matter of fact, the room is getting a little crowded.

How in the world did I get these people to come here? she thinks. *Was it really just because I asked them?*

They've come for intervention training. The counselor is explaining the importance of being specific with the alcoholic. *Just like in the book,* she notes. *But it feels different because he's talking about my husband.*

Her mother-in-law sits across the room. *God, it was hard to convince her that her baby boy had a drinking problem,* Mary Louise thinks. *But give her credit—she's here.*

She looks over at her friends Tony and Marie, who live next door and have been watching her husband get drunk at parties for nearly a decade. *And I never once talked to them about Jack's drinking. I guess I was just so ashamed of it, as if somehow it reflected badly on me . . .*

Her eldest boy Jason arrives, gives Mary Louise a hug, and takes a chair. He's twenty minutes late. She tries to be angry with him but can't manage it. *I'm just so happy he's here,* she tells herself. *He could have died that night. And he hasn't touched a drop in four months, goes to a couseling program and everything . . .*

She thinks back to that night of Jason's driving accident. *I know it sounds funny, but I'm almost glad everything came to a head. If Jason hadn't been in that accident, I probably would have put off doing anything about his father . . . I'd never have seen this counselor or gone to Alanon or learned anything about alcoholism, and I suppose I'd have stayed as ignorant and helpless and miserable as ever . . .*

The counselor is staring at her. "Is something wrong, Mary Louise?" he asks.

She doesn't understand the question. "No," she says. "Why?"

He gives her a funny look. "You're crying."

She puts a hand to her cheek. He's right. She grabs a handful of tissues from her bag.

"I'm all right," she apologizes, blotting furiously at her face. "Go ahead, go ahead. Really."

God, how embarrassing, she thinks. *They must think I'm crazy. But what could I say. That I'm just so damned happy?*

How do you explain to them what it's like to be here, after all these years? To think that somehow—finally—there may actually be a way out? A way to help Jack, and to help ourselves?

We didn't forget Sylvia Benton. She's in a crowd, too. There are twenty-five other people at her Wednesday night Alanon meeting. She's been going for a month, just watching and listening, not ready to speak.

Tonight, though, is her big night. She's going to tell the group her story.

Nervously, she describes her husband's behavior, and her response. "So what do you think?" she asks. "Is he an alcoholic? A problem drinker? Or what?"

One of the other women looks puzzled. "I don't see what difference it makes," she says. "I mean, he's drunk, you're unhappy—what more do you need to know? The real question is what can you do to change that?"

Ben Dreyfuss would have been at that meeting, too, except he was at the hospital, picking up his son. The kid, much to Ben's surprise, agreed to a twenty-eight-day treatment program.

All I had to do, Ben thinks as he waits for the boy to be discharged, *was stop getting angry and start getting educated. Set some boundaries and stick to them. I can't believe I wasn't able to figure that out for myself.*

Jennifer Strong has the phone number of a treatment center on the nightstand next to her bed. She was careful not to write the name so her husband wouldn't know she had gone behind his back.

She's getting ready for bed. Alone, as usual; her husband is out somewhere, "with friends." In one more month the baby will arrive. *What will I do then?* she wonders. *I can't have him bringing those people around when the baby is here.*

She tries not to cry. *As soon as the baby is born, I'll go for help,* she promises herself. *Nothing will stop me. But I just can't face it now . . .*

Don't worry about Jennifer. She'll figure it out soon enough.

But it's true that for most people the solution is in front of them all along. It's hard to see sometimes, but it's there. The key: *If you can't change the addict, then change yourself.*

You'd be surprised at the results.

Hopefully, this book has shown you a bit of light at the end of the tunnel. Perhaps you're already over the biggest hurdle—that feeling that nothing you do will have any impact.

Most importantly, you should at least realize that you don't have to *wait.* You don't need to wait to seek professional guidance and direction. You needn't wait for support and advice from people like yourself. You can begin changing your enabling and provoking behaviors *today.*

And lastly, you don't have to wait for the alcoholic or addict to change first.

Hundreds of thousands of people have already begun the process of recovery. Some will have an easier road than others, and their paths may diverge along the way. But that's always true in life, isn't it?

If you're interested in the process of intervention, contact your local treatment facility and ask them for assistance. We've provided a simple **Intervention Workbook** to help you guide your group through the various steps. See also the **Suggested Reading** list for further references.

That's all we have to say, for now.

Are you still waiting?

Intervention Workbook

To prepare for a structured confrontation, follow the directions below. As you do, refer back to Chapter 3 on how to get someone into treatment for further explanation and instruction.

Step One: Review the Enabling Syndrome

1. Read the sections on the patterns of addictive disease and identify the pattern you are dealing with. If more information is necessary, turn to the Suggested Reading list for additional suggestions.
2. Using the information, identify the stage of addictive disease. What symptoms can you list to justify your conclusion?
3. Who are primary and secondary enablers? List examples of their enabling behavior.

Step Two: Identify Probable Defenses

1. List the principal objections this addict would have to entering a treatment program.
2. Make a list of answers that can offset these objections. Note which objections seem most difficult to deal with.

Step Three: Analyze Flaws in Previous Approaches

1. Examine previous attempts to get the alcoholic or addict into treatment. Give specific examples if possible.
2. Describe briefly what you believe caused previous attempts to fail. How would you correct these weaknesses?

Step Four: Begin Preparation for Session

1. Make a list of examples of problems in the following areas. Be specific in describing incidents.
   a. Episodes where drinking/drugs interfered with behavior or ability to function.
   b. Evidence that drinking/drugs are contributing to health problems.
   c. Instances where alcohol/drugs have been used in excessive amounts, at inappropriate times, or in inappropriate places.
   d. Signs of drug /alcohol-related memory loss, personality change, hiding or sneaking behavior.
   e. Problems on job, within family, with marital relations, with law, related to alcohol/drugs.
   f. Other relevant problems.

Step Five: Identify Potential Leverage and Influence

1. Who might influence the alcoholic toward treatment?
2. Who might be able to provide actual leverage if addict refuses treatment?
3. Are those persons available to participate in confrontation? Do they feel that confrontation is advisable in this case?

Step Six: Select the Intervention Team

1. Who will participate in your confrontation?
2. What can each participant offer?
3. Is there anyone who should *not* participate in the session?
4. Select *moderator* for session.

Step Seven: Rehearsal

1. Have one person play the addict. Have each team member present a statement just as he or she will during the actual confrontation.
2. Identify the weaknesses in any person's presentation. How might it be made more convincing?
3. Anticipate problems. How will the team ensure that the alcoholic is willing to listen to the information they present?

Step Eight: Select Time and Place

1. Choose when and where the session will take place.
2. Decide how the team members will get the addict to the session.

Step Nine: Have Treatment Options Prearranged

1. Have treatment program reserve bed or interview time coordinated with time of confrontation.
2. Handle all financial or insurance questions prior to confrontation.
3. Solve logistical problems, such as who will care for patient's business, home, and so forth, while in treatment.

Step Ten: Action

1. Discuss with other team members and counselor your last-minute questions about:
    a. presentation
    b. your role
    c. leverage or influence
    d. how you'll deal with objections
    e. other issues.
2. Do it. Go ahead. Take your best shot.

GUIDE TO ADDICTIVE DISEASE

FREQUENTLY ABUSED DRUGS

Alcohol tops the list as America's most abused drug. But of the many other drugs frequently abused, both illicit and doctor-prescribed, only a few such as cocaine, heroin, or marijuana are almost universally recognizable. Otherwise, America's drug habit is fed by a bewildering pantheon of brand-name and generic substances, making it hard for the uninitiated to separate and understand such sound-alike but very different drugs as Demerol, Dalmane, or Desoxyn (respectively, a narcotic, a sedative, and a stimulant).

If you want to read more about a specific drug in the Guide to Addictive Disease but are uncertain which section has the information you need, the list below of frequently abused drugs will help. For example, the drug Xanax is found under the general family of Sedatives, Hypnotics, and Anti-Anxiety Agents; you would turn to the section in the Guide entitled "Sedatives" to learn about the general effects and problems associated with the abuse of a drug like Xanax. Drug names marked in boldface mean the Guide's pertinent section comes under that name (for example, you'll find the general topic of stimulants under the heading "Cocaine").

STIMULANTS
Benzedrine
Biphetamine
Cocaine
Dosoxyn
Dexedrine
Methedrine
Ritalin

NARCOTICS
Codeine
Darvon
Demerol
Dilaudid
Fentanyl
Heroin
Methadone
Morphine
Percodan
Talwin
Stadol

SEDATIVES, HYPNOTICS,
AND ANTI-ANXIETY AGENTS
Amytal
Ativan
Dalmane
Doriden

Halcion
Librium
Nembutal
Placidyl
Quaalude
Restoril
Seconal
Serax
Tranxene
Tuinal
Valium
Xanax

HALLUCINOGENS
LSD
MDA
MDMA (Ecstasy)
Mescaline
Psilocybin

DISSOCIATIVE ANESTHETICS
Ketamine
PCP

CANNIBIS
Hashish
Marijuana
Sinsamilla

Alcoholism

Despite the attention paid to cocaine, heroin, and PCP, it's helpful to remember that alcoholism probably kills more people annually than all illicit drugs combined.

Ironic, isn't it? That we've accepted, even encouraged the use of a drug which is in many ways more harmful than any other? In fact, it's been noted that if alcohol were discovered today (instead of 10,000 years ago) it would never make it past the Food and Drug Administration. "Are you kidding?" they'd laugh. "Legalize a major central nervous system toxin so that restaurants can serve it with dinner?"

From a strictly medical viewpoint, there's only one common substance that does anywhere near the damage alcohol does. That's tobacco.

As you've noticed, we legalized that as well.

This paradox—that we've somehow accepted drugs which have proved more damaging to our health than those we banned—is instructive. Just as many of our attitudes toward alcohol make little sense once you examine the nature of the drug, so too are most of our attitudes toward alcoholism the product of tradition and superstition rather than rational examination. Because of this, the average person seeking to understand alcoholic behavior begins not with an open mind but with a well-developed system of beliefs—many of which are misleading, and some of which are downright destructive.

Let's take a moment to look at a few commonly held beliefs about alcoholism and alcoholics, and at how the modern chronic disease approach contradicts them.

Myth: You have to drink a lot over an extended period to develop alcoholism.

This represents the old myth of the "self-induced" disease, and it's one reason why doctors frequently fail to diagnose alcoholism in younger people. "He's only been drinking for a few years," the physician reasons. "He can't be alcoholic yet." In reality, alcoholics develop symptoms of alcoholism early in life. These symptoms cause them to drink more, and to drink more often.

Myth: Alcoholics are basically weak willed or they'd be able to control their drinking.

Nothing could be further from the truth. Alcoholics respond abnormally to alcohol, somewhat as diabetics respond abnormally to sugar. As a result, the alcoholic's urge to drink becomes much stronger and more persistent than the nonalcoholic's. Over time, the alcoholic's willpower grows to be the servant of the addiction, dedicated to keeping up the flow of alcohol and to holding back the tide of associated problems. Think of it this way: if alcoholics were weak willed, it would be a lot easier to get them into treatment programs.

Myth: Alcoholics have underlying psychological problems that cause them to drink excessively.

Long-term studies that span decades indicate that those who become alcoholic are no more likely to suffer from an underlying psychological disorder, prior to the onset of alcoholism, than are nonalcoholics. As the disease progresses, alcoholics begin to exhibit signs of depression and other psychological problems, but these appear to be the results of alcoholism rather than its causes.

Myth: The roots of alcoholic drinking are in the alcoholic's relationship with his parents.

Adoption and twin studies have indicated that the roots of the susceptibility to alcoholism are probably genetic. Alcoholics do frequently have poor relationships with their parents, but that may be because:
1. The *parent* was impaired by alcoholism—it runs in families, after all.
2. The alcoholic's drinking or drug use began very *early* in life, negatively affecting maturation and relationships.
3. Alcoholism aside, the alcoholic just didn't get along very well with his parents. Remember: there are probably millions of people in the world who would describe their childhoods as "unhappy." Only a small percentage develop this disease.

Myth: Treatment is useless unless the alcoholic really "wants" to quit drinking.

Most alcoholics enter treatment in a state of profound ambivalence. On the one hand, they don't want to give up drinking; on the other, they don't want to suffer as a result of it. Attitude fluctuates from one extreme to another on a daily (sometimes hourly) basis. It's only after they've been sober for awhile—and had a chance to experience its rewards—that this ambivalence begins to lessen. In one sense, treatment itself is a way of motivating the alcoholic to stay sober long enough to get to like it.

Now, let's take a look at how alcoholism works.

The Maintenance Pattern

Alcoholism features both the maintenance and loss of control patterns, often at different times in the life of the same alcoholic.

For example, here is the story of a forty-two-year-old man who progressed through maintenance drinking into a pattern where periods of abstinence were interspersed with extended drinking binges.

"I come from a family where there's a lot of alcoholism, and to a certain extent, I'd say it has affected my life since I was a kid. My grandfather had a pretty severe problem, and he lived with us until his death when I was twelve. I liked the old guy, but I thought he was crazy even then. I mean, why did he put himself through that? Wasn't he ashamed of himself? I knew I'd never do anything like that.

"Anyway, I didn't do any serious drinking until I was in college. Then after graduation, I went into the restaurant business. I had to drink with the customers, and pretty soon I was putting away eight or nine drinks a night. But I spaced them out over five or six hours, and I was careful never to get drunk, so I didn't see how it hurt. I could hold my liquor pretty good.

"After a couple of years, I started to have some trouble sleeping. I discovered that a couple of shots of whiskey put me back to sleep. But then I noticed I was pretty hung over in the morning, so I took to starting the day off with a beer or two. Nothing serious, but it cleared my head.

"To make a long story short, by the time I was thirty, I was drinking every day, and often late into the night. My wife started to complain about it. I thought she was exaggerating. Sure, I put away a lot of booze, if you counted every drink—but how was it hurting? She admitted she'd never once seen me really drunk. Still, she nagged, I got mad, and things between us went downhill.

"The first time I ever went on what you might call a binge was on a trip to Mexico. We were with some friends who liked to drink, and the party got going and just never slowed down. My wife went back to the States and I stayed another week. Finally, I got sick, and had to go to the hospital. I spent three days puking my guts out. When I went home, the house was empty. She'd moved out.

"I went on the wagon for a few weeks, but I was pretty unhappy. I started drinking again, and boy! it seemed like something had happened to my self-control. I just couldn't keep from getting into trouble. I'd have a couple of drinks with the intention of laying off, and somehow I'd just keep going on into the night. I missed a lot of work and got fired. I got picked up for being drunk in public—I don't remember the circumstances, but I think I took off my clothes in a coffee shop—and when they let me off, I went on another toot! This time, I tried to stop and couldn't. I called a friend of mine, and he took me to Detox.

"Nowadays—my first detox was six years ago, and I've been through it three times since—I notice that no matter how long I stay on the wagon, when I drink again, I get drunk immediately. Even on a small amount of alcohol! I used to drink a bottle a day, and go to work, and nobody would even know I'd been drinking! Now, I'm like some old lady who can't hold her liquor. Or worse: I'm like my grandfather."

This case illustrates the *progression* of the disease. The appearance of *elevated tolerance*—the ability to consume more than most persons without obvious intoxication—is evident early in his drinking career. This is why he didn't regard drinking as harmful. Like most people, he equated alcoholism with drunkenness and, in the absence of such episodes, concluded (erroneously) that he did not have the disease.

Tolerance serves two purposes. First, it allows the alcoholic to drink more than others before showing the signs of intoxication. Second, it encourages consumption since smaller doses will not produce the desired effect. Note how later in this man's drinking career, his protective tolerance deserts him—leaving him vulnerable to episodes of uncontrolled intoxication, even though the amount he drinks may be considerably less than earlier in life.

Many early-stage alcoholics experience alcohol primarily as a *stimulant* rather than as a depressant. Unlike their nonalcoholic counterparts, they report that alcohol improves their functioning at work, in school, or at play. "Drink to relax?" one alcoholic scoffed in our hearing. "If I want to relax, I'll take a nap. I use alcohol to give me a *boost* when I need it." Accordingly, they learn to drink in a fashion that maximizes this stimulant effect and minimizes its depressant qualities. They'll drink until they begin to experience the initial sensations of intoxication—"till I start to feel that buzz coming on"—then slow down, adding more alcohol only as the previous dose begins to wear off. This in fact sets the stage for the maintenance pattern, which emerges with the onset of withdrawal symptoms.

Withdrawal, like nearly everything else in alcoholism, is progressive in severity. Early symptoms—episodes of anxiety, nausea, irritability, insomnia—are dismissed as the flu or a hangover. Later, we see the onset of symptoms normally associated with physical dependence:

Tremors, which are most severe when the alcoholic tries to
    write or pick up a glass
Panic attacks, where the alcoholic experiences disabling anxi-
    ety for no obvious cause
Vomiting, even when no food is in the stomach ("dry heaves")
Fractured sleep, where the alcoholic awakens frequently, often
    covered with a layer of sweat, and has difficulty falling
    asleep again.

These and other symptoms produce a critical change: the transformation of alcohol from a *recreational* to a *medicinal* substance. Why does alcohol provide the fastest, most effective relief? Because *lack of alcohol* is the hidden source of discomfort.

The advent of withdrawal signifies the appearance of the middle stage of alcoholism. Changes in behavior may be subtle at first and center around the central issue of meeting the body's increasing demands for the drug.

There are several ways to provide one's body with additional alcohol. One is to *increase the size* of a given dose (there are a lot of alcoholics who mix drinks in peanut butter jars). Another is to *increase the frequency* of drinking (in other words, reduce the intervals between drinks). Still another involves switching over to a *stronger form* of alcoholic beverage (such as whiskey or vodka). It's also common to find drinkers adopting practices that maximize the effect of each drink, such as *drinking on an empty stomach* (food slows down absorption), *gulping drinks* rather than sipping them, and *avoiding mixers* which might interfere with impact. Behaviors that indicate an increasingly important role for alcohol—such as counting off the minutes to Happy Hour, or making a drink the first priority after work—correlate strongly with the appearance of addiction. When a person begins *sneaking* drinks—perhaps in the kitchen while he or she cooks, or volunteering to fix another round for everyone at the party—the situation should be obvious. The alcoholic has become aware that his or her drinking differs from other people's, to the point where it must be hidden from their eyes. Still others "prime the pump"—drink *before* a party in order to limit themselves to one or two drinks while people are watching.

Why is it necessary to increase the amount of alcohol? Partly because the alcoholic's elevated tolerance forces him to consume larger than normal amounts to alleviate discomfort. Partly because a greater amount is now required for the the alcoholic to feel "normal"—that is, comfortable. And the level at which withdrawal symptoms begin *increases* as time passes. Figure 5 illustrates this phenomenon.

Note that the alcoholic's elevated tolerance protects him or her from appearance of obvious intoxication even when the blood alcohol level is high. Note also that the level at which withdrawal symptoms begin is above .00—and in fact, may reach the point where the alcoholic has difficulty consuming enough alcohol to completely eliminate his or her discomfort.

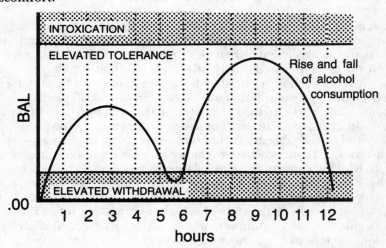

Figure 5. In the maintenance pattern, withdrawal starts above .00 BAL. Alcoholic must keep BAL above the point withdrawal begins by drinking, yet not drink so much that intoxication is reached.

This is the genesis of the *maintenance pattern*. Maintenance drinkers use alcohol to medicate withdrawal and rely on a combination of tolerance and their own not inconsiderable willpower to protect them from problems that would normally attend those who drink in these quantities. Eventually, the drinking begins to infiltrate parts of the day which are reserved for other activities—the middle of the night, working hours, breakfast and lunch—and the amounts consumed over a twenty-four hour period can be phenomenal. It isn't unusual to encounter alcoholics who drink in excess of a quart of liquor, a half-gallon of wine, or a case of beer over that span.

Still, typical maintenance drinkers have sufficient control to confine consumption to times and places where it is least risky. They may avoid drinking at work or during regular working hours, which encourages them to further overdrink when outside those boundaries. An example, from a woman who visited us for assistance in getting her husband into treatment:

"I don't know if you could call him an alcoholic," she explained. "He gets up in the morning and goes right off to work, and he doesn't call in sick very often. The problem is when he gets home. He's usually in a bad mood—you can tell by his face—and he doesn't want me to talk to him till he has something to drink. He'll go right to the refrigerator and get a beer, and he'll stand there and drink it. He won't even close the refrigerator door! By the end of the evening, he'll have finished off a couple of six-packs. Sometimes more. He doesn't get what you'd call drunk, where he stumbles around or falls down, but he gets different— sort of mean and impatient. I hate to say it, but the kids have gotten to the point where they just avoid him. And frankly, whenever I can, so do I."

Examine this situation and you'll see a good illustration of the mechanics of the maintenance pattern. People assume that alcoholism affects the alcoholic only when he's drinking. In fact, alcoholism—in the form of withdrawal—may affect the alcoholic's behavior more when he's not drinking than when he is. This man resists his craving for the drug during the day but "loads" his system with alcohol as soon as he gets off work. He then drinks heavily into the evening, to the exclusion of any other activity. This leads us to believe that he's not too pleasant to be around on the job, either. He's no doubt *irritable, tired, tense*—due to withdrawal. Of course, while we can see that it is a natural consequence of his drinking pattern, he would blame his mood on the imperfections of his co-workers or family. And when the boundaries of work are removed—on the weekend, for example—his drinking no doubt quickly expands to fill the empty hours, like air rushing into a vacuum.

Imagine how his consumption would increase if he were laid off from his job, or retired . Yet he would no doubt blame the change on boredom, or depression over unemployment.

A key point: despite the negative impact on her life, this man's wife remains unsure whether her husband is alcoholic. That's typical of the maintenance pattern—in the absence of certain problems, those around the drinker hesitate to identify the disease.

Remember that the life of the maintenance drinker will differ markedly from that of the alcoholic who obviously loses control. Maintenance drinkers tend to keep their jobs rather than lose them. They maintain the appearance of stable family life, though not without extensive damage to their relationships. They may avoid drunk driving arrests and other alcohol-related problems. They exercise extreme self-discipline in their use of alcohol for years (or even decades).

Because of this, the families of maintenance drinkers respond very differently than those of drinkers who lose control. They are invariably *less* aware of alcoholism and particularly of its negative effect on their own lives. Over the years, they *adapt* to the disease.

Lastly, it's important to understand that maintenance drinking may actually produce more physical damage than binge drinking. This is because the maintenance drinker experiences a state of chronic, low-grade alcohol poisoning (often accompanied by numerous vitamin deficiencies) that may last for much of his lifetime. So even though this drinker avoids losing job and family to alcoholism, he nevertheless may sacrifice a number of years from his life expectancy.

The situation of the maintenance drinker is analogous to that of the heavy smoker. Tobacco addiction produces few identifiable social "problems"—although that too seems to be changing—but somewhere along the way, the smoker may well drop dead of lung cancer.

Accordingly, some maintenance drinkers are first identified through medical tests that unearth elevated liver enzymes or other common indicators of alcohol-related physical deterioration. Unfortunately, the average physician doesn't perform these tests during a routine physical examination, and so most alcoholics go undiscovered.

The psychology of the drinker reflects the peculiar characteristics of his pattern. The maintenance alcoholic worships at the altar of "functioning." Principal defenses include:

"I function, don't I?" This claim is based upon the misconception that alcoholics are people who can't function at all. The drinker may not be operating at a very high level, however. Hidden alcoholism often leads to lost promotions, frequent job change, personality conflicts with supervisors, and poor performance ratings. Additionally, keeping one's family intact does not mean that family is happy or healthy—as anyone who grew up in an alcoholic family knows.

"My drinking isn't affecting anyone but myself." The most blatant sort of denial. Alcoholism affects everyone near it, to a greater or lesser degree. Nevertheless, those around the drinker may be complicit in this denial by avoiding confrontation or by falling into useless nagging.

"You hardly ever see me drunk." The slogan of the alcoholic with a high tolerance. Again, this mistakenly equates alcoholism with drunkenness. Episodes of uncontrolled intoxication may not appear until the late stages of the disease.

Loss of Control

Eventually, most alcoholics lose control over drinking in the usual three areas:

Amount

The alcoholic drinks more than he intends. For example, a male alcoholic goes to the local bar to have two or three drinks with "the boys." Instead, he stays late into the night, spends most of his money buying booze, and gets in trouble with his wife when he returns home. There is an increasingly *compulsive* quality to his drinking: one drink, instead of satisfying him, seems to increase his desire for more. This will lead to episodes of evident intoxication. Rather than stopping short of the upper limit of his tolerance, he'll drink past that level and become obviously drunk.

Time and Place

Drinking will slip outside the boundaries the alcoholic has set for it. If a woman executive has a longstanding rule against drinking at work, something will happen to make adherence to that boundary impossible. For example, suppose that she has a presentation to deliver and she's badly hung over from last night. She knows she can't go in front of her superiors in that condition. So she sneaks out at lunch and has a couple of quick drinks, chews 250 breath mints, and sails through the presentation with flying colors. "What was I so paranoid about?" she asks herself later. "Nobody suspected a thing. I was just nervous. Anybody would have had a drink under those circumstances." She doesn't notice that she's broken her own longstanding rule—and left herself vulnerable to a whole new set of possible problems if, in the future, her drinking is discovered.

Or suppose the problems of another alcoholic, a year or so further along, have progressed to the point where his wife is now threatening to leave. To placate her, he promises to abstain on weekends and stay home with the family. There's only one problem: without alcohol, he feels terrible. So he sneaks off to the liquor store, buys a pint of vodka, and hides it in the garage.

He spends the rest of the weekend finding excuses to visit his stash. "I'd better check the lawnmower," he says. "Better make sure the lid on the trashcan is closed."

In both instances, the ability to confine drinking to certain times or places is sabotaged by the disease.

Duration of Episode

Suppose, another alcoholic has reached the point where he's had to go on the wagon to save his marriage. Let's say he's been sober a month.

His wife is planning to visit her mother in New Jersey over the weekend.

He thinks: "She'll be gone from Friday evening to Sunday afternoon. What's to stop me from picking up a six-pack and having a little party while I watch the ball game on TV? I'll still have Saturday and most of Sunday to recuperate. She won't know anything about it."

So he buys the beer and settles in to watch the game. She returns two days later. Where is he? Asleep on the couch. Empty beer cans all around. Ashtrays overturned and cigarette burns on the rug. Road-Runner cartoons on the TV. She files for divorce.

Was this his intention? Of course not. His plan was to conceal his drinking. He fell victim to the onset of the *binge* pattern—round-the-clock, compulsive drinking, interspersed with periods of abstinence.

It's essential to understand that loss of control generally occurs over an extended period. Episodes of unpredictability are interspersed with periods of ostensible control. This fools the drinker into thinking that his problems are situational in origin.

Let's look at a hypothetical case. Suppose Alfred the Alcoholic has been drinking in typical maintenance fashion for a number of years. He's clearly addicted, but up to this point has managed to avoid the kind of problems usually associated with alcoholism. Then his boss invites him to the wedding of one of his daughters. Alfred has too much champagne, gets boisterous, and insults the bride's mother. The next morning, he doesn't recall all of what he said or did. His wife gives him the gory details. He is deeply embarrassed. "I don't know what came over me," he worries. "That champagne went right to my head—I'd better stick to whiskey in the future."

So he goes back to maintenance drinking, which seems to restore everything to its proper order. Then, just when he thinks he has everything under control, his boss invites him to the wedding of his second daughter. Alfred goes. His resolve: stick to whiskey. Avoid the champagne

The following morning, his wife relates an even more incredible story. Apparently Alfred got drunk at the reception, told the bride's mother she resembled a "fire hydrant in pink satin," then fell asleep under the hors d'oeuvres table. He remembers nothing of this.

Alfred is horrified. "What is happening to me?" he asks. "Am I losing my mind?" So he strictly rations his intake of alcohol. He measures, times, and counts his drinks. And just when he thinks he's got it back under control, his boss—let's say for the sake of argument that this gentleman does not learn from experience—invites Alfred to the wedding of his third and last daughter.

This time, Alfred—who's resolved not to touch a drop at the reception—allows himself "just an eentsy little one" for the purpose of appearing "sociable."

He wakes up a week later, in a detox ward in Phoenix. He's kidnapped the bride. Nobody knows where he left her.

We could diagram Alfred's experience as shown in Figure 6.

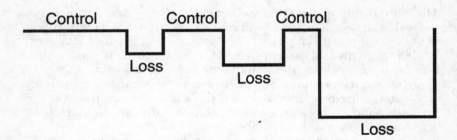

Figure 6. Episodes of loss of control increase in duration as drinking career progresses.

Note how the periods of control grow shorter while the episodes of loss of control become more severe. Everyone around Alfred will be pointing to his binges. Alfred himself will be obsessed with the apparent unpredictability of his behavior. "Why is it," he will wonder, "that sometimes I get in trouble, and sometimes I don't? There must be something in my environment that is causing these problems."

Thus the alcoholics who are experiencing such difficulties turn to *defenses* to provide acceptable alternative explanations. They *deny*, they *rationalize*, they *externalize*, and they *minimize*.

When you filter reality through such defense mechanisms, you take away your motivation to change. If it's not really a problem—or better still, if it's somebody else's problem—then what's your worry? There's certainly no reason to give up alcohol. So you continue drinking, the disease continues to progress, and you experience still more problems. Which require still more highly developed defenses. And so on and so forth, until conventional reality is a dimly remembered concept, and structured intervention is required just to get the alcoholic to perceive the obvious.

One way of identifying the drinker who is losing control is through the appearance of various *strategies for avoiding overdrinking.*

One of our former patients—a longtime maintenance drinker who coincidentally happened to be a behavioral psychologist—concluded that the reason he drank a case of beer every day was because he bought beer by the case, to save money.

"If I purchase no more than two cans at a time," he reasoned, "and keep nothing at all in the house, I'm sure my consumption will be greatly limited."

So he adopted the practice of walking from his home to the nearest convenience store—a distance of three blocks—buying only two cans of beer, and walking back home before drinking it.

At the end of a month, he was making fifteen trips a day to the store and had worn out a pair of shoes.

Ironically, there exist programs that avow to teach the alcoholic to control his or her consumption. These programs are based on a "conditioning" model; they insist that the alcoholic "learned" to drink excessively and so can be taught to drink within acceptable social boundaries. Of course, with the support and encouragement of the program, some alcoholics are able to return to what appears to be "controlled drinking" for extended periods. Nevertheless, studies done on graduates of these programs indicate a high rate of recidivism as time passes, accompanied by obvious loss of control.

If you stop and think, the absurdity of such a quest seems apparent. The struggle, the sacrifice, the expense, the sheer devotion expended in this direction might be put to better use at almost any other task. Alcoholics Anonymous has long held a tolerant view of attempts by its own members to regain control over alcohol; it's called "rejoining the research division." The fact is, the great advantage of abstinence is that despite its demands, sobriety is ultimately easier for the alcoholic to achieve than any other solution.

Cocaine

First, let's take a look at cocaine itself. Cocaine is the active alkaloid in the coca leaf, a plant that has absolutely nothing at all to do with chocolate. Coca has been cultivated and used by natives of the Andes mountain region of South America—now the nations of Peru, Columbia, and Bolivia—for about the last five thousand years. There may be as many as four million habitual coca chewers among the native tribes today.

Americans have their own, lesser versions of coca chewing: we consume enormous amounts of nicotine, in the form of tobacco, and caffeine, in coffee, tea, and soft drinks. These drugs are also stimulants, with secondary appetite suppressant effects.

Have you ever watched someone at the breakfast table, cup of coffee in one hand, cigarette in the other? First a sip of coffee, then a puff on the cigarette; followed by another sip and another puff, and so on, until she's gone through several cups of coffee and several cigarettes.

What's she doing? Stimulant loading: getting the level of stimulants in her brain and bloodstream up to the point where she feels "awake." Why is she doing it first thing in the morning? Because the previous day's loading dose of stimulants has worn off (we've yet to devise a way to smoke and drink coffee while asleep) and she needs to alleviate her marked feeling of fatigue. She'll periodically replenish these stimulants throughout the day to "maintain" a comfortable level. Whenever she does something that causes this level to fall—goes without a cigarette for an extended period, has a large meal, etc.—she'll experience a "spontaneous" craving for a smoke and a cup of coffee.

We mention this because it illustrates the extent to which stimulants—long regarded as nonaddictive—produce dependence. Think of all the people you know who've had trouble giving up smoking, or even caffeine. This discomfort—much magnified—is what occurs when cocaine addicts attempt to give up their drug of choice.

When you isolate the alkaloid cocaine from coca, and snort it up your nose through a straw or a $100 bill (depending upon your station in life), you magnify the stimulant and appetite suppressant properties while adding still another primary effect. Cocaine in this form is a powerful euphoriant: a drug that produces pleasurable feelings. If you're familiar with computers, you might think of it this way: cocaine accesses the pleasure hardware of the brain without having to do a lot of programming. It's fast, easy, and above all, it works.

Now you understand why people experiment with cocaine: to obtain these feelings. Note that you don't necessarily have to feel bad to begin with in order to want to feel better. It's a mistake to assume that people who experiment with this drug necessarily suffer from depression or low self-esteem, or even succumb to peer pressure. Our guess is that if you somehow miraculously eliminated depression, poor self-esteem, and peer pressure from the world, you'd still have a market for cocaine. Simply because it works.

There are two other things to learn about cocaine. First, because of its effectiveness, it's a powerful *reinforcer*. That's a fancy way of saying that once you try the drug, you may discover you really want to try it again.

To illustrate: take a laboratory monkey. Hook it up to an apparatus that administers a premeasured intravenous dose of cocaine whenever the monkey presses a lever. The animal will learn to perform this task within a few repetitions. Then, once the behavior has been ingrained, try to interrupt it. Electrify the floor of the cage so that the monkey gets irritating shocks; it will scream and cry and make a horrible fuss, but it will probably not forget to get the cocaine every so often. Because the drug tells the monkey's brain it isn't hungry, the monkey will ignore food; in some cases, it will starve itself to death. It won't do that for heroin, but it will for cocaine.

The second important quality is that when cocaine wears off, it doesn't simply return the nervous system to its normal level of activity. Instead, the brain drops into the *depressed* range, leaving the user fatigued, enervated, foggy (see Figure 7).

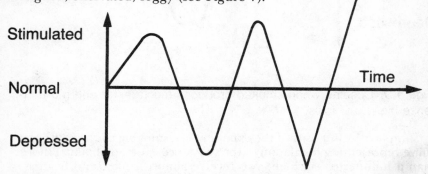

Figure 7. Cocaine's negative effect—after each "high" comes a plunge into depression.

As the drug wears off, the user experiences the first inklings of cocaine's negative side. Note that the reactive depression felt by the cocaine snorter is significantly greater than that experienced by the coca chewer. This is because the drug is delivered to the nervous system in a more potent fashion. Just as the high is more intense, so too is the low that follows on its heels. And note also the relatively brief duration of effect that marks cocaine inhalation. This is a practical rule of stimulant ingestion: the higher the high, the lower the low, and the briefer the effect, the greater the addictive potential. In other words, snorting the drug is more likely to create addictive problems than chewing it.

Smoking and the New Cocaine Epidemic

The practice of smoking cocaine has further contributed to the rate of addiction among users.

Cocaine hydrochloride, in its inhalable form, is difficult to smoke. Its melting point is too high. By the time you get it hot enough to give off vapors you can inhale, it's so hot it burns up. The way around this is to treat it with a solvent, converting it into a "paste" which can be allowed to dry and smoked in a pipe. This has a lower melting point and therefore can be smoked. When you smoke cocaine, you greatly intensify its effects (see Figure 8).

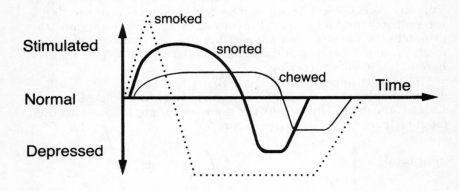

Figure 8. Cocaine when smoked produces much faster and more intense highs and lows.

Compare the intensity of the experience of smoking cocaine with the curve representing inhalation of the substance. Instead of taking more than a minute to feel high, you receive almost instant gratification. Instead of lasting for twenty minutes or more, you drop out of the euphoric phase and into reactive depression (or "crash") in three to eight minutes.

One of our recovering cocaine patients compares this to "having an orgasm and walking directly off a cliff."

The original smoked cocaine was called *freebase* and was usually made with ether. A newer variant is popularly known as *crack* and is made with baking soda solution. The difference between ether freebase and crack is a bit like the difference between hamburgers at fancy restaurants and those you get in fast-food places: one takes a little longer to prepare and is probably a bit higher quality. The product, however, is essentially the same.

We seldom see anyone smoke cocaine for any length of time without developing obvious symptoms of addiction. Alongside smoking stands *intravenous (IV) use,* which also delivers the drug to the system with tremendous intensity and produces a curve of stimulation and depression similar to that of freebasing. IV users often share needles and that, of course, puts them at risk for a particularly nasty consequence: AIDS.

The Syndrome of Cocaine Addiction

The behavioral symptoms of addictive disease are expressed quite clearly in cocaine addiction. Loss of control appears to be the dominant pattern among cocaine addicts.

Perhaps the most striking feature of cocaine addiction is the *compulsive quality* that accompanies use.

Having ingested a small amount, the addict finds his desire for cocaine *increases* rather than lessens. It therefore becomes difficult for him to predict exactly how much he'll use at a given session. Sometimes he'll be able to save a little for later occasions; at other times, this will be nearly impossible.

Cocaine is expensive, so most addicts (unless they're also suppliers) are forced to use it intermittently. Frequently, family members ask: "Can she be an addict if she goes a week or even two between episodes?" The answer is yes, if these episodes are characterized by compulsiveness. Addicts may also use other drugs—alcohol, marijuana, sedatives—during the intervals between binges. Remember: it's one thing to go a few days without cocaine. It's another to be drug free.

Signs of Loss of Control

Over Amount Consumed. As the disease progresses, addicts tend to fall into a pattern of purchasing as much cocaine as they can afford, then using it until it's gone. If the addict has cash—or if someone else is dumb enough to lend it—he or she will go looking for still more. This is how cocaine addicts get into debt. Here's one young man's story:

"I thought of myself as somebody who had 'cash-flow' problems—meaning I didn't have enough cash to buy all the coke I wanted. One day I hit on a great solution: I approached my supplier—a guy named Eduardo—and offered to go to work selling his coke on 'consignment.' If he'd give me five grams, I'd sell four, give him the money, and keep one gram for myself as payment. He said okay, and I became a vendor.

"This worked fine for the first few weekends. Then one night I got the five grams from Eduardo and took them home. My routine was to wait for it to get to a certain hour—maybe eleven o'clock or midnight—and then I'd go over to the club and unload the stuff. I went ahead and did up my gram, figuring I'd get high so my customers could see how good the coke was. Unfortunately, it didn't work; I hardly got high at all. This was real frustrating—here I was with about two hours to kill and no more coke to do. That's when it hit me: why don't I do a second gram, and sell the remaining three at a markup?

"But once I did that, I kinda went nuts. I figured: why not do another gram, and find some rich sucker to buy the remaining two for an arm and a leg? It made perfect sense to me at the time.

"Anyway, about three that morning, I realized all the coke was gone, and I had absolutely no cash to show for it. I was in the area of deficit spending. Only my creditor was not a bank. It was a guy named Eduardo, who carried a .45 in the glove compartment of his Lincoln Continental."

Over Time and Place Where Cocaine Is Used. The addict begins using the drug at times or in places where it will cause problems. This signals a dramatic increase in craving. For example, here's the story of a sixteen-year-old high school student:

"Toward the end, I would sometimes do coke right in class. I'd keep it in a little vial around my neck, and when the teacher would turn her back, I'd pull it out, put a little on a knuckle, and snort it up my nose. It was crazy. Everybody in class would sit there and watch me use it. I knew one of them would turn me in. But I just couldn't help myself. Some days, I couldn't get through a forty-minute class without coke."

A twenty-eight-year-old woman, who worked for one of those high-tech firms with three letters in its name, described herself as so careless she would not only freebase cocaine at her desk, she would on occasion leave the pipe out where people could see it. News stories have related how athletes would use cocaine immediately before, after, and even during games, despite the obvious danger of discovery.

Over Duration of Episode. At first, cocaine use is confined to a given evening. Later on, it may extend into the night or even the following morning. Sleep patterns are severely disrupted, and the *binge* cycle appears: extended periods without sleep, followed by a "crash" of exhaustion.

"I tried to keep it to Saturday night," said one woman, "but Saturday night kept turning into Sunday morning, and I wouldn't start to come down till about five o'clock on Sunday afternoon. I would still be so wasted I had to call in sick on Monday, or I'd be late to work. Maybe I'd be on time but so irritable they would wish I stayed home."

Such binges contribute mightily to the appearance of symptoms of *cocaine toxicity,* which causes the addict to behave in new and strange ways.

Continued Use Despite Adverse Consequences

Where cocaine-related problems might cause the casual user to rethink his position, they often spur the addict on to further use, in even greater amounts, in spite of the difficulties he or she experiences. Even life-threatening situations aren't sufficient to stop drug use. Here's an example, from the fellow who got his drugs on consignment from his "friend" Eduardo:

"My methods got me deeper and deeper into debt. Within six months, I owed about $50,000 to a number of people. The one that really worried me was Eduardo, because he was even crazier than I was. I started avoiding him, which was hard because I had to go to work every day, and sometimes he'd park across the street from my building and just sit there for an hour or more, just to psych me out. I was pretty paranoid by then, anyway. One day, I go to my car, which is in the underground garage, and Eduardo is waiting for me. He starts waving his gun around and yelling at me, and his English is so bad I can't even understand what he's saying. Finally I panic and run away, and the son of a bitch starts shooting at me! I scramble under a parked car and pray he doesn't find me. I was so scared I threw up, right on the spot. Eventually, the cops come and haul him away, kicking and screaming in Spanish. I crawl out from under the car and I can't even stand up, man, I am so weak with fear. I remember sitting there against the wall and saying to myself, over and over: this is never gonna happen again. I am through with drugs. I learned my lesson.

"Ninety minutes later, I'm looking for somebody to sell me some coke. I'm thinking: no way I can handle this without something to help me cope."

Note how the drug-related crisis, no matter how much it frightens the addict at the time, serves to motivate further use rather than abstinence. This is why so many cocaine addicts require structured intervention to get them into treatment. The addict's thinking is so distorted that he can't recognize the obvious: the drug that he thinks "helps him cope" is the source of the problems he must cope with.

Tolerance and Dependence

Cocaine addicts experience varying degrees of tolerance to cocaine, which contributes to increased use, since smaller doses are no longer effective. Another way to meet the demands of increased tolerance is to use better quality cocaine—in other words, move a step up the supply line, where the concentration of cocaine is higher. Or, as many users do, switch to a more potent method of delivery: smoking, or injecting the drug into a vein.

Cocaine addicts experience a different withdrawal syndrome than alcoholics or narcotics addicts. Here's what happens following a cocaine "binge":

The Panic. Phase One: Two to four hours after last use. Depression, anxiety, agitation; extreme, persistent hunger for the drug.

The Crash. Phase Two: Four to thirty-six hours after last use. Exhaustion, severe depression (perhaps accompanied by suicidal thoughts), interrupted sleep, absence of strong craving for the drug.

The Honeymoon. Phase Three: Twenty-four hours to seven days after last use. Elevation of mood, sense of recovery, relatively low craving.

The Craving Returns. Phase Four: One to two weeks after last use. High craving linked to conditioned cues (seeing friends who use, etc.) and emotional excitement; mood swings, anxiety, sleep disruption. Most addicts relapse here.

Emotional Augmentation. Phase Five: Two to five weeks after last use. Cycling moods, continued craving on erratic basis.

By comparison with alcohol, cocaine withdrawal is relatively benign. Because of its persistence and the intensity of craving, however, it presents problems in treatment. Without some kind of structured program, the addict will probably relapse during this withdrawal period.

Cocaine patients report *protracted symptoms* and cravings long after cessation of use. These vary tremendously from individual to individual, in both nature and intensity. Food cravings in particular may lead to pronounced weight gain and unhelpful "crash diets" (see chapter on recovery). Some addicts report persistent headaches, insomnia, sexual dysfunction, even acne and other skin problems, all of which seem to improve spontaneously with time. Mood swings and dramatic fluctuations in energy level, which are characteristic of recovering addicts in general, are perhaps more acute for the cocaine addict. One patient described it as follows:

"For about five months, my body and my brain seemed to be on a predictable schedule. I'd be real low during the week—sometimes I'd have to drag myself to work—and then I'd begin to feel better when Friday rolled around. But by Saturday, I'd start having all this anxiety and nightmares, and I'd break out in cold sweats sometimes, and it would be all I could do not to go out and buy some coke. Then I'd be depressed for some reason all day Sunday and I'd go to bed about 6 P.M. I would toss and turn all night, and get up exhausted on Monday, and drag myself off to work. By Tuesday, I was depressed again, and the whole thing would start all over.

"It drove me crazy. I would sit around for hours and try to figure out why I was depressed. And if I wasn't depressed, I'd try to figure out why not. I thought it was all due to problems in my life, you see. It wasn't until later that I figured out my body was *still following my coke schedule*—depressed all week, up for the weekend, go nuts on Saturday, crash Sunday night, drag through Monday. It's like I trained my nervous system to operate on this cycle, and it took it about five months to figure out I wasn't doing that anymore "

Cocaine Toxicity

Once binges emerge, they're often accompanied by the phenomenon known as cocaine toxicity. This dramatically alters the behavior of the addict.

Some of the symptoms of toxicity:

Paranoia. Cocaine use, once an occasion for socializing, becomes an isolative experience. The addict may in fact be unwilling to spend time with other people (unless they're providing the cocaine).

One classic picture of a cocaine addict in the later stages: sitting by himself in a room, lights dimmed, door locked, shades drawn, alone with his pipe. There may be a gun close at hand; some cocaine addicts turn their houses into armories. Every so often he gets up and goes to the window, parting the shades so he can study the cars across the street. *Was that Ford parked there yesterday?* he wonders. *Are they watching my house?*

Still another classic portrayal is one of insane jealousy. "He started to get suspicious whenever I was gone for more than thirty minutes," one woman related about her cocaine-using husband. "He started accusing me of sleeping with his buddies, whom I hardly knew. Then there was the time I came home and he had a bunch of my panties spread out on the kitchen table. He told me he was going to take them to a lab and have them tested to see if there were traces of other men's sperm."

Hallucinations. The characteristic hallucination produced by cocaine toxicity involves *bugs*. The sensations might be both visual and tactile (you can feel them as well as see them) and can take on a remarkable reality. One woman told us a story about moving into an apartment she believed was infested with fleas. After having the exterminator out several times, she realized the "fleas" were really the product of her freebasing.

Aggressive or Assaultive Behavior. Toxic addicts sleep poorly (if at all), spend a lot of time in paranoid fantasy, are extremely irritable, and have very little impulse control. This can make them dangerous.

One woman told how her husband began dropping hints that he regarded her (and not cocaine) as the "real cause" of his unhappiness and suggested that if she really cared about his welfare, she'd commit suicide. He would leave loaded guns about the house to encourage her.

Sexual Dysfunction. Oddly enough, given this drug's reputation as an aphrodisiac, the great majority of cocaine addicts seem to experience some degree of sexual dysfunction. In males, this is expressed as difficulty reaching orgasm, and eventually by periodic or chronic impotence. In women, one finds retarded orgasm or inability to reach orgasm at all.

In both sexes, sexual desire seems to decrease as cocaine involvement increases. "I just figured I wouldn't be able to get it up, anyway," one man reported. "Who has time for sex?" said a woman. "Unless of course it's to get at some guy's stash of coke."

A twenty-six-year-old woman describes it more vividly: "I was a coke whore," she said. "Basically, it's just like a regular prostitute, except you sleep with coke dealers and you take your payment in cocaine. I was actually proud of it at the time, because I was getting my coke without money. I thought that was pretty smart. Then one day, I met this guy I really liked, and I went to bed with him because I wanted to—and I *still* couldn't feel anything. Somehow, I'd screwed up my system. The only thing that made me feel good was coke. Nothing else worked."

Which brings us to another common symptom of toxicity: *anhedonia,* or inability to experience pleasure from normally pleasurable activities. Probably the result of dopamine depletion, this condition further reinforces dependence on cocaine. Not only does the drug "work" better and faster than other sources of gratification, it gradually erodes the user's ability to experience pleasure from anything *but* the drug.

Use of Other Drugs. Cocaine toxicity is painful. You don't sleep, you may hallucinate, you're paranoid, have no appetite, are panicky and easily irritated. One solution is to use a depressant drug—alcohol, for example—to bring yourself down to a more manageable level. The problem, however, is that as cocaine addicts "come down" from the toxic phase, their exhausted brains slip right into the depressed phase—which may feature, after an extended binge, suicidal ideation.

The following chart in Figure 9 illustrates the phenomenon.

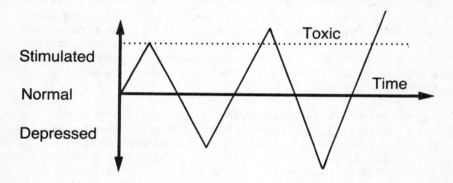

Figure 9. The "elevator syndrome" associated with cocaine.

When depression begins to hit, the addict is strongly tempted to use more cocaine. As he does, however, he may pass quickly through euphoria into the toxic phase—bringing back the discomfort associated with that condition. So he uses more alcohol, drops rapidly back into depression, which leads to more cocaine use, and so on. This is sometimes called the "elevator syndrome."

The addict's goal is to stay close to the "normal" line, but that becomes increasingly difficult.

One way to "smooth out the ride" is to inject a combination of cocaine and a narcotic (heroin or Dilaudid, for example). This practice is called "speedballing."

Even when cocaine addicts finally recognize the severity of their problem and enter treatment, they often play down the importance of their involvement with other drugs. "Cocaine really ruined my life," they admit. "But alcohol? It was just a temporary solution. It never caused any problems. I can keep drinking."

This turns out to be of central importance in recovery. In our experience, the best single predictor of relapse—a return to cocaine use—is whether or not the patient attempts to continue drinking. And one great problem in treating cocaine addiction involves getting the addict to abstain from all drugs.

Marijuana

Marijuana—or more properly, cannabis—is one of the world's most widely used drugs. Smoked in a pipe or rolled cigarette, marijuana reached the height of its popularity in the 1960s when it was widely regarded as safer and more enjoyable than alcohol. Many of today's parents grew up smoking the occasional joint and regard it as no more harmful than a can of beer or a glass of wine.

Indeed, among the pantheon of illicit drugs, marijuana is one of the least socially offensive. Though marijuana does adversely affect health and the ability to perform common tasks like driving, few smokers wind up in detox units because of marijuana withdrawal or get "stoned driving tickets." As a result, the general attitude toward marijuana among those under the age of thirty-five is one of amused tolerance.

Unfortunately, this attitude doesn't accurately reflect the potential hazards of marijuana addiction. Depending upon a number of variables—susceptibility, age, quality of marijuana used—cannabis can be incorporated into an addictive syndrome and thereby create a number of difficulties for the user.

The Addictive Syndrome

One of the most enduring conflicts in the field of drug abuse concerns the issue of whether or not marijuana is physically addictive. As we noted earlier, the point is of little practical importance. Determining that a given symptom is either "physical" or "psychological" in origin is difficult if not impossible where drugs are involved. The important point is that marijuana users can and do experience elevated tolerance and a withdrawal syndrome, and that these symptoms create an addictive pattern.

It's funny, though. For a number of years, Americans heard very little about marijuana as a drug of abuse. Among substances, it was considered a weak sister. We don't know how many times we've heard parents breathe a sigh of relief when they discovered their teenager was "only smoking pot."

"Jeez, we were worried he was doing *drugs*," they'd say.

Now, in the past few years, people are again beginning to talk about marijuana addicts.

So the question arises: what happened? You almost get the impression that the Sixties pot smoker must have been stronger or smarter than the Eighties version—that marijuana addiction is a relatively recent phenomenon, reflecting some kind of hidden change in cultural values or a weakening of the national character.

But in fact, marijuana addicts have probably been around forever.

It's just that in the Sixties, people were so blasé about pot—and so many people in a certain age group smoked so much—that it was difficult to pick the addict out from the crowd. They simply weren't recognized by their peers.

We went to college in the late 1960s and early 1970s, an era when marijuana use was, in our circle, at least as socially acceptable as drinking beer. In every dorm lived one or two kids who supplemented their student loans with income from dealing grass. A party that didn't include marijuana was considered a bad party. We saw nothing unusual when someone lit up a joint at ten in the morning, between classes. It didn't matter to us that the college was surrounded by a conservative Midwestern community with strict laws against this sort of behavior. We believed that marijuana was harmless—especially in comparison with the alcohol favored by our elders.

Even then, we were aware that some of our classmates smoked more than others. Still, we would have been hard put to find someone who didn't smoke at all.

Curiously enough, we lost interest in marijuana as we grew older. It wasn't that we made a conscious choice not to smoke it—we simply lost the desire. We knew fewer and fewer people who indulged, and therefore, opportunities for using grass gradually disappeared. We certainly weren't fond enough of the drug to go to the trouble of meeting some stranger in order to buy it. We just drifted away from smoking. There were other things to do.

Years later, an old friend from college called to invite us over for a "mini-reunion." He was a schoolteacher who'd just completed a book of his own and wanted to share experiences. We arrived at his house at nine o'clock in the morning and immediately noticed that something was wrong with his behavior. In the first place, he was amazingly nervous; he seemed to have difficulty sitting still, much less carrying on a conversation. Despite the fact we hadn't seen each other in ten years, he seemed totally disinterested and kept looking distractedly about the room, as though wondering how he could get us to leave. After half an hour of fidgeting, he suddenly said: "Say, want to see my study? Where I wrote the book?"

He led us up to a loft, which held the predictable tools of the writer's trade: table, chair, and typewriter. There was, however, one significant addition. On the table next to the typewriter sat a large water pipe, obviously for smoking marijuana or hash. We noticed our friend was grinning.

"Wanna get stoned?" he asked.

"No, thanks."

His face fell, then brightened again.

"Mind if I do?"

"It's your house," we said, with some resignation.

The results were amazing. Within five minutes, it was as if we were talking to a different person. He had magically become warm, relaxed, personable. Our status as guests had changed from boring to endlessly fascinating.

"Sorry I had to drag you up here," he apologized. "This is the only place in the house my wife lets me smoke. She doesn't want the kids to see it."

"She wants you to stop?"

"Oh, yeah," he said. "Remember what a pothead she used to be? She's really changed since college. Gotten real straight. She thinks I'm addicted to dope, which is crazy, of course. I've read everything there is on marijuana, and I can tell you, it isn't addictive."

Later on, he told us about a trip to the mountains, during which his wife had secretly thrown away his stash of grass in an attempt to get him to stop. Within three days, she was begging him to start smoking again. "I was practically a lunatic," he joked. "Couldn't sleep, couldn't hardly eat, mean as a snake. She'll never try that again."

"Sounds like you're addicted," we pointed out. "Look what happened when you went without it for a few days."

"But that was just psychological," he insisted. "It's not like I'm hooked on the stuff. As it is, I'll probably quit someday. I just don't feel ready yet. Meanwhile, it isn't harming me or anything. I was Teacher of the Year at my school, man. I'm getting a book published. It's just that smoking dope is one of the few things left in my life I can honestly say I enjoy."

For us, this visit served as a mini-lesson in addiction. Clearly, in any situation (or age group) where a large number of people are using a drug regularly, some of them are going to develop addictive disease. But because drug use is socially acceptable, it will be hard to differentiate them from anyone else. Remove them from that environment—or give the majority time to mature out of their drug-using phase—and the addict will stick out like a sore thumb. Because he or she won't grow out of it. It will, in fact, get worse.

Pattern One: Primary Marijuana Addiction

If you've learned something about addictive disease, you should be able to identify the maintenance pattern in this example, with its trademark use of a drug to medicate withdrawal and rationalizations concerning the addict's ability to function in spite of his addiction. Again, our friend emphasized his achievements rather than the problems he experienced: discord at home, marked discomfort when he didn't have access to the drug, dependence on it for everyday functioning.

The marijuana withdrawal syndrome is relatively mild in comparison with alcohol or heroin, but then again, so is the tobacco withdrawal syndrome, and look how that affects people's behavior. Symptoms may include loss of appetite, diarrhea or other bowel irregularities, tremor, irritability, nausea, sweating, cramps and muscle ache, insomnia, and episodes of anxiety. As with any form of drug withdrawal, symptoms vary widely between individuals as to extent, duration, and severity.

Much of the marijuana available today seems to be of higher quality than that commonly found in the 1960s. Several new forms—lumped together under the name *sinsamilla*—are stronger in concentration than the marijuana we smoked as college students and are therefore more likely to produce addictive symptoms and physiological consequences. In some areas, weak varieties of cannabis are misted with liquid PCP and sold surreptitiously at a higher price.

There are over four hundred chemical components in cannabis, but the most important psychoactive ingredient is thought to be Delta-9 THC. Following ingestion, this substance is absorbed readily by the fat cells and released into the bloodstream over an extended period. In infrequent users, traces of marijuana can be detected as long as thirty days following a single use. As you can imagine, a drug that remains in the system for that long can produce a number of cumulative, chronic effects.

These include:

Increased Risk of Lung Disease. Some marijuana cigarettes contain as much as five times the amount of tar found in an ordinary cigarette. Thus if someone smokes four joints, he may consume the equivalent in tar of a pack of cigarettes. This would seem to increase risk of lung cancer or other lung disease. And of course, nobody wants to get lung cancer—the recovery rate is almost too low to publish.

Sexual and Hormonal Changes. This occurs particularly in adolescence, which is a time of considerable biological upheaval. Chronic marijuana use may interrupt normal hormonal secretions and produce irregular menses or changes in secondary sex characteristics.

Changes in Cognitive or Intellectual Functioning. This is of course the subject of interminable debate, partially because it's so difficult to establish causation in these areas. A number of researchers believe that chronic marijuana ingestion can lead to an *amotivational syndrome* (loss of interest in activities normally pleasurable), *memory deficits* (particularly in the area of short-term recall), difficulties in *purposive activity* (completion of intellectual tasks), and *conceptual skills* (formation of concepts to link information in coherent patterns).

Of course, from a practical perspective, the last person to be aware of this sort of deficit is the person who suffers from it. Whenever we talk with a group of students, there are always two or three in the back of the room who raise their hands and openly admit to smoking heavily for at least two years. "And it hasn't affected my intelligence," one will insist.

"How do you know?" we'll ask. "You don't seem so bright to us."

"I was always this way," he'll proclaim. "Even before the drugs."

Pattern Two: Marijuana in a Polydrug Pattern

As a number of experts have pointed out, marijuana also serves as a "gateway" drug for adolescents who later become involved with much "harder" substances. The reason for this is simple. It's the easiest illegal drug to obtain.

It's even easier to get than alcohol in some cases. If you're thirteen and you want beer, you have to steal it from your parents, or get someone to buy it for you. On the other hand, there's probably a kid selling grass in the boys' bathroom at school.

As a result, kids who later develop drug problems usually start with marijuana. By the time they develop a full-blown addictive syndrome involving another drug—alcohol, cocaine, a narcotic—they may use marijuana only infrequently. When they do use it, it's to alleviate or counteract some of the sensations associated with other drugs. If they're tense or nervous, marijuana is a calming agent. It may not be as potent as some other substances, but like alcohol, it's cheap and it's there.

Later on, when they complete a treatment program, they find a desire for marijuana returns in the absence of stronger substances. Thinking nothing of it—after all, grass never caused any problems, did it?—they begin using marijuana once again, to relax, to socialize. Soon enough, they discover the craving for cocaine or alcohol returns, and they are unable to resist it.

This is why treatment programs place a premium on abstinence from all drugs. And because the addict's involvement with marijuana may be the lengthiest of all, it may be the drug he finds hardest to abandon.

PCP

Perhaps no drug is as widely feared as PCP. Even today, many people associate PCP with psychotic behavior, mass murder, and permanent insanity. Take our word for it—if everyone went mad whenever they smoked PCP, very few people would be using it. Though PCP can induce psychosis and other forms of organic brain dysfunction, it often does so *slowly*, over an extended period. There are PCP *addicts* who go to work or attend school along with the rest of us, at least until addiction makes normal functioning impossible.

PCP is difficult to classify. It possesses some of the characteristics associated with sedatives, stimulants, and hallucinogens. It's easiest to think of it as a *dissociative anesthetic*—a drug that temporarily "distances" the user from awareness of painful stimuli.

The general public has trouble understanding why medical science invents drugs like PCP, which then turn out to be the source of so many problems. Of course, the scientists who developed PCP weren't looking for a drug of abuse. They were searching for an anesthetic which blocked pain without excessive suppression of heart and respiratory function.

You may have heard that one of the principal hazards of modern surgery involves the use of *general anesthesia*. Such anesthetics are necessary—the patient wouldn't permit the doctor to operate without them—but they carry a degree of risk. Think of it this way: prior to surgery, the patient is put into a state where little is operational but his heartbeat and breathing. Then, the surgeon opens him up and messes about with his internal organs. Can you see the potential for an undesirable medical complication—such as death?

This is equally true in veterinary medicine. Large, expensive animals are known for their delicate constitutions and unpredictable response to medications.

PCP promised an ideal solution. There was a problem, however. Sometimes, when the drug wore off, the subject went through a period of agitation and restless excitement which included visual disturbances and delirium—not an ideal condition for a patient who has just undergone major surgery.

As PCP lost favor in the medical community, it found its true audience on the streets. The principal "street" method for ingesting PCP is by smoking it. Liquid or solid PCP is sprayed or sprinkled on marijuana, parsley flakes ("green"), or plain cigarettes. When inhaled, the user gets the *dominant* acute effects of the drug, which include:

Euphoria. Yes, PCP makes people feel good, temporarily. This is why they use it.

Perceptual Distortion. Some users report "funhouse mirror" distortion of body image. "I always feel like my hands are bigger than they should be, and when I look down, my feet are too far away," said one girl. Others experience hallucinogen-like distortion of light and color. A number of our patients have described a "sensation of being almost weightless, of not being able to feel the ground under your feet," which sometimes results in "moonwalking," of the Neil Armstrong (not Michael Jackson) variety.

Difficulty Communicating. This is especially noticeable at higher doses. The user may have trouble articulating words or putting down ideas on paper. "When I first started smoking boat (PCP)," one user reported, "I thought I'd write down my experiences, like I did on acid (LSD). But it was really strange—all I could get out were single words or short phrases. It was like something was blocking my brain. And I was an English major."

Agitation or Restless Excitement. This is what PCP is famous for—a period of agitation and confusion, which in some cases produces the spectacularly bizarre behavior of legend. For most users, this experience is the exception rather than the rule. If it happened more often, they'd probably avoid PCP and switch to some other drug. When it does occur, however, it has been known to lead to behavior up to and sometimes including acts of criminal insanity.

Reduced Response to Painful Stimuli. This drug is a superb anesthetic. To understand the effect on behavior, imagine you're a sixteen-year-old "doper" who's out using drugs with his buddies. Now remember that sixteen-year-old dopers don't use one drug—they use a variety of substances, depending on their availability. So let's assume this kid has been smoking marijuana laced with PCP, and drinking beer, and smoking a little crack, and all this is sloshing around in his brain cells. As a result, he's feeling numb, energized, and more than a bit agitated. And suddenly for no particular reason—maybe he remembers something critical his teacher said earlier in the day—he wheels around and smashes his fist, as hard as he can, into the brick wall behind him.

What sensation should he feel? Pain, of course. Immediate, attention-getting, behavior-stopping pain.

But suppose he doesn't. Suppose that the pain he experiences is no greater than, say, punching your fist into your opposite palm.

What's he going to do? He'll hit the wall again.

Why?

Because one of the only things that keeps people from hitting walls when they're angry is pain. Remove pain, and you remove one of the great natural inhibitors of stupid behavior.

Now view it from the perspective of a police officer. It's two in the morning. You come across a kid in his underwear, obviously blitzed out of his mind on something, standing at the curb and looking as though he plans to run out and play "dodge 'em" with the traffic. You grab him; he panics and begins struggling; you try to restrain him, he struggles harder; you rap him on the head with your stick, he struggles harder still.

Can you see how this could escalate to the point where someone gets shot? And there's no shortage of policemen with eyewitness accounts of PCP users who take several bullets and keep coming.

Chronic Toxicity

The effects of PCP aren't limited to periods of direct influence. After several months of regular use, we begin to see symptoms of chronic toxicity, which linger even during periods of abstinence. These include:

Residual Distortion of Perception. Or the "flashback" experience. Distortions of color and light, which interfere with essential tasks like driving a car.

Auditory Hallucinations. Some users report occasional episodes of hearing voices—even to the point of carrying on conversations. One former patient, a telephone operator, was brought to the hospital with the report that she'd shown up at work, put on her headphones, and begun answering calls, only to have her supervisor discover that she hadn't plugged the headphones into the switchboard. Ergo, the calls were not coming from outside. This phenomenon seems to be relatively short-lived, and normally disappears shortly after detoxification.

Speech and Language Deficits. Again, there is debate as to how widespread these deficits are, and as to how long they may persist. The most common are:

Blocked Speech: Difficulty articulating the spoken word, so that it has to be "forced" out, something like what occurs with victims of mild left-hemisphere stroke.

Sparse Speech: Giving excessively brief responses to questions that normally require elaboration, as in:
Question: "How do you feel about the prospect of nuclear war?"
Answer: "Okay."
(Of course, lots of parents tell us their teenagers talk this way, even without drugs.)

Stuttering: In persons with no previous history of speech defects.

Since oral communication precedes written language, any such deficits will carry over to reading and writing, as well.

Perhaps this is why PCP users tend to fail in school. Unbeknownst to them, their drug use is interfering with essential cognitive functions, making schoolwork more difficult even when they're not stoned.

Memory Deficits. PCP users may find that their ability to retain new information is severely impaired, even when they haven't used the drug for several days or weeks. This deficit, once established, may continue well into recovery.

Depression, Mood Swing, and Paranoia. Chronic users often experience the kind of persistent, "low-grade" depression that makes life a burden and everyday activities a motivational challenge. Some users report cyclic mood swings in which they alternate between extreme, unrealistic self-confidence and unrelenting self-hatred. Still others report the onset of paranoid thoughts and feelings, which lead them into isolation that deepens their depressive state, and sometimes into violence.

Psychosis. A psychosis is a state of severely disorganized thinking which is traditionally associated with brain diseases such as schizophrenia. However, PCP seems capable of inducing psychotic states in two ways:

Toxic Psychosis: This is an adverse reaction to a given dose (or overdose) of the drug, and usually produces bizarre behavior requiring psychiatric hospitalization. As the PCP leaves the system, however, the psychosis abates and the patient returns to normal.

Drug-Induced Psychosis: In some cases, PCP use—even a first-time dose—can produce a psychotic state which lasts for weeks or months after the drug is discontinued. There are probably certain people whose brains are susceptible to this phenomenon, and the PCP simply puts them over the edge. The problem is we can't reliably predict when, where, or to whom the drug-induced psychosis will strike.

PCP's dubious reputation has even spread to the street, where standards are not particularly high. Its street names include "Hinkley" and "Captain Stupid." Nevertheless, it's become a primary drug for thousands of addicts.

Narcotics

Narcotic drugs—our principal painkillers and the basis for much of modern medicine—also produce one of the most troublesome forms of addictive disease. People are introduced to narcotics in two ways:

Use for Intoxication

Narcotics are powerful euphoriants. The sensations they produce—supreme relaxation, absence of anxiety and discomfort, a "golden glow" often compared to floating on a cloud—have been described by poets throughout history. Where our nineteenth-century ancestors drank laudanum or smoked opium, modern users seek out heroin, Dilaudid, and Demerol for the pleasurable sensations they bring. Severe criminal penalties have by no means eradicated these drugs from society; in almost every major American city, there is an underground community of narcotics users and traffickers who make the drug available to anyone who is willing to go to the trouble of finding it.

Here is a typical example of someone who became addicted through use of illegal narcotics for purposes of intoxication (a twenty-seven-year-old man):

"I saw heroin for the first time when I was sixteen. My older brother knew these guys from when he was in the service. One night they brought some smack (heroin) over to the house when my mama was out. I watched them smoke it, and it seemed like they were having a real good time. So later on that year, when I met a kid at school who had some dope, I let him turn me on to it. The first time I used it I got sick, but the second time I had a real good ride. From then on, I just kind of naturally drifted in with the doper crowd at school. They turned me on to lots of things—grass, loveboat (PCP), blow—but my favorite was heroin. It's funny—most people start with grass and work up to smack, and I was just the opposite. No matter what I tried, I always remembered how good that heroin felt. Nothing like it, in my estimation.

"The first time I shot heroin was the night I graduated high school. I wasn't going on to college—I wasn't much for school, and they just passed me though my senior year to get rid of me—and my plan was to join the Army after I partied around for awhile. But I didn't know how good that needle was going to feel, man.

"At first, I was working construction, making good bucks, but it was all going to dope. My connection worked the same job, so I could cop whenever I wanted. Plus, he let me do errands for him—carry dope to customers and that stuff—so even if I was short of cash, I could always get my hands on some drugs.

"But all good things must end, right? He got busted. There I was, with a hellacious habit and no steady source, no credit, no nothing. I tried to lay off, but I couldn't. I was so sick I had to call in all the time, and the foreman fired my butt. I knew then I had gotten in over my head. I decided to kick. I went off to some cheap motel in the boondocks for three days and sweated it off. It wasn't that bad—like having the flu, I guess.

"Then I says to myself, 'You got to change your life, boy.' So I went down to the Army recruiter, tried to sign up, and got thrown out on my tail. It never occurred to me that they'd check me for needle tracks.

"I went out immediately and got loaded. Then I went on a run like I'd never been on before. I ran out of money real soon, so I had to start stealing from people—first my mama, and my brother, then I started breaking into people's houses. I got thrown out of my parent's house, then I got busted for B&E and possession of a firearm. My brother got me a lawyer, and he pleaded me to a drug program. I went a few times, but the program was so lame I dropped out. I never stopped using, anyway, so I don't know what good it was doing.

"The rest is pretty boring. My family won't have nothing to do with me. I've pretty much been living the street life for the last seven years, except for the time in the joint.

"It's funny. In spite of all I've been through, I feel like nothing has happened since I first picked up heroin.

"Like my life stopped right there. Not that I died or anything—I'm still kicking—but it's like when you play the stereo and the needle gets stuck. It just keeps playing those same few notes, over and over. That's what my life is like. The same thing, over and over again."

Medicinal Use

A far greater percentage of the population is introduced to narcotics through medical treatment, since narcotics are far and away our best *painkillers*. A visit to the dentist or back specialist may produce a prescription for *codeine, Percodan,* or *Darvon.* An accident or surgical procedure provides introduction to Demerol or Dilaudid. Though most people cease use as their medical problems fade, a certain percentage develop addictive disease.

This is the story of a thirty-one-year-old woman who became addicted to prescription narcotics:

"When I was about fifteen, I fell off a horse and broke my arm. The riding instructor called my parents and they dragged me off to the hospital. The doctor gave me a shot of Demerol. I've never forgotten it—it was the greatest sensation I ever had. Like being in a warm bed under a big, thick, soft blanket. I hardly noticed my broken arm. After they set it, they gave my mother some codeine to take home. I remember I used it all up in a few days. I didn't touch another narcotic till I was almost twenty. But looking back, I suppose you might say I already had a taste for them.

"In college, I began having trouble with my back. I was told I had a disc that was disintegrating. I went through every known form of therapy—each one seemed more painful and useless than the last—but nothing worked. Finally, they performed surgery. In fact, they operated six times in the space of three years.

"Of course, I had a lot of pain, on a more or less constant basis. I was on medication of all different kinds. Nothing seemed to remove the pain entirely, but I was able to function, at least. Then one of the surgeons started to get nervous about how much medication I was taking. He thought I was in danger of overdosing. I tried to tell him that I could probably take twice as much as he gave me and still have some pain, but he didn't believe me. He talked to my other physicians, and they decided to wean me off some of the narcotics. At that time, I was mainly taking Demerol and codeine, with some Valium to relieve muscle spasms and to help me sleep. It was a lot, I admit, but I felt I was managing admirably given my special circumstances.

"The effort to wean me off was a total disaster. I have never experienced pain like that in my life. Worse than right after surgery. I *begged* them to increase the dose. They wouldn't give in. Finally, I got so desperate I went to another doctor on the side, and he gave me a prescription for Percodan. I used those—supposedly a two-week supply—in two days. I decided to try still another doctor for another prescription. I thought that if I saw several doctors, I wouldn't draw as much attention, and they wouldn't suspect how much I was using. I didn't like being dishonest, but I felt they were forcing me into it.

"Eventually, I was going to as many as thirty different doctors, using four or five different phony stories to get narcotics. I had a notebook with a schedule in it, and I kept notes on each doctor—how he responded to a certain complaint, whether or not he seemed suspicious of me, things like that—it was unbelievably complicated.

"One day, I made a very bad mistake. I went to a doctor I had visited before, and in my haste I told him a different story than I had used on the first visit. He got suspicious, and after I left, called around to pharmacies. He tipped off the police, and a few weeks later I was arrested in a drugstore, trying to fill a scrip for Demerol. That led to conviction, and I was remanded to a drug program."

The Addictive Syndrome

We take the time to describe both patterns because people so often assume that addiction to a prescription drug is substantially different from addiction to illegal substances. In reality, the addictive process is virtually the same.

Note the presence of an *elevated tolerance* in both cases.

Then the obvious burden of a *withdrawal syndrome:* one compares it to a "bad flu," which reaches the point where he can't make it to work, while the other notes that her pain was "worse than the day after surgery." Whatever the reason for their initial use, as addiction progresses both come to view narcotics primarily as a way to stave off withdrawal. Whatever pleasure the street user experiences from shooting heroin fades, to be replaced by an overwhelming need for the drug in order to "function" on a daily basis. Similarly, the legitimate pain of the back patient is augmented, then eventually surpassed, by the discomfort of withdrawal.

Thus the basic pattern is one of *maintenance* use. The narcotics addict lives from day to day, manipulating the environment to provide a steady supply of drugs, manipulating himself to keep going in the face of a seemingly endless, circular struggle, from hour to hour and from fix to fix.

Narcotics addicts experience profound loss of control, particularly over the time or place where use occurs. This is due again to developing withdrawal; the addict knows that using a narcotic at work is dangerous, but if she doesn't use, she suffers for it. She may hold out as long as she can, but eventually, withdrawal overwhelms her resolve. During the brief periods when she's without the drug, she finds a pronounced craving dominates her thinking. She alternates between two states of consciousness: either stoned, or planning how to get stoned. *Efforts to quit on her own fail;* even if she goes cold turkey for a few days, she quickly relapses. She becomes a living illustration of the addict's willingness to continue using despite adverse consequences: her life may be threatened, she could be arrested, she might end up in jail—yet none of this is sufficient to motivate abstinence.

The addict develops that remarkable *self-centeredness* that is characteristic of addiction. Her relationships begin to disintegrate, simply because she is no longer paying attention to them. People become important only to the extent to which they affect her ability to use drugs. She concentrates on manipulating rather than relating to others. She sees little and understands less, blinded by her own discomfort and the overwhelming need to relieve it. When dangers arise—the possibility of arrest, divorce, AIDS—she denies, rationalizes, externalizes, or minimizes them.

Narcotics addicts frequently report a variety of health consequences related to their drug use. One of the most common involves loss of sexual desire, often accompanied by impotence in men and lack of orgasm in women. Others involve the dramatic increase in risk of infection due to drug injection, and related consequences such as hepatitis and, of course, AIDS. Combined with the risk of overdose and the general poor attention to health and nutrition among users, lifespan can be dramatically reduced.

"They say that alcohol is worse for you than heroin," said one addict. "Maybe it is. But you see a lot of old alcoholics running around. How many junkies do you see past the age of fifty?"

Sedatives

Sedatives are drugs used to relieve tension. *Hypnotics* are sleeping medications. Since anxiety and insomnia are two of the most common complaints in medicine, this is an amazingly popular category of drugs. And because they are largely dispensed by prescription, a physician frequently plays a key role in any addictive syndrome.

At one time, the *barbiturate* drugs dominated the sedative category, primarily through the popularity of four short-acting barbiturates: *Seconal, Nembutal, Amytal,* and *Tuinal.* But over time, these drugs proved to be both addictive and dangerous, since it was potentially easy to go over the lethal level of dosage as tolerance grew and sedative effect waned.

Later, during the 1940s and 1950s, a number of nonbarbiturate sedatives were introduced as "safe" and even "nonaddictive." There was *meprobamate,* introduced under brand names like Miltown and Equanil. There was *methaqualone,* better known as Quaalude, which garnered an undeserved reputation as an aphrodisiac. In each case, it was found that the drug was only marginally superior to the barbiturates in terms of risk.

But the search for an effective sedative produced the most phenomenally successful group of drugs in pharmacological history: the *benzodiazepines.* You know them better by their brand names: Valium, Librium, Dalmane, Ativan, Xanax, among others.

These drugs became so popular because they appeared to avoid the problems that haunted their predecessors. The lethal range was so far from the therapeutic dose that it was nearly impossible to die by overdose. Where tolerance developed quickly to barbiturates, benzodiazepine users seemed to continue getting effective relief without dose increase. And when, in a testing situation, the drugs were abruptly terminated, there was little evidence of withdrawal.

For the most part, it worked out well. The majority of patients were able to use the benzodiazepines without mishap, for the purposes intended. Nevertheless, the initial hope that we'd at last found a "nonaddictive" potent sedative was groundless. Because people can and do become addicted to the benzodiazepines.

And that addiction, once established, is one of the most difficult and painful to interrupt.

Here's an example:

Mrs. P., a forty-eight-year-old woman, had been using benzodiazepines for six years. The drug was originally prescribed for chronic back pain. It seemed to work well initially, but after six months of daily use, she began to experience unexplained episodes of anxiety, characterized by rapid pulse and dizzy spells. She consulted her orthopedist, who took her off all medications for a period of one week. Her back pain returned in full strength, and her anxiety actually seemed to increase, to the point that she was afraid to leave her house. She also complained of persistent loud ringing in her ears. The orthopedist put her back on the benzodiazepine and referred her to a psychiatrist, who diagnosed her as suffering from panic disorder of uncertain cause. He increased the dosage of sedatives and added an antidepressant medication. This seemed to produce initial relief, but after another few months, the symptoms began to reappear, this time complicated by sleep disruption. Mrs. P. had to be strongly encouraged by her family to leave her home at all, even to visit her doctors. The psychiatrist admitted her to a psychiatric hospital for two extended periods, during which time he tried different combinations of anti-depressants and benzodiazepines, along with daily psychotherapy. Each time, she would improve enough to be discharged, but within a month, would be worse than before.

Finally, in desperation, her psychiatrist called in for consultation another physician who incidentally had experience in addictions treatment. He recommended removing her once again from all drugs, and when he saw the severity of her response—which included pronounced tremors, cramps, muscle ache, and even minor visual hallucinations—decided to completely detoxify her. Over the course of six weeks in the hospital, her symptoms gradually abated.

This is a somewhat unusual case of benzodiazepine dependence. For one thing, Mrs. P. herself did not increase the dose; she became physically dependent on doses that were close to the therapeutic range. Nevertheless, her withdrawal experience was profound and consisted of symptoms that could not be traced to other causes. The "panic disorder" diagnosed by her psychiatrist looks in retrospect to have been mostly drug withdrawal.

Note also the unusually long course of benzodiazepine withdrawal. She was still experiencing vivid symptoms six weeks after detoxification began.

We hope you noticed how the physicians in this case misidentified drug withdrawal. The orthopedist knew that his patient's symptoms might be related to the drugs she was taking and so terminated them; however, when the symptoms persisted for a few days, he immediately assumed there was an underlying psychiatric cause and referred the patient on for psychiatric consultation. This psychiatrist looked at the same symptoms and assumed them to be the product of a panic disorder, which he medicated with still more benzodiazepines. It was only the intervention of a third physician which led to the correct treatment.

This is a classic case of *maintenance* addiction. Other addicts may experience more profound loss of control, leading to behavior very much like that of a cocaine addict. One sedative addict exhibited classic signs of manipulative behavior; a doctor at a local detoxification center who investigated, learned that she had been obtaining Valium from no fewer than *eleven* physicians in her area under false pretenses. According to the addictions specialist, she consumed as many as thirty pills *daily* and had left another state in order to avoid prosecution for prescription forgery.

Because the withdrawal syndrome from these drugs is so dramatic, let's examine a few of the commonly reported symptoms:

Panic Attacks. A panic attack is a more severe episode of anxiety. Often for no apparent reason, the user is afflicted with crippling, immobilizing fear, accompanied by rapid pulse, nausea, headache, and cold sweat. Of course, because so many patients were originally placed on benzodiazepines for anxiety disorder, it's extremely difficult, if not impossible, for patient or physician to differentiate this aspect of drug withdrawal from a worsening of the original anxiety disorder. As a result, this symptom is often treated with increased doses of tranquilizers—which provide temporary relief, only to be followed by still worse attacks.

Perceptual Disturbances. These might include distortions in color and light, or a blurring of vision, especially around the periphery. Some addicts report the appearance of "night blindness" which further encourages them to avoid going out.

"Hot Flashes." Again, since so many benzodiazepine users are middle-aged women, these are often associated with menopause, and it is extremely difficult to differentiate the cause of the symptom.

Headache. Pain of migrainelike persistence.

Muscle Cramping. Aches, pains, and cramps are characteristic of withdrawal. There are literally dozens of other symptoms that could be described, but perhaps the best summation is that benzodiazepine withdrawal represents a seemingly endless "uproar" in the nervous system, resulting not only in its own direct discomfort but in the augmentation of any other nervous or physical discomfort the body may be experiencing.

The key issue in sedative withdrawal is not only the severity but the *duration* of the withdrawal period. It is not uncommon to encounter sedative addicts who are experiencing what appear to be acute withdrawal symptoms several weeks after their last dose. And when you include *postacute symptoms*—which are less painful but still disturbing—the withdrawal syndrome can sometimes seem to last for months.

Curiously, despite the extended discomfort of withdrawal—or maybe because of it—recovery rates for detoxified sedative users appear to be among the highest of any addiction. With proper detoxification, education, and with alternative treatments for whatever disorder brought them to sedatives in the first place, the prognosis can be excellent.

Mixing and Matching Drugs

Suppose you're a maintenance alcoholic, in the grip of withdrawal. You confine your drinking to evenings because you're afraid someone will smell alcohol on your breath in the daytime. But some mornings you find yourself nervous, irritable, given to unexplainable fits of anxiety. At a friend's urging, you consult your doctor. You "forget" to mention your alcohol consumption; after all, the problem isn't when you're drinking, but when you're not. The physician decides you're under too much stress and prescribes a tranquilizer. You discover the medication miraculously alleviates your discomfort. As a result, you decide that when you're having a particularly bad day, you can rely on a pill instead of alcohol. That way, drinking remains confined to the "safe" hours of the evening.

Or imagine you're a cocaine user. You've recently discovered your nervous system doesn't tolerate coke as well as it did. Instead of that euphoric rush you once experienced, you feel fidgety, restless, on edge. You complain to a friend, who offers a practical solution: mix cocaine with a drug whose effects are to some extent the opposite—a narcotic such as heroin, for example. Inject both at the same time, and notice how your nervousness disappears. The "rush" is back.

Or perhaps you're a teenager, fascinated by the romantic image associated with drug use. You hang around the outlaw crowd at school, using anything anyone offers you, just to see what happens. During a given month, you may assault your nervous system with a dozen different substances of varying effects, in varying amounts, in combination or separately. From your view, you're just "having a good time." To those around you, the effects on your behavior are bewildering.

These are just three examples of *multiple drug* use among persons with addictive disease. This phenomenon falls into the following general categories:

Drugs Used to Potentiate or Antagonize Other Drugs

This is what happens in the second example, where heroin is combined with cocaine because its effects on the central nervous system are generally opposite. Though heroin is not a true "antagonist" (a drug that blocks cocaine's action), it is nevertheless a depressant where cocaine is a stimulant, and therefore serves to counteract some of cocaine's more pronounced stimulant properties. Cocaine, in turn, offsets some of the excessive sedation associated with heroin. As a result, some users believe they obtain a "smoother ride" than through using either drug by itself.

The practice of combining a stimulant with a sedative or narcotic for this purpose is called "speedballing." The ingredients need not be heroin and cocaine; many other substances will interact in a similar fashion.

Sometimes, drugs are combined because the similarity of their effects produces a *synergistic* or "potentiating" result. One user told us why he mixed Quaalude with alcohol. "It's the best little sleeping pill in the world," he insisted. "Sometimes I'll have been up all weekend, and I'll want to go to sleep, and I can't seem to do it. My brain just won't relax. So I'll drop a couple of 'Ludes and wash them down with vodka, and go out like a light."

Here, the similar depressant qualities of alcohol and Quaalude produce an additive (or in some instances, multiplicative) effect. The sedation produced in combination is greater than might have been achieved by larger doses of one drug alone.

This, however, can be dangerous. We can imagine a morning when the young man who mixed "the best little sleeping pill in the world" simply never wakes up. In fact, it's one of the major factors in accidental overdose among addicts. Mixing drugs sometimes produces a degree of potentiation that overcomes even the addict's elevated tolerance.

Drugs Used to Substitute for Other Drugs

In our first example, a tranquilizer was used to substitute for alcohol in a maintenance drinking pattern. In part, tranquilizers were developed to do some of the same things alcohol does (calm nerves and induce sleep) in a more precise fashion and without the negative side effects for which alcohol is known.

Quickly, alcoholics learned to incorporate sedatives into their addictive pattern. Often, this was done with the encouragement of their physicians.

For decades, doctors received little or no training in the mechanisms of alcoholic behavior. One result was that physicians often failed to diagnose alcoholism in their patients even when it was obvious to everyone else around them. Another was that physicians fell into a pattern of substituting prescription drugs for alcohol in the vain hope that the alcoholic would be able to use these "safe" substances to medicate whatever discomfort drove him to drink.

Put yourself in the place of a physician confronted with an alcoholic patient. You know the fellow drinks too much. The funny thing is, your patient acknowledges it, too. But, he insists, there are reasons. He's overworked, and his wife and he don't get along. He's under a lot of obvious stress. You want to advise him to eliminate drinking—or at the very least, you decide, "cut way back"—but he presents you with a challenge. "If I give up alcohol," he asks, "how am I going to handle the pressure? I won't be able to sleep at night. I'll have anxiety attacks again."

What to do? You decide to compromise: if he slows down or stops drinking, you'll provide a sedative to help him "cope," and a sleeping pill for restless nights. That way, you believe, you've eliminated his need for alcohol. Now, he can use a medication instead of booze.

Of course, the physician has just made an essential error. In reality, the alcoholic has been using a medication all along: alcohol. And he shows signs of dependence and of loss of control. The sedative the doctor prescribes will alleviate withdrawal, because it so precisely duplicates the effects of alcohol. But then, what is to prevent the alcoholic from developing the same problems with these new sedatives that he did with alcohol? What prevents him from developing yet a second addictive disorder, which complicates and worsens his present condition?

The answer: not much. And in fact, many alcoholics fall into exactly that trap.

There has been a lot of adverse publicity about the addictive potential of sedative-hypnotic drugs. This has resulted in greater awareness of their dangers and lowered incidence of prescription where the patient has an identified alcohol problem. Still, whenever a new sedative is introduced—usually with considerable publicity claiming it is "safer" and "less addictive" than previous models—the temptation for physicians to use it is strong.

Use of a Wide Variety of Drugs

This pattern, as in our example, is most common among teenagers and those in their early twenties. We call it the "Garbage Syndrome," and persons who fall within it "garbageheads."

Adolescence is the age of experimentation—in almost every area of life. So we suppose it's understandable that teenage drug users assault their brains with many different substances.

Taking a drug history from such a kid can be an adventure. Here's a history given by one seventeen-year-old drug abuser who was asked to: "List the drugs you have used in the past three months."

Beer	3–4 times weekly
Grass	every day
Bottle vodka	five times
Wine coolers	3–4 times weekly
LSD	10–15 times
Crack	30–40 times
PCP	30–40 times
Caffeine pills	twice weekly in large doses
Mom's sleeping pills	5–6 times
Heroin	twice
Percodan	twice
Gasoline	10 times
Glue	10 times

As you might imagine, this young man's behavior is rather unpredictable. Sometimes, according to his parents, he's a "nice kid, even too quiet." At other times, he's "irritable, and sullen, and defensive." On several occasions, he's become irrationally violent; once, when he was stopped by the police for driving erratically, he tried to steal the officer's gun and was nearly shot down. He remembers nothing of this incident. His school attendance is poor, his grades have fallen precipitously, and he has few close friends.

Sometimes, people like this young man are characterized as suffering from an emotional or mental disorder rather than drug abuse, simply because they don't use enough of any one drug to be perceived as addicted to that substance. We think this is a misunderstanding. Think of it this way: where is it written that people have to develop problems with one drug at a time? Why wouldn't we expect to find individuals who evidence a dramatic susceptibility to a wide range of addictions?

Later on, perhaps—when he's older, and the seemingly endless experimentation with chemicals loses some of its allure—we'll see a primary drug emerge. Meanwhile, the effects of this assault on the nervous system may be remarkable.

Suggested Reading

It's sad but true: there are a number of very misleading books on alcoholism and drug dependency. If you are not careful, you can become hopelessly confused. We can't tell you what to *avoid*, so we'll simply advise you where to find useful information we know to be trustworthy.

Alcoholism

Under the Influence: A Guide to the Myths and Realities of Alcoholism. James R. Milam and Katherine Ketcham. Seattle: Madrona Publishers, 1981.
   Start with this book for a real education about the disease of alcoholism.

Cocaine Addiction

800-COCAINE. Mark Gold, M.D. New York: Bantam, 1984.
   Includes an excellent self-test for addiction.

Treatment

Don't Help: A Guide to Working with the Alcoholic. Ronald L. Rogers and Chandler Scott McMillin. Seattle: Madrona Publishers, 1988.
   Our earlier work which describes in detail a task-centered approach to addictions treatment.

Family

Getting Them Sober: Parts One and Two. Toby Rice Drews. Bridge Publishing, 1980.
   Good, practical advice for the family member.

Intervention

Intervention: How to Help Someone Who Doesn't Want Help. Vernon Johnson. Minneapolis: Johnson Institute Press, 1986.
   Includes examples of confrontation sessions.

Twelve Step Programs

The Twelve Steps Revisited: AA and the Disease of Alcoholism. Ronald L Rogers, Chandler Scott McMillin, and Morris Hall. Seattle: Madrona Publishers, 1988.

How to use the Twelve Steps from the perspective of treating a chronic disease.

Nutrition

The Self Healing Cookbook. Kristina Turner. Grass Valley, California: Earthtones Press, 1988.

A solid, well-written guide to alternative nutrition as a way to regulate mood and health.

Publications of Alcoholics Anonymous and Narcotics Anonymous

Alcoholics Anonymous. Bill W. and others, 1955.

The "bible" of AA. Includes the all-important chapter, "How It Works."

Twelve Steps and Twelve Traditions. Bill W., 1953.

The "official" interpretation of the Steps and Traditions of AA.

Living Sober. 1975.

Practical advice for the first days of recovery.

Narcotics Anonymous. 1982.

NA's version of AA's "bible."

Recovery

Eating Right to Live Sober. L. Ann Mueller, M.D., and Katherine Ketcham. New York: Bantam, 1986.

Nutrition and diet for the recovering alcoholic.

Recovering: How to Get and Stay Sober. L. Ann Mueller, M.D., and Katherine Ketcham. New York: Bantam, 1987.

Basic review of intervention, treatment, and recovery.

Glossary

Aftercare. Follow-up care for persons who have successfully completed inpatient or outpatient addictions treatment. Usually includes group therapy.

Alanon. Self-help organization for those who care about an alcoholic. Also uses a Twelve Step model.

Alcoholics Anonymous. A self-help organization whose primary purpose is to reach the suffering alcoholic. Uses a Twelve Step program of recovery.

Alcoholism. "A chronic, progressive, potentially fatal disease characterized by tolerance and physical dependence, pathologic organ changes, or both; all of which are the direct or indirect consequences of the alcohol ingested."

Anhedonia. Difficulty experiencing pleasure from normal activities. Common among cocaine addicts and others.

Antagonist. A drug that blocks (completely or partially) the effects of another drug.

Binge or Episodic Pattern. Periods of uncontrolled use of alcohol or drugs interspersed with periods of reduced consumption or abstinence. Usually the result of *loss of control.*

Blackout. Amnesia for events which occured while drinking or drugging. Not to be confused with *passing out.* During a blackout, the person is awake and does not realize he or she will not recall events the following day.

Chronic. Long lasting.

Co-dependency. A syndrome featuring ongoing mutually destructive relationships with the sick, including persistent enabling and provoking behavior and continued involvement despite adverse consequences.

Comparing In and **Comparing Out.** Alcoholics *compare in* when they identify symptoms of alcoholism in their own experience. They *compare out* when they stubbornly avoid recognizing these same symptoms.

Crack. A form of cocaine which can be smoked.

Crash. The reactive depression that follows a cocaine binge.

Craving. Spontaneous desire for a drug. Can be *free-floating* (unrelated to outside events), *linked to emotional excitement,* or *conditioned* (related to environmental cue such as watching someone else drink).

Defense Mechanisms. Irrational thinking designed to relieve negative feelings brought on by unacceptable actions.

Dependence. Withdrawal symptoms appear with decreasing or ceasing consumption of a drug.

Disease. A morbid process with characteristic identifying symptoms. It is not necessary that the cause or likely outcome be known.

Elevator Syndrome. The practice of using a sedative (such as alcohol) to counteract the toxic effects of a stimulant (such as cocaine). Also sometimes called *elevator cocktails.*

Emotional Augmentation. Increased emotional response to normal stress, brought about by acute or postacute withdrawal. Anger may become rage, sadness may become depression, relief may become elation, etc. Often mistaken by those around the addict for mood or personality disorder.

Enabling. Behavior on the part of others which protects the alcoholic or addict from the consequences of his or her drinking or drug use.

Flashback. Recurrence of certain symptoms associated with drug use long after the drug has left the system. Includes perceptual distortions and anxiety, among others. Harmless in itself but frightening to the addict.

Influence (in intervention). Strong direct encouragement to seek treatment from concerned persons whom the alcoholic or addict trusts.

Intervention. Organized efforts on the part of those around an alcoholic or addict to get him or her into treatment. Often includes a *structured confrontation* with the alcoholic.

Leverage. Actual consequences that interveners will bring to bear should the addict refuse treatment. Usually centers around withdrawal of enabling behaviors.

Loss of Control. An inability to consistently predict the *amount consumed, time or place,* or *duration* of a drinking/drugging episode.

Maintenance Pattern. Daily or near-daily consumption of alcohol or drugs in such a fashion as to stave off withdrawal symptoms and permit the addict to function in everyday life.

Narcotics Anonymous. Twelve Step program modeled on AA and focusing on recovery from addiction to drugs as well as alcohol.

Pathologic Organ Change. Deterioration or adaptation of organs (such as liver) which indicate exposure to toxic effects of alcohol or other drugs. Usually identified through laboratory tests.

Provoking. Behavior on the part of others which directly encourages the alcoholic or addict to drink or use drugs. Ranges from offering or sharing substances with the addict, to participating in useless arguments which the addict uses to justify relapse.

Recovery. The process of getting well. In addictions, it is viewed as an extended process featuring numerous biological, attitudinal, and lifestyle changes.

Relapse. Return to drinking or drug taking.

Resentment. Anger held over an extended period (sometimes years), and usually centering around an event where the addict felt *betrayed, victimized, prejudiced against,* or *taken advantage of.* Resentments are fuel for relapse and for problems in sobriety, and are a major focus of the AA and NA programs.

Significant Others. Those involved with an addict whose behavior may have appreciable impact on his or her recovery.

Slippery People and **Slippery Places.** Relationships or environments conducive to relapse.

Sponsor. An experienced AA or NA member who develops a personal relationship with a newer member for the purpose of assisting him or her in recovery—particularly in working the Steps.

Stigma. In addiction, negative connotation that surrounds diagnosis of alcoholism or drug dependency. Encourages addict to do everything in his power to *avoid* the diagnosis and thereby interferes with treatment.

Susceptibility. Degree of risk for developing a given disease. For example: children of alcoholics are more susceptible to alcoholism than those without this background.

Synergism. When two drugs of similar effect are combined, the resulting effects may be additive or multiplicative. Common factor in accidental overdose.

Tolerance. Reduced response to a drug over a period of exposure. Caused by brain and liver adaptation. The addict or alcoholic experiences tolerance as the need to increase dose or frequency in order to obtain the desired effect.

Withdrawal. Signs and symptoms experienced by the addict when consumption ceases or is curtailed.

Index

About the Authors

Ronald L. Rogers has been clinical director of numerous addictions treatment programs and is currently a consultant of New Beginnings at Warwick, Maryland. He is a member of the adjunct faculty of the University of Virginia and has been an instructor for the Maryland Office of Addictions Education. He is a member of the Maryland Addictions Counselor Certification Board. His expertise in the areas of group therapy and program development is widely recognized and sought, and he speaks and lectures frequently in the greater Washington, D.C., area.

Chandler Scott McMillin is director of the Addiction Treatment Center of Suburban Hospital in Bethesda, Maryland. He is also a member of the adjunct faculty of the University of Virginia and an instructor for the Maryland Office of Addictions Education. A very popular speaker on the subject of addictions, specializing in the process of intervention, McMillin is the general editor of the If It Runs in Your Family series.

Together, McMillin and Rogers have authored six books on addiction, including *Relapse Traps: How to Avoid the 12 Most Common Pitfalls in Recovery; If It Runs in Your Family: Reducing the Risk of Alcoholism; The Twelve Steps Revisited;* and *Don't Help: A Guide to Working with the Alcoholic.*

OTHER BOOKS OF HOPE AND HEALING FROM PERIGEE

Freeing Someone You Love from Alcohol and Other Drugs
by Ronald L. Rogers and Chandler Scott McMillin
A step-by-step program of intervention and treatment of alcoholism and other drug addictions based on the principle that addiction is a hereditary, progressive, chronic disease.

Healing the Wounds of Childhood
A Recovery Guide for Adult Children of Dysfunctional Families
by Dennis J. McGuire, Ph.D.
A powerful and informative book that describes for the first time exactly where adult children are going in the process of recovering from a difficult childhood, and what they should expect along the way.

Reach for the Rainbow
Advanced Healing for Survivors of Sexual Abuse
by Lynne D. Finney, J.D., M.S.W.
A ground-breaking book that has become the classic on the topic of sexual abuse and incest—for survivors, their loved ones, and their therapists.

Available at your local bookstore or wherever books are sold. Ordering also is easy and convenient. Just call 1-800-631-8571 or send your order to:

The Putnam Publishing Group
390 Murray Hill Parkway, Dept. B
East Rutherford, NJ 07073

| | | | Price | |
			U.S.	Canada
_____	Freeing Someone You Love from Alcohol and Other Drugs	399-51727-8	$12.95	$16.95
_____	Healing the Wounds of Child- hood	399-51615-8	9.95	12.95
_____	Reach for the Rainbow	399-51745-6	12.95	16.95

                                            Subtotal $_____
                          *Postage and handling $_____
                                           Sales tax $_____
                                     (CA, NJ, NY, PA)
                           Total Amount Due $_____

Payable in U.S. Funds (No cash orders accepted). $10.00 minimum for credit card orders.
*Postage & handling: $2.00 for 1 book, 50¢ for each additional book up to a maximum of $4.50.

Enclosed is my ☐ check ☐ money order
Please charge my ☐ Visa ☐ MasterCard ☐ American Express
Card# _____ Expiration date _____
Signature as on charge card _____
Name _____
Address _____
City _____ State _____ Zip _____

Please allow six weeks for delivery. Prices subject to change without notice.